Christopher St. George Clark

Of Toronto the Good

A Social Study - The Queen city of Canada as it is

Christopher St. George Clark

Of Toronto the Good
A Social Study - The Queen city of Canada as it is

ISBN/EAN: 9783337192778

Printed in Europe, USA, Canada, Australia, Japan

Cover: Foto ©Andreas Hilbeck / pixelio.de

More available books at **www.hansebooks.com**

OF TORONTO THE GOOD.

A SOCIAL STUDY.

The Queen City of Canada as it is.

BY

C. S. CLARK.

"Not necessarily Toronto alone but every city in America."

———•———

Toronto as a Social Study was brought prominently before the World by the remarks of Canadian delegates to the Social Purity Conference at Baltimore, and the World's Convention of the Women's Christian Temperance Union, held at Toronto in 1897.

———•———

MONTREAL
THE TORONTO PUBLISHING COMPANY.
1898.

COLES CANADIANA COLLECTION

Originally published in 1898
in Montreal
by the Toronto Publishing Company.

Facsimile edition reprinted by
COLES — the Book people! Toronto.
© Copyright 1970

CONTENTS:

	PAGE
Toronto	1
City Government	6
Police Force	11
Society	27
The Press	32
The Stock Exchange	51
Financial Enterprises	54
Business in Toronto	62
The Detectives	64
Hotels	67
Restaurants	71
Boarding Houses	73
Holidays in the City	76
City Parks	77
The Public Schools	79
Street Boys	81
The Social Evil	86
Street Walkers	131
Lodging Houses	137
The Poor of the City	142
Pawnbrokers	142
Gambling Houses	143
Drunkenness	143
Imposters	144
Pickpockets	145
Crooks	145
Thieves	146
Assignation Houses	147
Churches and the Clergy	147
The Bar	188
Music and the Drama	191
Quack Doctors	198
Situation Agencies	204
Swindlers	205
Conclusion	209

TORONTO.

"Toronto the Good" and beautiful is one of the finest cities on the continent in point of beauty, wealth and intelligence, as it is unquestionably the leading commercial city of the west. It supplies to a large extent the requirements of Manitoba and the North West, and promises to seriously rival Montreal in the extent of its wholesale trade. Situated in the centre of the Province, and commanding the leading position on Lake Ontario, it is essentially a point of importance.

It has some of the handsomest streets on the continent, and is really well laid out. Jarvis street with its elegant pavement is in summer a most attractive thoroughfare, and the same may be said of Bloor, Sherbourne and Spadina, but the extreme east end, and the west end east of Parkdale are the abode of poverty to a very great extent, and are commensurately less desirable.

The city extends from the Bay northward to a line scarcely definable, and this is also the case with the east and west. Real estate men and companies have opened large tracts of land, and farms have been converted into building lots, and as the fact of their being in the city limits increases their value, it becomes therefore, most desirable that they should be incorporated as soon as they are so divided.

It was in the year 1883 that Toronto became land hungry and began to stretch forth ambitious hands to seize adjoining sections of the County of York. Bear in mind that up to this date Bloor street on the north, Dufferin street on the west, and virtually the Don on the east marked the boundaries of our city, whose area was 6,771 acres. In 1883, Yorkville threw in its lot with the Queen City and became St. Paul's Ward. Its area was 543 acres. Its eastern boundary was Sherbourne street, and its western a line just east of Bedford road. In 1884, St. Matthew's and St. Mark's ward were born, a total increase to Toronto's area of 2.346 acres. For just three years the city remained content, and then came the addition of a strip 200 feet deep on the north side of Kingston road (now Queen street), containing 57 acres, the new annex of 209 acres, 99 acres of Rosedale quickly followed in the succeeding year; 1052 acres, including Seaton village, 91 acres between High Park and the west limit of Parkdale, and about 68 acres which carried St. Paul's hard up to the top of the hill above the C. P. R. Hemmed in by the city on three sides, Parkdale next joined fortunes with Toronto and in 1889 added St. Alban's Ward, a fair-sized debt and 650 acres of land to the municipality. This was the last accession to our area, excepting a small strip of 35 acres on the east side of Greenwood's line, which was acquired in 1890. Toronto now discovered that she had grown even too strong, and that she had acquired enough territory to hold all the citizens we are likely to have for the next fifty years. Hand in hand with this tremendous extension of territory went the local improvements and the increase of our debenture debt, and for the last six years citizens have been wondering what all the territory was ever wanted for, and have been execrating the insane speculative mania which sewered and block paved and sidewalked the grassy swards of the county of York's farm lands.

Recapitulating then we see the growth in area of the city of Toronto as follows :

1834 to 1883............	6,771 acres.
1883........	7,315 acres.
1884...	9,661 acres.
1887	10,528 acres.
1888...	11,239 acres.
1889...	11,889 acres.
1890 to 1896..	11,924 acres.

That is to say, we have in a period of seven years almost doubled our area. Those best qualified to speak authoritatively see in this large extension of territory all the woes in the way of taxation which now afflict the city. Had there been added not thousands of acres of what has been fitly designated goose pastures, but, say, Parkdale and Yorkville and its suburbs, we should now have a compact city, light taxation, land valuable, and a better and more prosperous population. And it would also have been infinitely better for those sections which came in by reason of land speculation during the seven fat years when Toronto's sober population became land-crazy and speculation-mad.

Among the men who have been brought down by the collapse of the real estate boom in Toronto, comparatively few can be classed as lenders. A few, and, compared to the majority of borrowers, a very few, have been financially prostrated by lending injudiciously. The sufferers among the lending class have been mainly widows and orphans, whose money was advanced through the agency of some rascally lawyer upon worthless second mortgages. The sufferings of these unfortunates have been grievous enough, but adversity has found most of its victims, not among those who lent, but among those who borrowed injudiciously. The men who have come to grief are the men who sank all their own money in land, which was pledged as security for further loans. While the boom lasted the lenders reaped a harvest of heavy interest from the borrowers. When the boom was breaking the lenders in most cases saved themselves by sacrificing the borrowers' property. It is quite evident, from the current rates of interest, that borrowers who think they can get rich by paying more for money than they can earn with it, are becoming scarcer. The enterprising borrower in Toronto has paid dearly for his fondness for speculating with other people's money. In some cases the other people who supplied them with money have suffered. In most cases the borrower has been the sufferer, and the present over-abundance of money is proof that lenders have become cautious, or that borrowers have become scarce.

Toronto's population is, two hundred thousand nearly, and this does not include the immense throng of visitors for business or pleasure, who arrive and depart daily. During times of more than ordinary interest such as some great religious or edueational convention, the Industrial Exhibition or some special attraction, these arrivals are greatly increased The population is made up from almost every nation, though Canadians prodominate as they should.

It is the goal of almost every youth's ambition in the province to become eventually a resident of the Queen city. Its universities, than which there are on the continent none better, attract students from all parts of the country and the United States as well, while the convents, business colleges, veterinary college and similar educational institutions are composed almost entirely of out of town people of both sexes. To succeed a young man must set to work to build up a reputation for he will be taken for just what he is worth and no more.

In point of morality the people of Toronto compare with those of any other city quite favourably, and if the dark side of life is to be seen here, one may also witness the best. In its charities Toronto stands in the front rank of Canadian and American cities. The various religious denominations spend annually thousands of dollars and private contributions towards charitable institutions amount in the aggregate to sum that are almost princely.

To a certain extend the people are liberal in matters of opinion, and as a rule men do not seek to influence the opinions of others except in so far as they are privileged to do so, but any faddist no matter how absurb or ridiculous his theories may be, will find converts in Toronto who will be surprised at the lack of intelligence on the part of those who do not fall in love with them. As an illustration of the susceptibility of Torontonians the conversions made by Prince Michael of Detroit, among the religiously inclined, may be cited as a fair example of what others may do or have done.

Strangers coming into the city are struck with the existence of the extremes of rich and poor. Living in the city is very expensive, the poor are obliged to live in the skaky, tumble-down houses of Centre, Elizabeth, South Jarvis and Lombard and Bathurst and some other streets, while the middle classes and those of only moderate means reside in the suburbs, or a considerable distance from the business part of the city. They come down every morning to business in crowds between the hours of seven and nine, and literally pour out of it between the hours of four and seven in the evening. In fair weather the inconvenience of such a life is trifling but in the winter and especially after a heavy fall of snow it is very great, and should the street cars be obstructed the annoyance is considerably increased.

A considerable number of people own their own houses, though this circumstance may be a questionable advantage. House rents are comparatively high, particularly in the heart of the city, and many people of moderate means are compelled to let furnished rooms or take boarders to supplement their slender incomes.

That owning a house is a desirable boon is not by any means certain. When the real estate boom was in its zenith property changed hands at prices that were an unmitigated gratification to those who sold them, but those who bought are not so well satisfied. It is really comical some of the ideas people have of the value of their land. To trace this matter up I wrote to a firm of real estate agents in reference to a house on Charles street. It was not by any means a new house, but it was rented for sixteen dollars a month and taxes. Price three thousand two hundred dollars. By the fairest calculation in mathematics, it will be seen that to pay six per cent. one hundred and eighty dollars are required, taxes forty eight dollars at least, and then your chances of profit are only contained in the remote contingency of the property increasing in value. Three thousand dollars at six per cent would be infinitely preferable to a house of the description I have mentioned. This is not by any means an exceptional case. I could give you similar ones by the score.

In spite of all these drawbacks, however, Toronto is a delightful place to live in. Its boating is unsurpassed. The bay on a summer night, is one mass of skiffs and sail boats, and there is scarcely a youth in the city who has not experienced the delights of rowing, and a large number are owners or part owners of boats.

Some years ago a number of baths were presented to the city by a one time resident at a cost of some $5000.00, and they were certainly a boon to the boys of the city. A storm, however, destroyed their utility and for a long time there was only the beach where they could go, including the sand bar opposite Queen's wharf. It is currently reported that some stately lady used to sit at the hotel window and survey the boys in bathing through an opera or field glass, until she made a complaint with the result that bathing without trunks was prohibited by the police. Like all such prohibitive legislation, however it is to be remarked that it was regularly and systematically set at defiance. On Sunday mornings in summer the sand bar was alive with boys and young men who strip themselves and throw their clothes in a boat. If a policemen looms in sight they take to the boats and I have never heard that anyone has been arrested yet.

During the past summer, Mr. W. J. Gage made an offer to the city council to build a swimming bath in a central locality, if the city would furnish the site. A special committee was appointed to consider the matter, and confer with Mr. Gage, and recommend to council such plans and methods as they may find practicable and desirable to secure the best possible results from the liberal proposition made by Mr. Gage.

The Mayor's experiment, by which the city provided a steam tug to ferry the boys of the city across the Bay to the sand bar for bathing lessons proved a huge success. On one Saturday no less than 3000 boys were taken over, and as there was an experienced swimmer in charge, and all necessary appliances on hand also at the expense of the city, the bathing is absolutely safe, and the departure is proving an immense boon to the boys in the hot weather.

Besides the bathing afforded by the island it is the terminus of all the boats that leave the slips at night. All the water front comprises interminable lengths of boat houses both private and public, and the houses owned by organizations such as the Royal Canadian Yacht Club are perfect palaces in their way. Aquatic sports comprise very largely the principal diversion of Toronto's men and boys, and there is scarcely a boy in the city whose sympathies are not enlisted in some of the great summer events.

This seems to be a matter which is the legitimate outcome of events. The bay seems to be the only place belonging to the city that is not consecrated. The parks are for walking in, not for athletic sports, the streets for traffic, and woe to the boy who is caught desecrating them by playing upon them. If he is under the age of sixteen years, and enter a billiard room, he is liable to arrest again, so that his opportunities for enjoying life are very limited indeed, and with the restrictive legislation passed for his benefit, he has not much opportunity for playing, with the result that pernicious amusements are at a premium.

A child eleven years old appeared in the Police court charged with the offence of playing ball on Sumach street. The ball, a small rubber affair, was produced in court and the boy when asked why he did not bring the bat also, explained that he had no bat, and was playing with the ball and a piece of a stick when the policeman interrupted him. There was no question as to the guilt of the accused. Hugh Miller, J.P., fined the boy $2 or ten days in goal. A good hearted justice of the peace like Mr. Miller could not go against the by-law, but the by-law forbidding ball playing in the street should be enforced against children with a good deal of discretion. By-laws that deal with graver offences than ball playing are not enforced at all. The child who was playing with a soft rubber ball on Sumach street was doing nobody any harm, and the city has something else to do with its money than to pay policemen to run down children who in their innocence think it no sin to try and enjoy themselves.

A squad of boys, the oldest of whom was thirteen, were playing ball in front of their home on Victoria street, opposite the Normal School grounds, when Police Constable 195 ordered them to desist and took their names. The officer did his work civilly enough, and the protest is not against him, but rather against the folly of employing policemen for the persecution of small boys. Not that the Toronto small boy is an angel. By no means. He is rude and mischievous. His mania for damaging trees and defacing property may be explained by the fact that it is unsafe for him to attempt to enjoy himself in any more innocent way A hundred property owners can bear witness that the police have not come between the small boy and his enjoyment of the game of tearing down fences or breaking the windows of vacant houses. But let a few children start a game on a quiet street with a lawn tennis ball such as those boys on Victoria street used and immediately a policemen interferes. When the street becomes the playground of youths or grown men some body is liable to get hit with the hard ball they use. It ought to be easy to avert this danger without perpetuating a by-law which permits the police to exclude children from the streets and to terrify them with threats of Police Court prosecution for the heinous offence of playing with a soft ball.

CITY GOVERNMENT.

The city is governed by a mayor and twenty-four aldermen who receive $300 per annum who are elected annually, though the mayor, as an act of grace, is usually permitted to have a second and sometimes a third term. His salary is three thousand dollars per annum.

In the Municipal Amendment Act of 1896 a radical change has been made by the creation of a Board of Control, which applies practically only to the city of Toronto. The Board consists of the Mayor and three aldermen, the latter to be elected by the Council. The tenure of office is yearly. Salaries to the limit of $700 each may be fixed by bylaw. The duties are to prepare the estimates, deal with and award contracts, inspect all municipal works, nominate to the Council all heads of the various civic departments and recommend the salaries, and no official or clerk shall be appointed without the consent of the Board, except on a two-thirds majority of the Council. Power to dismiss employes, and to regulate the work of the various departments, are some of the other duties of the Board.

It shall also be the duty of the Board, subject to the approval of Council, to regulate and supervise all matters connected with expenditure, revenue and investments, and recommend such measures to the Council as may be deemed necessary therewith;

To have supervision and control of all books, documents, vouchers and securities belonging to the corporation;

To see that persons in office and to be appointed to office shall give and maintain the necessary security for the performance of their respective duties;

To carry out the orders of the Council, and for that purpose to direct and control all heads of departments in the execution of the duties of their offices;

The Board shall, as soon as may be, provide the necessary funds for any expenditure recommended by two-thirds of the members of the Council present and voting, and the yeas and nays on sach voting shall be recorded and forwarded to the chairman of the Board;

The Board shall hold regular meetings, in time to allow the presentation to the Council by the Board of all reports of the Select and Standing Committees, transmitted to the Board three days previous to the meeting of the Council;

The Board shall appoint one of their number as vice-chairman, who shall act as chairman in the absence of the Mayor, having first been notified by the Mayor in writing of his intention to be temporarily absent from his duties;

Reports of all Standing and Special Committees shall be presented to the Board of Control for transmission to the Council.

Reports of the Board of Control intended for the consideration of Council shall be transmitted to the members of Council one day previous to the meeting of the Council.

A new clause in the section defining the duties of the Committee on Legislation provides that all agreements for franchises, etc., shall be considered and reported upon by that committee.

At the municipal elections held on the 3rd January, 1898, John Shaw was elected Mayor over Mr. E. A. Macdonald by 4000 majority. This is Mr. Shaw's second term really, he having been elected Mayor in August, 1897, by the City Council, when Mayor Fleming was made Assessment Commissioner. With regard to Mr. Fleming, I am much pleased that he has received this appointment, though I know him only by reputation. I have watched the course of civic politics in Toronto from a distance, and I never heard of a more dirgraceful campaign than that waged against him when Mr. Warring Kennedy defeated him by something under fifty votes, excepting, perhaps, the one just closed, in some minor points. The speech made by Mr. Macdonald at the nominations, according to the Globe's report was an intellectual treat. Mr Shaw and Mr. F. S. Spence were treated to such a scathing denunciation that the Globe headed its report " Running in the Mud." When Mr. Fleming and Mr. Kennedy were the candidates, it was not sufficient that their public records should furnish the basis of argument, but the press supporting Mr. Kennedy did not tire of referring to him as the " successful business man ", while the reverse was said of Mr. Fleming. But amongst the most disgraceful things said in a most disgraceful campaign was the comparison drawn between the two men as to their relative positions in the Methodist Church. Would it not have been the act of a gentleman, let alone a Christian for Mr. Kennedy to have protested against such tactics ? Yet when one Methodist Minister from his pulpit expressed his intention of supporting Mr. Fleming he was promptly called to order by these same papers, and treatened with dire consequences if he persisted. Does the Omnipotent sleep ? Was it not Almighty God who said "Vengeance is mine, and I will repay ?" Mr. Kennedy did not serve his term, however, for the house of Samson, Kennedy & Co., " the successful business men " made an assignment. Was not that the hand of an avenging Providence? Had Mr. Kennedy possessed any of the qualifications that entitled him to the position of Mayor, one might have condoned the mud throwing by the press that was indulged in, but his messages to council were compared by one journal to a comic song or a burlesque, and not unreasonably so. When he sent a message of condolence to the widow of Sir John Thompson, he informed her that Sir John possessed an exuberance of intellect that was highly polished, as though he were speaking of a shirt front. When the Globe saw fit to adversely criticise some of his acts, they were sent a letter informing them that as they saw fit to criticise His Worship they would get no more advertising. So there ! That must be about on a par with what a school boy of ten would do. But perhaps, about the most ridiculous thing was when Mr. Kennedy cabled his regrets as Mayor of Toronto at the death of the Russian Emperor—an act that provoked from the Evening Telegram a most excellent caricature. In my next edition, I may give miniatures of these caricatures, if I can get the consent of that paper.

Some years ago, chiefly owing to the influence of the News, which was at that time specially influential in both temperance and labour circles, Mr. W. H. Howland, the nominee of this combination, was elected, and during his regime, and with the influence of the News, the ring that seemed to have been formed to swindle the water-works department was exposed and the guilty parties brought to justice.

This exposure was the lever that commenced the idea of a strictly moral city, which should be consummated by restrictive legislation. A more fatal mistake was never made. Mankind in general have a passive regard for public opinion, and unwritten laws regarding morality, and can usually be trusted to give a moral support to usages that have a tendency to elevate their fellows, but once make this unwritten law take the form of restrictive legislation and this same mankind will most emphatically rebel. In support of this assertion, let me say that I have in easy recollection the names of quite a dozen women of unquestionable reputation, members of different churches, who will visit American cities and smuggle into Canada hundreds of dollars worth of merchandise and declare to the preventive officer that they have nothing dutiable when if he were to make a search he would find that they were telling him the most barefaced falsehoods. Make any law which is regarded as restrictive and which does not receive the moral support of the people, and men who would never dream of breaking it before it became law, will take a delight in doing so simply to show their contempt, and because they consider it interferes with their rights. This was what happened in Toronto, and finally culminated in a most complete and over-whelming defeat to the party supporting it. Mr. Howland knew that he dare not face the electorate and ask for re-election a third time, but Mr. Elias Rogers was prevailed upon to do so by those who stood beside Mr. Howland, and a veritable Waterloo was the result to them, in spite of the fact that the prayers of the righteous were implored on behalf of their candidate. Had Mr. Rogers been opposed by the most unmitigated blackguard in Toronto, there can be no doubt that he would have been defeated, or elected by such a narrow majority that it would have been tantamount to defeat. The people were simply waiting an opportunity to rend them.

It is simply the repetition of history.

We are informed that the Puritans, when in the ascendant, had with an iron hand crushed down many amusements, the desire of which is a natural appetite of man, and thus created a hunger and a longing for the forbidden things, which became an unappeasable frenzy when the Restoration brought a change. The nation plunged madly into the opposite extreme. An utter absence of shame marked the mode of life in that most wicked age. The blush of innocence seemed almost forgotten in the court circles in England. Almost all the duties to God and man in the theatres were held up to public mockery. Virtue in every form especially truth and modesty came in for the comedian's jeering, and the loudest applause was brought forth from the audience by the triumph of the profligate and the ridicule cast upon the victims of his success.

On a lesser scale was the Puritanical rule exercised in Toronto. We did not have any such crazy names as "Praise God Barebones," or others equally ridiculous, but we had suppressing laws being introduced, and attempts made to carry them out. The populace were absolutely incensed, and the Government was ruthlessly overthrown, and justly so.

Mr. Edward F. Clarke was nominated by those who were opposed to this state of affairs, and it may be mentioned that he had the support of the News, which was, I believe, the only paper in the city supporting him, while Mr. Elias Rogers was the nominee af those who wished to see a continuance of Mayor Howland's policy. Arrayed on the side of Mr. Clarke were the leading business men of the city, and Professor Goldwin Smith moved his nomination.

The battle raged long and fiercely and was not without its humourous side as well. Aarrayed on either side were the forces of practical common sense, and on the other a sentiment to make people religious and moral by "Act of Council". Another element in the contest was a by-law reducing the number of licences, and the arguments used against Mr. Clarke were that if he were elected there would be no possibility of carrying this law into effect. It promised to be a rich harvest for the newspapers in the way of advertising The W.C.T.U. announced in black heavy heading letters "For God, Home and Country", that Mrs. Youmans would address the eleclors in such a place at such a time, and some Alliance made an equal if not more brilliant show. The other side carried on the warfare without this amount of advertising, but having the sympathies of the people their work had a lasting and radical effect. Mr. Clarke was elected, I believe, by nine hundred majority,

The first sign of open rebellion against the people who intended by act of council to keep an eye on the morals of the city came when Mr. Howland attempted to give effect to a by-law making it a misdemeanor to hire a horse on Sunday. The matter was brought into the courts, and when Mr. Clarke was elected it was allowed to drop. The city had become heartily sick of paying for legal services to give effect to the whims of Mr. Howland and his clique, and since that time we have had no such attempt to introduce radical measures for the purification of the common ruck. But those who were with Mr. Howland have attempted in various ways to bring in other restrictive legislation, and with most disastrous results. After two defeats a by-law permitting the running of street cars on Sunday has passed by a good substantial majority, and to-day we have Sunday street cars, where ten years ago, a man was prosecuted for letting out a horse on Sunday. Again it would appear, have the Righteous come to grief. The prayers of different people were asked that God might decree that the by-law should not carry. Apparently God did not take much heed of their prayers for the by-law carried. Coercing morality into people is pretty much like fighting a wolf. If you keep up the fight gradually and fire a shot into him occasionally, you will in the end succeed in killing him. But once you start to make too short work of him and drive him into a corner, then look out for squalls. He will turn and with the energy of madness destroy the man who might have killed him, had he been less in a hurry. Now there is to be another horror in store for Toronto. It is stated that the steamship companies are to run their boats on Sunday from Toronto to some American port. It may be not out of place for me to observe that on the first Sunday that cars ran in Toronto, the city survived the shock, and was not visited by any land slide, earthquake, or tornado, but seems to be in the same old place doing business as usual.

I am indebted to the kindness of Mr. R. T. Coady, City Treasurer, for the following figures :

MEMO OF ESTIMATES OF SALARIES, 1897.

CITY OF TORONTO.

Aldermen	$ 7,800
Assessment Department	14,340
Audit	2,950
Board of Control	2,800
City Clerk's Department	10,376
City Surveyor & Assistant	3,225
Court of Revision	1,500
Engineer's Department	20,000
Fire Department	109,665
Isolation Hospital	5,000
Jail	13,450
Law Department	13,300
License Receiving Office	760
Local Board of Health	15,820
Mayor	3,600
Mayor's Office	2,000
Messenger City	624
Parks and Gardens	2,025
Police Court Officers	8,572
Police Department	207,229
Property and Markets	11,585
Public Library	12,465
SCHOOLS, Collegiate Institutes...........$ 48,050	
Public Schools............ 353,114	
Separate Schools.......... 24,533	
Technical " 6,856	
	432,553
Tax Collectors	8,800

Treasurer's Department.. 19,200
Water Works—Rating and Revenue Branch, (under
    City Treasurer).. 22,647
Water Works Department, (under City Engineer)... 41,500

        Total..$993,786

For the year 1896 the receipts of the city from all sources, including the balance on hand at the beginning of the year, amounted to $7,336,710.92 and the disbursements to $5,559,633.24 leaving a balance on hand and in banks of $1,777,077.68, including $1,245,652.60 of Sinking Fund moneys. The statement of current assets and liabilities shows liabilities for the year $1,650,122.57 and assets $1,586,047.15 leaving a debit balance of $64,075.42.

TORONTO'S DEBENTURE DEBT.

The debenture debt of the city on 31st December, 1896, was as follows :—

General debenture debt.......................................$13,053,653.05
Local improvement debenture debt..................... 7,653,763.18
Toronto Railway... 1,067,328.57

        Total gross....................................$21,775,145.80

Deduct cash and debentures at credit of various sinking funds as follows:—

Cash...$1,245,652.60
City debentures, purchased with sinking fund
    money 3,672,330.44
Invested in Dominion of Canada stock............... 486.67

        Total...$4,918,469.71

Leaving a total net debenture debt of $16,856,676.09.

The value of property owned by the city is estimated at $12,000,000, exclusive of all public works and services of the city.

POLICE FORCE.

I am indebted to the courtesy of Lt. Col. Grassett, late the Prince of Wales Leinster Regiment, Chief Constable for his Annual Report for 1896, from which I take the following statistics relating to the force: There were 8,329 persons apprehended or summoned during the year, being 671 more than in 1895. Breaches of City By-laws represent 539 of the increase. Lost property shows a decrease of $4,570 and stolen property an increase of $9,017. The percentage of lost and stolen property recovered was $8,407 and $407 respectively—the difference in the latter being accounted for through identification being rendered impossible by melting plate, jewellery, etc., and by disposing of goods outside the city.

OF TORONTO THE GOOD.

DETECTIVE DEPARTMENT.

The records of the criminal cases dealt with by this Department, taken as a whole, show an increase of 151 over those of 1895, but as petty larceny represents an excess of 140, the more serious offences total about the same.

COMPARATIVE STATEMENT.

Nature of Offence.	1895.	1896.	Increase.	Decrease.
Murder..	7	4	......	3
Burglary	32	26	......	6
House-breaking	188	189	1	......
Highway robbery	13	13	......	......
Pocket picking	80	100	20	......
Horse stealing	4	3	......	1
Larceny	1,423	1,563	140	......
Total	1,747	1,898	161	10
Miscellaneous cases attended to	2,690	2,636	......	54
Occurrences reported	4,430	4,530	100	......
Committals for felonies	798	799	1	......
Value of property recovered,	$18,252	$15,436	......	$2,812
Arrests made	667	734	67	......

MURDER.

The four cases under this heading comprise, two of infanticide by persons unknown, one of a man who killed another and was acquitted by a jury on the grounds of self-defence, and the fourth a jockey who died from the effects of a murderous assault committed for the purpose of robbery. All hope has not yet been abandoned of placing the suspected parties on their trial for this crime.

In addition to the foregoing there occured three instances of manslaughter. One caused by a fall on the street due to a collision with two unknown men; another a fratricide of which the accused was acquitted, and for the third a man awaits trial.

BURGLARY.

There were six fewer cases of burglarious entry reported than in 1895, and the amount stolen, apart from the large sum obtained by the thieves at the Toronto University, was rather under that of the previous year. In one instance the burglar resorted to firearms to effect his escape.

HOUSEBREAKING.

The number of reports classified under this heading are about the same as in the preceding twelve months, but the loss sustained was larger by $900.00. Nearly all the men who committed most of these depredations were eventually arrested and are now in prison.

OF TORONTO THE GOOD.

HIGHWAY ROBBERY.

While the number of cases was the same this year as last, the amount stolen was larger, nearly all of which came from the pockets of drunken persons.

POCKET PICKING.

This class of offence being easy to commit and difficult to detect has been on the increase, and the pecuniary success attending those engaging in this sort of thieving is represented by $1,571 in cash, as compared with $935 in 1895.

Out of 100 instances reported, 25 occurred in the streets, the remaining 75 in places of public resort, such as shops, churches, markets, etc.

LARCENY.

A considerable increase is to be noticed under this head both in the number of cases and the amount stolen, the figures respectively being 120 and $5,238. They cover thefts of infinite variety, the new code classification being more comprehensive than the old.

CHANGES IN THE DEPARTMENT.

	Chief Constable.	Deputy Chief Constable.	Staff Inspector.	Inspector of Detectives.	Inspectors.	Sergeants.	Patrol Sergeants.	Detectives.	Acting Detectives.	Constables.	Total.
Remaining last year..	1	1	1	1	6	15	12	6	4	219	266
Appointed during year.							1	6			
Retired on pension							1				
Dismissed.										3	
Resigned								1		3	
Remaining	1	1	1	1	6	15	16	6	4	207	258

Appended is the usual statement of receipts and expenditure taken from the books kept in the Orderly Room.

	Estimate.	Expenditure.
Salaries	$206,948 05	$204,741 54
Clothing and equipment	8,051 71	7,578 14
Miscellanous sundries	6,833 00	4,736 40
Ambulance service	1,115 50	991 56
Mounted service	1,485 00	1,260 13
Patrol wagon and signal service..	4,314 50	4,029 08
Van service	442 00	449 18
	$229,189 76	$223,786 03
	$223,786 03	
Balance	$ 5,403 73	

STAFF INSPECTOR'S DEPARTMENT.

The reports received and attended to by this Department are recorded as 2,439, being 26 less than in 1895. The cases brought into the Court were as under :—

	1895	1896	Fines Imposed. 1895	1896
Houses of ill-fame	46	45	......	......
Disorderly houses	36	56	$ 140	$ 315
Liquor cases	74	87	1,345	1,763
Cruelty to animals	139	118	326	276
Miscellaneous	369	444	801	282
Total	687	750	$2,612	$2,636

HOUSES OF ILL-FAME.

While houses of ill-fame with regular inmates are not more in evidence than they were a year ago, loose women have scattered themselves about, living in rooms where they can receive men without police interference, often to the annoyance of the more respectable neighbors, who object to their presence, and desire their removal. The police, however, find it no easy matter to deal effectively with this class of persons. Enticing men from windows and doorways, being safer than solicitation on the streets, has been resorted to in some localities.

GAMBLING.

If gambling is carried on with the usual outfit and equipment necessary for the purpose and in rooms accessible to anyone who wants to join in a game, the police claim to be unaware of the fact. Two raffles, two lotteries, some Chinese playing fan-tan on Sunday, and boys shooting craps in the streets, include all the cases before the Court under this heading.

LIQUOR CASES.

The returns show a slight decrease in the number of prosecutions for a violation of the Licence Law. The result has been, no doubt, contributed to by the granting of a license at the Island. The illicit sale of liquor there has almost ceased. There has been no relaxation in the efforts of the Department to enforce observance of the law.

CHARGES AGAINST MEMBERS OF THE FORCE.

2 Constables were Absent from duty without leave........Dismissed.
2   "   "   "   "   "   " ....Fined.
1   "   "   "   "   "   " ....Admonished.
1   "   "   Assaulting a comrade..................Fined.
1   "   "   "   citizen .... "
2   "   "   Allowing a prisoner to escape.......... "
1   "   "   Being found coming out of a brewery
                           while on duty..................... "
1   "   "   Being found coming out of a licensed
                           hotel while on duty...............Reduced.
1   "   "   Being found coming out of a licensed
                           hotel while on duty...............Fined.
1   "   "   Borrowing money from a hotel-keeper... "

1 Sergeant	for	Intoxication	Severely reprimanded.
1 Constable	"	"	Admonished.
5 "	"	"	Fined.
1 "	"	Making false statements to a superior officer	Dismissed.
9 "	"	Neglect of duty	Fined.
2 "	"	"	Admonished.
1 "	"	"	Allowed to resign.
1 "	"	Neglecting to report important information communicated to him by a citizen	Reduced.
1 "	"	Soliciting money for services at a cricket match	Fined.
22 "	"	Violation of the Rules and Regulations of the Police Department	"
14 "	"	Violation of the Rules and Regulations of the Police Department	Admonished.
1 "	"	Violation of the Rules and Regulations of the Police Department	Allowed to resign.

The city is governed in police matters by three commissioners, the Police Magistrate, the Mayor, and the County Judge, but any complaint against the force is made to the chief constable, and investigated by the commissioners, who also deal with the officers offending, or who are to receive any special mark of approbation.

Besides having a sure thing in the way of their pay, the police seem to have the privilege of doing other work besides, as will be seen by the following correspondence :

SIR,—Can you give the public any information how it is that the police of this city are allowed to take contracts when they are off duty? I think they get enough without taking the bread out of the mouths of the poor mechanics. I have seen two of them shingling houses in St. John's ward more than once. I think the sooner it is stopped the better. If they are not satisfied with their pay why not leave like men ?—Fair Play and Justice.

The correspondent in his communication directs attention to a matter that should receive the prompt attention of the Chief constable and the Board of Police Commissioners. It should be fully investigated. The constables referred to in the latter are said to be two brothers named Tripp, one of whom has only recently joined the force, who, if they are doing the work, are guilty of violating one of the regulations of the police department. The regulations in question prohibit members of the force from engaging in any business, either themselves or their wives. The regulations strictly define that a constable is required to devote his whole time to his business as a policeman. If he engages in any other employment he should be held accountable to the Board of Police Commissioners for insubordination and breach of discipline. It is no secret that not a few constables do not scruple to carry on speculations and operations in real estate while they are supposed to be doing their duty. The matter affords the Board a wide scope for an investigation, whereby they might easily ascertain just how many, if any, members of the force are growing wealthy by side dealings in real estate, and how many of them practically carry on profitable real estate agencies.

While there is a bare possibility that some salutary reforms may be made, it is safe to say that the probabilities are very remote. In the following observations given by different people, it will be seen that one man makes the charges that Staff Inspector Archibald has appealed to religious bodies and has been able thereby to perpetuate the system. In his address to the electors in his first campaign, Mr. Fleming is reported as saying :

I want to say a word about our heavy police expenses. Now do not misunderstand me. I am not criticising our policemen. I believe, and I do not say this for any other purpose but of fairly giving credit where credit is due, I believe there is not another force on this continent that will compare with ours.

A voice—At drinking lager.

Mr. Fleming—No, I do not think there is a force of men in America who drink as little lager as our police. Neither is there a lot of policemen who as seldom enter a saloon. (Laughter). No, they are a sober lot of men.

A voice—What about Archibald and his Morality Department.

Mr. Fleming—When I become Mayor I will investigate that. Now I do not think we ought to have so many drunks at the police court. Arresting a man when he is simply drunk, when he is walking quietly home never does any good. It swells the number of cases. It gives our police court needless work. It often causes the unfortunate offender to lose more time than he would have lost if he had been allowed to go home and get to work the next morning. Then his suffering family suffer still more. It gives our city a worse name than it really deserves, and it never does the arrested man a particle of good. You never knew one dollar and costs to cure one single case of drunkenness. The shame of the police court often does incalculable harm to the man who has been overtaken by his evil appetite, that after all, our present social customs and laws really foster. As a rule the first offender, after spending his night in the cells, among thieves and hardened characters, alter the anxiety caused by his absence from home, after the loss of his half day, and the humiliation of the police court, simply has his case dismissed. I think that if it is necessary sometimes to arrest a man who is helpless, for his own protection, the inspector of the station could very well be empowered to record his arrest and set him at liberty when he gets sober. Mind, I am not advocating leniency with hardened drunkards, I am simply pointing out the fact that we are wasting time and money, and badgering citizens, with no benefit to anyone and with positive injury in many cases. (Loud applause). Then we have too many police court case of violation of city by-laws. I think laws ought to be enforced and respected, but it is pretty hard to see the city with such disgracefully dirty streets as some of our leading thoroughfares are to-day, prosecuting citizens who have not had sunlight enough to melt a little snowfall off his sidewalk before ten o'clock in the morning, or whose cow has committed the unpardonable offence of grazing for a few minutes on a vacant lot, at the storekeeper whose barrel of apples has stuck out an inch and a half too far on the sidewalks. Laws should be made to protect us, not to worry us. Policemen should be for our protection, not our annoyance. I want to see a little less expenditure of public money, and a little more use of common sense. (Loud applause).

At a public meeting the Rev. Father Geoghegan, of Hamilton, seconded a resolution in a speech pregnant with valuable ideas on the subject of juvenile treatment, and in the course of his remarks said :

Our policemen don't put themselves out to treat our boys with ordinary decency. I have seen policemen on Saturday night who could not notice men coming out of the side door of a saloon, run at a lad who was catching a ball on the street, and threaten him with arrest. But the boys had no votes which could control the aldermen who put the coat on the policeman's back, while the bar-room loafers had. At this there was great applause.

In support of the contention of the Rev. gentleman, a case occurs which is somewhat analogous, and demonstrates the difficulties civilians have in maintaining their rights. The newspaper report says :

Inspector Stephen, of No. 1 Police Division is engaged in investigating a charge against P. C. Duncan (145) of having committed an assault on a young man named Wm. Robinson, of 72 Gerrard street, west. Robinson states that he was standing near Hubbard's livery stable on Nelson street, in company with a friend when Duncan addressed him in an ungentlemanly manner, and afterwards struck him three or four blows in the face leaving bruises there. He states that he and his friend were returning from a party at Brock avenue, and in this way accounts for his presence on the street at that early hour of the morning. Duncan gives his version of the affair as follows : Robinson and his companion had knocked at the door of a disreputable house at No. 16 Nelson street He was on special duty watching the place He admits speaking to them, but denies having used any insulting language. Robinson clutched him by the arm, and all the force he used was only necessary to loosen his hold. The Inspector will make his report to the Chief Constable, who will likely refer it to the Board of Police Commissioners.

On the following day the same paper said in connection with this case :

Among the members of the police force there is considerable speculation being indulged in regard to the complaint that a young man preferred against P. C. Duncan. He alleges that Dnncan assaulted him and made a statement of the occurrence just as it transpired, to Inspector Stephen the day following. That report has not yet been forwarded to the Chief Constable by Mr. Stephen, and some of the constables are wondering if the Inspector has taken upon himself the authority of relegating it to the waste paper basket because the accused constable is one of his "pets" and likewise a countryman. The young man felt that he was harshly treated by the constable, and he does not intend to allow the matter to drop without being inquired into. In strange contrast another case is pointed out. P. C. Duncan made a trifling complaint against P. C. Childs (11), and Inspector Stephen forwarded his report on that case to Lieut.-Col. Grassett before the ink was dry on it. It appears that the young man who claims to have been assaulted by Duncan met Childs a few minutes later. He appealed to Childs for information, and the latter very properly advised him to report Duncan to his superior officers. Duncan and Childs had an exchange of compliments, in the course of which he called Duncan a "pet", or something like that. For this he is to be carpeted. Meanwhile, Duncan is not even reported.

Now let the reader for one moment contrast the treatment a civilian receives with the treatment a policeman receives if the former happens to be the culprit. The following is the newspaper report of an incident that will illustrate my meaning.

P. C. William Allan (184) was the victim of an unusually brutal assault at the hands of a gang of rowdies. He was patrolling his beat on River street, when two brothers named John and George O'Connell came together down River street. They were both apparently under the influence of liquor, John being very noisy, and using profane language. Allan arrested John when the brother interfered. Both men peeled off their coats, and proceeded to pound him with their fists and feet. George wrested the baton from the officer's grasp, and beat him with it, it is alleged, until his face was frightfully battered beyond recognition and frightfully disfigured. Allan struggled desperately with his assailants but they were assisted by a third man who came along. Allan was found in an almost unconscious condition by some neighb urs who came to render him assistance. The rowdies levanted as the newcomers approached, but later on George O'Connell was arrested. Allan was reported to be in a serious condition, so the prisoner was remanded for a week on the charge of assaulting the constable, bail being fixed in two sureties in $500 oo each

The above is the aspect of the case as first reported, and presented before the police court. The young men had the courage of their convictions, and carried it to the county court, and though I tried to get a copy of the actual judgment, I failed to do so, but I give you the following remarks from the Telegram on the subject :

The jury that judged between policeman Allan and his assailants are a credit to the city of Toronto and the county of York. It acquitted the innocent, convicted the guilty, and censured an officer who was summarily punished by the broken head that was the dividend he received for a large share in the authorship of the original scuffle. Their Honours the Commissioners assume that an officer, if infallible. They seldom chide the officious constable. This tolerance encourages tyranny and brutality, and finally uniformed bullies come to grief in the Assize court, where the common sense of a judge and jury affords the protection to the humlest of her Majesty's lieges !

The above will bear comparison with the following case, which still further shows the difficulties the public are compelled to contend against, in as much as the city seems to be compelled to defend a policeman, guilty or not guilty, and the other fellow must pay his own lawyer. It would seem only reasonable that both should be on terms of equality, if that were possible, in a case of this kind.

Wm. and Robert O'Reilly are brothers living on Power street. They were arrested by policeman John Welsh on Berkeley street, on a charge of being disorderly. They were put into the patrol waggon, handcuffed, put into the cells at No. 4, in a cold fireless room. The next morning the Magistrate discharged them after hearing the officer's statement, and they sued the policeman for $1000 damages for false arrest, cruel treatment and false imprisonment. Dr. Nattrass swore that he found Robert's back and ribs injured, which injuries, the boy swore were inflicted by Welsh jumping upon him with his knees. Charles Quinn, Patrick Milligan, John O'Donnell and Maggie O'Reilly told the story of the arrest in corroboration of the brothers' evidence. Officer Welsh said that Quinn and two other young men were acting as if drunk and used obscene language to him; Quinn struck at the officer who ran to arrest him, but he escaped; then he met Wm. O'Reilly, who was drunk and refused to give the officer his name; he was arrested for the refusal. Meanwhile Robert came up and interfered, when he, too, was arrested. In the westle both fell, and he did not jump upon the boy intentionally. One of the police regulations demands that any person who refuses to give his name may be arrested. Mr. Holmes who prosecuted the case said:

"Things have come to a pretty pass in this city if its citizens are to be treated in this way."

Judge Falconbridge very particularly enquired of Mr. Biggar who defended Welsh, by what authority these regulations were passed. The Solicitor thought by the municipal Act, but was not sure. Upon this point the doughty barrister got in a noted objection. In order to test the credibility of a witness Mr. Biggar asked him if he was not once in the dock on a serious charge, and what the charge was. The judge told the witness he need not answer unless he chose to do so; there was no truth in the charge. Constable O'Brien, one of the men who came with the waggon, said he handcuffed the boys by Welsh's order. Mr. Biggar argued against submission to the jury, but it went there.

A letter from Mr. Holmes to me said the verdict was for the plaintiff, county court costs set-off.

Again the following case is demonstrative that a purely vindictive spirit actuates the force in dealing with culprits:

P. C. Weston had a boy named John Connors before the court for drunkenness and having hit him on the head with a bottle. Mr. Baxter not having jurisdiction to try the assault case, a suggestion from the Deputy Chief that his Worship should deal out sufficient punishment to Connors on the drunkenness charge was acted upon. After hearing the evidence and learning that Conners had received a scalp wound from contact with the peeler's baton, Mr. Baxter imposed a fine of $3 and costs or 30 days. The Deputy Chief then said that he thought he would have to prefer the charge of assaulting Weston against Conners.

Mr. Baxter—But you led me to understand that both offences were to be dealt with at once.

The Deputy—So I did, but that small fine don't suit me

Mr. Baxter—I won't allow you sir, to criticise my rulings.

The Deputy—I want to lay the second charge.

Mr. Baxter—You can do that, of course, but it all goes to show that each case should stand on its own bottom. As you intend to swear to that other information, I will make the fine $1, or 30 days. Conners was remanded for a week on the assault case.

Of this Deputy Chief the Toronto News says:

The burglar who escaped from the cells at Police Headquarters pried his way out with a crowbar, but the entire staff armed with crowbars could not pry the deputy chief from the well paid job he fills so muchly that he overflows into judicial duties.

The following is another case of police espionage, and shows that where the defendant has the courage and the money to go on with his case, he will generally come out on top, and will be a cause for rejoicing to those who like to see every one get British fair play, and in striking contrast to the above case, where the Deputy Chief seemed to think that where the defendant was a common civilian and the punishment meted out was not a sufficient vindication of the majesty of the force he must institute another charge against the defendant. The following is taken from the Telegram:

James H. Bailey, the young man whose mother alleges that the boy was induced to plead guilty to a charge of criminal assault on Maudie Tyerell, a girl under the age of 14, by the representations of Detective Watson, is happy to-night. The details of this case are well known. Detective Watson, it is alleged, went to arrest the boy on the above charge, and told the lad and his mother that a conviction was sure, and that the sentence would be severe. It is also charged that the detective promised that if the boy pleaded guilty he would be let off, while if a plea of not guilty was entered the punishment would be terrible. These affidavits are attested by the affidavit of the prisoner and the prisoner's mother, while the circumstances of the case strongly indicate that such a promise was made by the detective. The boy pleaded guilty and the Magistrate sentenced him to five years at Kingston and 15 lashes. A certiorari was granted with a view towards quashing the conviction, and it was returnable before the common pleas divisional court over which Chief Justice Galt and Justice MacMahon presided. Mr. Holmes appeared on behalf of the prisoner. Mr. Cartwright, Q.C., Deputy Attorney-General sent word that the case was one which the crown deemed unworthy of their defending, consequently the conviction was undefended. Mr. Holmes read the affidavits and briefly outlined the case, whereupon Chief Juctice Galt said that the conviction of the boy Bailey was one of the most outrageous proceedings he had ever heard of.

"I am ready," he said " to issue a peremptory order quashing the conviction and restoring the boy to liberty at once."

"I concur," said Justice MacMahon.

The papers were immediately drawn up and signed by the judge annulling the conviction and setting aside Magistrate Denison's warrant of commitment. Afterwards the judges issued an order of protection to Magistrate Denison and detective Watson to shield them from an action for damages for false arrest, malicious prosecution, conspiracy &c.

The above decision will strike the averge reader as being in every respect a just one. In commenting upon it, the Telegram says:

One of the worst of Colonel Denison's judgments was reversed yesterday by their Lordships Chief Justice Galt, and Justice MacMahon. Their decision set a boy at liberty after a confinement of more than five months and saved him from spending five years in the penitentiary and enduring fifteen lashes. Seldom has there been on record a case that better illustrated the inhumanity of some detectives and the off-hand methods of Col. Denison. The boy was taken from his mother's house late one night He left behind him the assurance that everything was all right and that he would return in the morning. The next day the poor simpleton pleaded guilty. He was not allowed time to consult his mother, and the Magistrate sentenced him to five years in the penitentiary and fifteen lashes. The arrest, the trial; the conviction, the sentence were all alike disgraceful. Detective Watson must have urged the boy to plead guilty. Either under the pressure of advice from the detectives or in ignorance as to the nature of the offence, the prisoner admitted guilt. Surely it was Colonel Denison's business to warn the culprit that his plea wrecked all chance of liberty. But no. The detective was there to secure credit of a conviction, and the Magistrate was there to fill the penitentiary Why should they pause ? It only takes the court about three minutes to sentence a man to penitentiary for five years. It takes the man somewhat longer to serve the term. Fortunately for him the boy had a mother who was not too poor to retain J. G. Holmes. The lawyer made a good fight and finally freed the prisoner. There may be other boys sent to penitentiary under similar circumstances, who having no money to right the wrong are suffering the injustice done to them by a high-pressure police Magistrate. Colonel Denison is generally right, but the case in point is proof that he is not above trifling away a prisoner's liberty and ruining his life in order that he may get through the day's work before eleven a.m.

In the above case it must strike the average beholder that if Detective Watson possessed the first iota of manhood, he would have given the Magistrate to understand that it was through his instrumentality that the boy pleaded guilty, but it is only one more of my contentions that he who is able to fight his battle in a higher court will always come out with justice.

A correspondent of the Telegram, who had received a courteous reception from some of the officers, considered it such a remarkable occurrence that he felt that he must advertise it, and writes as follows, under the heading of "A rara avis indeed."

SIR,—You often and very justly find fault with the police of Toronto for their incivility to the public, but I want to say a word in their favour. To-day I went to the police station at St. Andrew's market to ask a question The se-geant on duty, a fine, well-built, red whiskered man, answered me so politely and kindly and gave me all the information I wanted in such a nice, pleasant and gentlemanly manner, that I feel that I ought to let it be known publicly, and show that not all of the police force are rude to the public. W.S.H.

Immediately after the election of Mayor Fleming, and when it was thought that a change would be made in the Morality Department the Telegram published the following:

> Hatred of what its name implies inspires much of the so-called hostility to the Morality Department. The outcry against it was started by rogues who are pinched by its vigilance. Their howls finally deceived respectable citizens into the belief that Inspector Archibald was an ogre at the head of the branch of the pnblic service especially designed for the protection of vice and the oppression of virtue. The truth is that the Department in question is the least expensive and the most humane branch of the police service. It pays for its support many times over in the penalties that might but for it never be enforced. How many children have been shielded from cruel parents and brutal guardians by its kindly interference the secret records could tell. Its officers have been content to go on quietly doing their duty and their silence has been misinterpreted as assent to the abuse that has been heaped upon the department. The crusade has gone far enough, and it is time for those whose sympathies are on the right side to speak a word for honest men who have fearlessly done their duty.

I do not for one moment doubt the sincerity of these remarks on the part of the Telegram, but I do emphatically question their truthfulness. From the character of the Staff Inspector I do not think he is the man to allow his light to be hidden under a bushel, and were there any such cases as those mentioned by the Telegram, I think the public would be made aware of them in some manner. It may perhaps be stated that I am one of those who are pinched by its vigilance, and without denying the trnth of the statement, I think I may consistently and truthfully say that there can be no such imputation laid to the door of the Hon. Mr. Meredith, who from his place in the House said:

> My attention had been called to the fact that the law and Order Society of Toronto had been discussing the morality department of Toronto, and passing resolutions eulogistic of the department. Mr. Archibald, the officer of this department, and Mr. Curry, the Crown Attorney had attended the meetings of this society and had frequently spoken there. I do not think this is a proper course for public officers to pursue. They should not be partizans nor attend any meetings, nor speak at them where they might become prejudiced. (Cheers). How would the Attorney General like to see Judges attending such meetings? Would it notbias their minds against prisoners who might come before them? These officers had no right to identify themselves with any such society and he wished to call the attention of the Government to the fact.
> Mr. Mowat said he had not heard of the matter before, but that he would look into it.

Mr. Meredith seems not to be alone in his opinion of the morality department, for in the course of an address at a meeting of the Ratepayers Association, Mr. R. Reynolds said:

> The Morality department is too costly an affair. It should be abolished, but Inspector Archibald and others, by appeals to religious bodies had secured sufficient influence to perpetuate the system. Only a few days ago Inspector Archibald in the excess of his zeal had arrested an innocent young man. There was far too much anxiety in the morality department to make out cases. The ordinary police could do all the work, just as effectually, and at less expenses. A most disgraceful affair had been reported of the efforts in New York of the moralists to amend morals. A clergyman and two of his deacons had under disguise bribed women to commit a sin. Any man who by a bribe tempted another to commit a sin no matter for what end, was equally guilty as the person tempted. (Applause), and Rev. Dr. Parkhurst had proved himself to be a low dirty blackguard, unfit to occupy a Christian pulpit. He had degraded himself and his calling in making terms with unfortunate girls. As far as Toronto was concerned they had heard a great deal about the so-called morality department, but who had ever seen any report from it? All they knew about it was from newspaper reports. It was a fact that in spite of that department *there were in the city to-day more unlicensed whiskey dives, more gambling dens, more houses of ill-fame than ever before.* The department was not worth the money spent on it.

If the public were given a fair field upon which to fight there would, peihaps, not be such cause for complaint. If a person is arrested, and then found innocent, he has no ground for damages, notwithstanding the fact that his character may be ruined by the arrest. The following cases will clearly demonstrate my meaning, and I leave the decision with the public as to the justice of giving such advantages to the police as they possess :

Counsel on behalf of the plaintiff in the case of Thomas Humphrey vs. Morality Inspector Archibald, Detective Charles Slemin and Walter Duncan made an application before the Master in Chambers to disclose the name of the person upon whose information he acted in arresting the plaintiff. This was followed by a second application to compel the inspector to attend for examination at his own expense. Humphrey, it will be remembered, it is the young man who was arrested for committing rape on Miss Agnes Barnes. The girl could not give the inspector a minute description of her assailant, but could only say that he had a small light mustache, drove a Gladstone rig, and lived with his father on Spadina avenue. This information, it was shown this morning was turned over to detective Slemin who failed in his attempt to find out anything further until one evening while standing on the rear of a Spadina avenue car he heard two men talking. From this piece of eaves-dropping he heard that this young man, Thomas H. Humphrey, had got into trouble with a girl and had skipped to the United States. Humphrey was promptly arrested, and in his defense showed that from the 23rd of April until December 12th, he was in the States, and on the very day when the offence was alleged to have been committed he was in Detroit. After a lengthy argument between Mr. J. G. Holmes and Mr. Mowat, the Master in Chambers ruled that it would be a great injustice to the police department.

Duncan and Margaret McLaren vs. Staff Inspector David Archibald.—This was an appeal by the defendant from an order of the action, the plaintiff having been three times non-suited at the Toronto assizes. Originally the action was brought against Inspector Archibald to recover $10.000 damages for false arrest, malicious prosecution and for trespass, McLaren and his wife having been arrested on a charge of keeping a house of ill-fame, but not convicted. The most notable non-suit of this action was by Chief Justice Armour who in very forcible language deprecated the action of the police in accepting the information of a woman about town upon the strength of which the raid upon McLaren's house was made. Each time the plaintiff has been non-suited he has moved for a new trial and each time has succeeded in setting aside the non-suit and obtaining the new trial. The fourth order for a new trial is the one now appealed against. Justices Hagarty and Osler dismissed the appeal, while Justices Burton and MacLennan allowed it. The court being thus evenly divided the appeal stands dismissed, and the action goes to trial again, in accordance with the judgment of the common pleas division court. In giving judgment on the above action Chief Justice Haggarty said:

"While we are sitting here as judges we cannot forget we are citizens of Toronto, and it was with great surprise that we learned the city was defending Inspector David Archibald. *To my mind it is the most disgraceful piece of presumption ever brought under the notice of this court.* I hope some person interested will enquire into this matter, and see if it is the general practice for the citizens to bear the expense of defending actions brought against individuals who may happen to be in their employ."

I do not think the public will be disposed the insinuate that Chief Justice Hagarty has any personal object in speaking as he did on the subject, and his remarks therefore, carry that much more weight. If contestants were to meet upon free and equal grounds there would be no such cause for complaint, but to see the city screening men who are palpably in the wrong, is a gross mis-carriage of justice.

Their interference with the public became such an aggravation that the following is taken from a city paper:

"The police interfere with the public enough already," Col. Denison remarked from the bench, as he was actively engaged in combatting the combined efforts of Mr. Curry and Staff Inspector Archibald to persuade him that certain authority was vested in the force that he was convinced did not really exist. Patrol Sergeant Robinson and P. C. Kennedy visited the cigar store kept by Alfred Beatty at No. 12 Queen street east, to search for liquor. There was no interference by the proprietor of the store, but when the officers wanted to enter the premises adjoining the store, Mr. Beatty demanded a warrant.

"I have none," replied the patrol sergeant.

"Then you cannot proceed any further," said Beatty, as he barred the door.

The police magistrate was asked to determine whether or not Beatty was guilty of obstructing the policeman in the performance of his duty. He decided the question adversely to the police on all points referred to him. By his judgment a cigar store is not a place of public entertainment, that 10 o'clock at night is not a reasonable time to make an inspection, that the by-law only empowers an inspection of the shop, and a search of the premises other than the shop cannot be made without a warrant. During the argument his Worship intimated that a by-law of the city could not override a federal statute regarding a search for gambling, and was, therefore, really impracticable. In illustrating his views the Magistrate asked if it was reasonable to infer that because a man kept a licensed bowling alley, billiard parlor or roller skating rink the mere fact of that license would empower the police to run all over his premises and break open. They must confine themselves, he said, to the place actually licensed.

Mr. Curry—Well, one thing can be come. The license department can be asked to cancel defendant's license.

The Magistrate—What has he done to warrant that? Should his license be cancelled because he has been acquitted, simply having stood on his rights? The case was marked dismissed.

The following case is clipped from the Empire :

Another serious blunder has been made by the officials of the morality department, and the mistake has been the cause of the arrest of a highly respectable young man on a very serious charge. Some days ago a little girl named Maggie Colestock went to the staff inspector's department and laid a charge of criminal assault. Charles Goodman was taken into custody and accused of the crime, but Inspector Archibald was surprised to find that he had made a mistake, having arrested the wrong man. Goodman was immediately discharged the Magistrate remarking that, he should never have been arrested.

The cause for complaint against the Police Force seems to date beyond all recollection. If you will go back to the Globe and consult it at the time that Messrs Bunting, Meek and others were indicted for conspiracy, you will read as fellows :

UNCIVIL AS USUAL.

It would seems from the behaviour of some of the members of the Toronto police force that it is part of their duty to be as uncivil as possible, and this impression has certainly been strengthened during the conspiracy investigation concluded at the police court yesterday. Soon after Mr. Kirkland came into court to hear the judgment of the magistrate, he felt faint and asked a policeman to get him a chair. He was roughly told that there was no chair for him, and he was obliged to stand until he finally fall on the floor exhausted.

In preparing the above cases against the police force, it may perhaps be stated that I have given them from a prejudicial standpoint, and to such a possible accusation, I am ready to acknowledge that it is perfectly true. The personal experience I give you below has been so salutary a lesson to me, that I say with perfect truth that if it were in my power to rescue a squad of policemen whose lives were in danger I would decline to do it, although I would not go so far as to say that I would like to see them in such position, yet I feel that a more contemptible set of ruffians never donned a uniform. Some years ago a young fellow of eighteen or thereabouts came to Toronto to see the Exhibition, and during his stay he wandered down to the union station to see if anyone came in by the train from his home, whom he knew. While walking up and down the patform, Mr. Smart Policeman grabbed him and on suspicion of his being a pickpocket or something else equally definite, took him into the water closet, and searched him, finding nothing of course.

"Now," said the illustrious guardian of the law, "clear out of this and don't let me see you again."

Outraged and humiliated the lad got out as quickly as possible but he had the good sense to make known his grievance where the effect would be salutary. He went to the Mail office and informed one of the reporters, who believed his story. He told how he had been insulted and disgraced before the crowd at the Union station, and the next morning the Mail contained an article on the subject. This had the effect of bringing the matter before the Police Chief. Unfortunately, however, the young man was obliged to return to his home before any investigation could take place, though the Chief asked him, I believe to remain. In relation to this case, I would like to ask. "What redress could the young man get?" Really none. By-laws innumerable are framed for the protection of the force, but the public who pay them must take their chances in cases of this kind. A city by-law we are informed by Mr. Biggar permits a policeman to arrest a man if he does not give his name.

It is still fresh in the minds of the people of Toronto how Rev. W. F. Wilson was outraged by one of the force, and how throughout the whole proceedings he was worsted in every court to which the case was carried, until finally he was refunded his costs by the council.

It is a matter that may fairly be stated that if the policemen were the immaculate guardians they are anxious to have the public believe they are, there might be some excuse for these outrages being perpetrated, but they are not.

I have seen men—proprietors of saloons present members of the force with something (likely water) in bottles quite frequently. The manner in which it is done is quite amusing. The landlord would stand at the door with his hands at his back, and look carefully up and down. By and bye a big policeman would loom up in the distance, and when the time was propitious the bottle would be handed to the stalwart guardian of the law. This isn't hearsay evidence either, it is what I saw myself, and while it would serve no good purpose to tell the name of this particular man, I may say that if anyone thinks himself aggrieved he might enter a suit for libel, and I will give the names with pleasure.

Some years ago some little lads were playing near some one of the wharves, and as it is contrary for some one of the multifarious by-laws of the city regulating boys, a policeman ordered them to come to him at once. As the hardened little wretches did not obey with sufficient alacrity and also had the supreme hardihood to smile at the majesty of the law, the policeman shot one dead. Now the peculiarity of this case was the fact that this policeman was arrested, tried, and though a master effort was made by Mr. Nicholas Murphy, Q.C., to have him discharged, a jury really had the hardihood to convict him of manslaughter, and to this day, I am pleased to say he is doing penance in durance vile for his act, or if he isn't he ought to be, yet I believe some time ago an effort was made to have him released, a prayer that was not entertained by the Department of Justice, with their characteristic good sense.

For the benefit of the public I give my own personal experience, and all the particulars connected therewith. On a certain street, the name of which is not a necessary adjunct to this work is a kind of restaurant, where it is rumoured that in addition to the eating and drinking allowed by law, there can also be obtained the drink not allowed by law. One Sunday night passing down this street, I had the good fortune or otherwise to see two policemen enter this place. The first one entered the door, and passed in, while the other took out a little book and made some entry therein, then making some remarks to the proprietress, also entered, and the three passed into some back room together. All this I saw myself, and the policemen remained there some eight or ten minutes. During the course of the evening I had passed through this street quite a number of times, and the officers had, doubtless seen me, and at midnight or perhaps a little later I passed down on one side of the street, while the two officers were coming up on the other. One of them crossed over, and demanded what my name, address and business were. I informed him very promptly that it was no concern of his.

"Here now," he exclaimed angrily, with a broad Scotch accent, "I want your name and address and yer business."

All of which information I declined to furnish.

"I want yer name and address now, or ye know the consequences," he again demanded in a passion. His voice, like his temper, was gradually rising to a high pitch that would have delighted an ambitious tenor singer.

"And I don't intend to give you either," I replied. "What right have you to stop me on the street like this? As a citizen of Toronto I claim the right to walk up and down any street in the city that I wish, and you have no right to intercept me as long as I am conducting myself properly. If I do wrong you have the right to arrest me, not otherwise."

However, he was inexorable, and again demanded my name and address, adding:

"Unless ye give it to me, I'll take ye to No. 2 station."

"On what charge?" I asked. "Vagrancy? That won't do, as I happen to have sufficient money on my person to pay my board for a month in the best hotel in the city."

Strange to say this latter remark was true.

"Do you know the character of the street you're on?" he asked. "Answer me that."

"I do perfectly well. I have been on this street scores of times and know it perfectly."

By this time he seemed to have grown out of patience, and demanded:

"Where are ye goin' now?"

"I'm on my way home, but I want you to understand that it is not that I met you that I am going."

"Well go on now. It's just such damned young toughs as you that makes the town what it is," and as I passed he made a pass at me with his closed fist.

Now that is the case exactly as it stands and and as it occurred.

I submit that if the policeman had any right to arrest me or even molest me, he would have taken me under arrest at once, but I am convinced that he was afraid that I had seen him and his friend going into the dive I have mentioned, and dared not face the consequences. Had they arrested me I should have certainly made known the circumstances I have just mentioned, but as it was I stated the case to the city editor of one of the city papers, who informed me that the policeman had no right so stop me on the street, and he strongly recommended me to make a formal complaint to the Commission, but my own reason dictated otherwise, feeling quite sure that I would have had my labour for my pains.

This view of mine is amply corroborated by the following from the Telegram:

> There are evil possibilities in this idea of allowing the police commissioners sitting in secret to cancel the license of a livery man who may, for reasons good or bad, be viewed with suspicion by the detectives. The experience of the average citizen who has had a difficulty between him and the police adjusted by the commissioners will not increase faith in the judgment of their worships. *The commission is a good deal of an automatic register for recording the decrees of our uniformed fellow citizens, whose word is often taken before the oath of citizens in plain clothes.* Too much officialism is a danger peculiar to this time. It is not well to give judicial powers to a body that is partisan in the sense that it is often on the side of the policeman and against the civilian. The possibility that thieves might be occasionally aided by a livery man is not a graver public danger than the probability that the commissioners may wrongfully cancel the license of a man who has given no just cause for complaint.

It is a matter of regret that those who are fined and imprisoned for taking their own part against the police of the city have not means to carry their cases to a higher court. If a judgment be given against them they will feel that it is just. If they receive judgment in their favour it will be for the same reason. The following case is one where the defendant had this courage, and received the just judgment of the court:

> The case of young Skeans against Inspector Stephen was resumed with Skeans in the box. He detailed the circumstances of his arrest, claiming that he should have been summoned. He testified that judge Macdougall when hearing the appeal, said that the Inspector exceeded his duty as a police officer by making the arrest when a summons would have answered. Arthur Crozier, the boy in the case, first witness for the defence, told how he and some others boys were throwing some banana skins, playing tag, swearing, etc., when Skeans came up, cuffed him, and kicked him in the stomach. Crozier swore that he, unlike Peck's bad boy, threw no sticks, broke no windows, fired "nothing at nobody", never annoyed the ticket agent at the wharf. The inspector testified that he saw Skeans knock Crozier down; Crozier swore that Skeans kicked, the boy cried, the officer arrested, a constable appeared, Skeans told who he was but the inspector thought it best to make the arrest, the constable escorted the young merchant, while the superior followed with the boy and the party went to No. 3. The boy received the full benefit of Skean's boot. Judge McDougall did not say that he (witness) exceeded his duty, though he thought a summons would have answered the purpose. Upon cross-examination the inspector said he didn't hear a policeman say that no other man on the force but himself would have made the arrest; neither would he swear that the boy didn't tell him he was badly hurt. Mr. Johnson put judge McDougall right the inspector said when Mr. Duvernet asked him if Mr. Johnson did not protest against the judge's censure of Stephen. Johnson defended, against the appeal in Judge McDougall's court. Charles Sheppard swore that the John Hanlan did not come to Brock street wharf that day; Crozier swore positively that it did. Sheppard is the ticket agent at the place Crozier was hitting gentleman with a stick and banana skins and swearing loudly. The jury returned a verdict giving $250.00 to Skeans.

It is circumstances of this nature that prejudice the public against the police force, and it is not too much to say that if a policeman gets into trouble and is likely to get overpowered, there is not one citizen in a dozen who would assist him voluntarily. I have seen men thrown into the patrol waggon by a policeman and if the prisoner lifted his head or perhaps did nothing at all he would find a pair of knees on his chest and he would be thoroughly belaboured until he was knocked into senselessness or reason. I have seen cases where the policemen have been hooted by a crowd of respectable citizens when they were putting some drunken wretch into the waggon, simply on account of their cruelty. To those who are too poor to employ counsel to fight their battles, it will be advisable to always submit to arrest whether you are guilty or not ; you are generally assumed to be guilty, and if you want any stronger evidence than my word refer to the cases of Allan or O'Reilly, and you will be convinced of the wisdon of my advice, and the judiciousness of complying with it, not to mention the possibility of being clubbed almost to death as in the case of O'Connor previously mentioned.

It will be remembered that the force on one night attempted to raid the house of one Lyons, and that the latter objected to be raided. So much so did he object that he was brought before the sessions charged with the crime of unlawfully attempting to shoot P. C. Wallace. Mr. Lyons, like the sensible man that he is fought it out in the court, and the following is the result, which confirms the advice given by me, that if you wish to secure your rights and are able to pay for getting them, make a fight for them, and the justice of the judge in charge will decide whether you are right or wrong :

When the general sessions opened Judge Macdougall proceeded to deliver judgment upon ob ections raised by Mr. DuVernet in behalf of Patrick Lyons charged with unlawfully attempting to shoot P. C. Wallace under circumstances already detailed. His honour dismissed the prisoner, holding that the search warrant under which Wallace was acting was invalid for two reasons. First, that the initials " J.P. " after the name of Hugh Miller did not properly designate that he was a justice of the peace, and duly qualified to issue the warrant, and second, that the face of the warrant did not represent that he was acting in the stead or at the written request of the Magistrate. "The warrant," said his honour, "is similar to the peculiar documents now being freely used by the police, and I feel bound to say that had Lyons shot the officer dead, he could not have been convicted of murder. The crime would not be more serious than manslaughter, because the officer was forcing an entrance at his peril with a bad warrant." Mr. Dewart requested his honour to reserve a case but the Crown attorney's request was not complied with.

I can only ascribe the tyranny of the police force to one cause. An overwhelming majority of them, knowing themselves to be the scum that they are, are aware that the only chance they have of speaking to a gentleman is to tell him to "move on," or to associate with one is to arrest him, seize upon every pretext to do either one or the other not knowing how long it will be before another opportunity presents itself. I have lived in Buffalo, Ottawa, Montreal and different American cities and I found the police in these cities at least gentlemanly.

I have given you these circumstances to demonstrate the truthfulness of my remarks, and I think anyone imbued with the first elements of justice will admit the reasonableness of my contention that there is very little chance of justice being done in the present condition of things. Take an as example the McLaren case against the staff inspector. A woman about town gives information and the house occupied by these people is raided, and they were not convicted. Disgraced beyond all chance of redemption, they seek for redress, and what a sarcasm it is on institutions that are visionarily democratic. This family sue the inspector for damages, and are compelled to employ counsel at a very great expense to themselves, while the inspector who happens to be employed by the city is defended by the city solicitor who is paid by the taxes from these people, when in all justice it would seem that he should be compelled to pay his own counsel. While it may be argued that it did not require much ability to fight the city solicitor's department, Mr. Justice Hagarty nevertheless, expressed himself in language that will receive pretty general commendation everywhere else where British fair play is appreciated.

Time, however that sovereign balm for all human sufferings, may perhaps assist us. It is a remarkably pregnant portion of ancient history, where holy write assures us that Providence having permitted his chosen people to be oppressed by the Egyptians for centuries, finally delivered them and vanquished their enemies, and also that Job, after being subjected to the most diabolical treatment that Satanic ingenuity could invent, was finally restored to his old time prestige and health by the intervention of a divine Providence, so we may hope to receive from the same Providence who sees and knows our sufferings that aid we stand so munch in need of. Augusta J. Evans Wilson informs us that every Gethsemane has its strengthening angels; the agonies of the graden, she says brought them to Christ. That there may some day be a deliverance is quite within the range of possibility. I regret to say that in the report for last year no deaths occurred on the force, but I have much pleasure in pointing out that two men have been sent to the Insane Asylum. However, a glance at the ages of the men on the force may give us hope, and that even if the Commissioners and the council fail to assist us we still have the leveller of all mankind, the grim reaper, to accomplish this relief. Some of us may not live to enjoy the repose afforded by the new order of things, but we shall, perhaps, receive the everlasting commiseration of coming ages, when the tradition of our long suffering is handed down to them, and who will feel thankful, at least, that the opinion that policemen, like annuitants, live forever, is not so.

SOCIETY.

In Toronto poverty is not exactly a crime, but it is sufficient of an inconvenience to make everyone very desirous of not possessing it. Society is pretty much in Toronto what it is everywhere else except that money is the chief requisite here. In smaller places men who can boast of respectability and a character free from blemish are welcomed into good society with perfect good grace and as much warmth as though they were millionaires. In Toronto an unprincipled knave, if he keep his wickedness from becoming absolutely notorious can secure entrance to the best social circles.

A large number of those who occupy mansions are those who have risen from the ranks, which is greatly to their credit, for every intelligent person takes pride in the fact that in this country it is in the power of anyone to rise as high as his abilities will carry him. Society is somewhat clannish, and the members of a certain church find their intimate friends in the congregation of the same.

Occasionally a man will be found coming from his distant English home and announce himself as the scion of some of the mobility of the British Empire, and he is received with open arms. If my memory serves me correctly some years ago a Mr. Ballantyne appeared like a miteor in our midst, and announced himself as the descendant of the much abused Irish landlords, who had been obliged to live somewhat abstemiously owing to the bad condition of landed property in that country. He founded, I believe, a club called the Dickens Club, and after a pleasant sojourn amongst us he left like the swallows for a warmer clime, and finally we heard of him in New Orleans where he was committed for something or other, and as is customary in such cases he laid the blame at the door of society—that society upon which he had lived for many a long day,

When a short time ago our city was honored with the distinguished presence of one of the members of the Royal family of France, the Telegram rose to remark concerning him :

JEROME OF MONTE CARLO.

If it be the true function of good society to recognize worth and ignore worthlessness, the good society of Toronto and other cities does not appear to particularly good advantage as the admiring host of Prince Jerome Bonaparte.

This effete heir to a great but evil name might be a good deal better than the general character of his house. He might be, but is he ? The family greed of Prince Jerome is not redeemed by valour, and his other traits are said to be Napoleonic in their meanness, if not in their influence upon the world's history

In Toronto and Ottawa the boss of Monte Carlo was received and honoured as if he were a prince and a great man in Israel. The society leaders who welcomed the prince were far from well employed, for surely Jerome's business is no passport to the esteem of Canada's best people.

There are two or three society events in the course of the season, St. Andrew's Ball ; the Royal Canadian Yacht Club Ball ; and the affairs at Government House, all of which bring out society's youth, beauty and wealth. The doings of society are chronicled every week in Saturday Night and in addition to the society of the city, the out of town events are also chronicled.

The following clippings are taken from that journal :

Mr. Grenville P. Kleiser, whose success as an elocutionist in Toronto is not forgotten, has met with very gratifying success in Portland, Oregon, and other western cities.

One of the most successful of the good Friday concerts was given in the Central Methodist church. Mr. Harold Jarvis sang beautifully, and a new elocutionary light, Miss Marguerite Baker gave a couple of recitations. *A vast crowd of nice people sat seriously in the cosy pews*, and the programme, being of a grave and almost entirely sacred character, was in harmony with the spirit of the hour.

A very sweet and lovely Toronto maiden has joined the ranks of the matrons, since Miss DeJones of Gloucester street because Mrs. Brown, last Wednesday evening.

The foregoing is a fair sample of what appears every week, and as it is a fair subject for criticism, I will ask the careful consideration of sensible people to some of the paragraphs I have copied. I have nothing to say against giving a simple chronicle of an event, but I'm sure a generous public must consider itself edified by such a notice as the following :

"A very sweet and lovely Toronto maiden has joined the ranks of the matrons &c."

I forbear giving the further particulars of the case, as the lady in question doubtless had little idea of the use that was being made of her name, and it occurs to me that people must be of a degenerate turn of mind, if they can appreciate such trash. The announcement of the Good Friday concert in the Central Methodist Church is on a par with the above announcement.

"A vast crowd of nice people sat seriously in the pews &c"

But for really charming originality I think the following taken from the Niagara correspondence of that journal caps the climax :

"Miss DeSmyth of Buffalo, whose beauty and grace are so much admired, has been visiting relatives in town."

If the young lady in question, whose name I have changed—from that feeling of Christian charity that always actuates me—possesses the good legitimate common sense that heaven usually endows earthly mortals with, she will scarcely feel flattered with this florid and inane compliment to her beauty and grace. Novelists, from their privileged position, are permitted to rave as much as they like, and we accept it as a matter of course, but in private life mankind is disposed to regard a notice like the above in the light of vapour from some water brained sycophant, rather than as the production of a sensible correspondent who deals with facts, and gives the movements of society in a manner that common sense would seem to demand.

I think the great majority of sensible people will come to the reasonable conclusion that such drivel as the foregoing sounds like the price a social parasite is paying for being tolerated in polite society, that is if they are invited to the houses of the people they write about, which is extremely doubtful.

The most sensible articles I ever read were published in the Saturday Globe, "sweet," "lovely" and similar gush were eschewed,—a simple chronicle being given. I took the following from the Empire during the Parliamentary session of 1894 :

One of the most winsome of women I have met in Ottawa is Mrs Schultz, the wife of the Lieutenant-Governor. She captures one's affections instantly just by her sweet womanliness and the great tenderness for all things human, the reverence for all things good that is in her.

Lady Thompson the wife of Canada's Premier is fair and placid, slow and gentle of speech and wins the regard of all who meet her by the simple kindliness of her manner which sets even the shyest stranger at once at ease.

Lady Caron is a very pleasant and unaffected little lady, with whom one feels instantly at home, and Miss Caron, a bright and graceful little demoiselle ably assists in the discharge of the onerous social duties.

Of Mrs Ives the wife of the President of the Council, who in the charming home they have chosen for the session, entertains so delightfully it were impossible to speak without enthusiasm.

Mrs. Costigan, wife of the Secretary of State, is full of motherly kindness and good nature, which, with her sincerity and originality of speech, wins her a very loyal circle of friends.

Madame Angers, the pretty winsome wife of the Minister of Agriculture, is a great favorite in Ottawa society circles, and upon reception days her drawing room is always well filled.

Mrs. Foster is one of the most attractive of the Cabinet Ministers' wives. A quiet, gentle, sincere little lady of more than ordinary culture and attainment.

Mr. McNeill is one of the nice members of the House; a man thoroughly liked and respected by his confreres. Of quiet effective speech, and equally quiet courtesy of manner—there are few, indeed, to be found who have an ill word for the member for North Bruce.

Mr. Sam Hughes is not only nice looking but one of the nicest members of the Commons. He is looked upon in the House as a clever young politician, albeit he is occasionally disposed to do some original thinking.

The galleries like Mr. Haggart, he looks so big and strong and determined, resolute and tempery as the great iron horse, whose comings and goings he regulates. Yet with the determination and the strength there is always a suggestion of kindness.

"He looks like a fighter—one who could hit hard," said the member's wife.

"He would make a strong enemy or a most loyal friend." I said.

It is said that this great strong man is really shy, especially of women. He wouldn't be if he knew how kindly they looked down upon him from the gallery.

I submit the above for the consideration of an unprejudiced public, desiring only to observe that if the writer were a candidate for the Civil Service and did not receive an appointment, the Ministry was but a crowd of brutes impervious to adulation.

At a representative public meeting held in one of the halls of the city, which had been called to commemmorate the history of some by-law in connection with the curtailing of the liquor traffic a gentleman employed by one of the city newspapers invited me to go and hear the addresses. Some thirty-five or forty people were on the platform, and my friend called my attention to quite a large number who were indebted to his paper, and who, he stated, were so situated that it was utterly impossible for them to collect the money from them.

"There is a man," he said pointing to a thick-set, sweet faced individual, "who owes us $3.45. When the Central Bank failed we were given to understand that it was on that account that he was unable to pay us. In strict truth that was the reason, but instead of being a depositor, the actual fact was that he was indebted to the bank itself, and therefore, when it closed its doors he was left without the means of paying the account, and the published statement of the debtors of the bank showed him to be very largely indebted to it."

"There is another man," he said, pointing to a clerical looking chap. "who used to be a preacher. Some time ago he had been in the habit of making visits to different parishes in connection with church work, I think it was, and in an evil hour when putting up at a hotel, he asked the proprietor to make out his bill and add a larger amount than was really due. This would be paid by the people interested, and the balance was to be refunded by the proprietor to the preacher. By an unlucky chance he met the wrong man for his purpose, and the hotel proprietor disclosed the whole thing."

"He is no longer in the ministry then?"

"No, when these matter came out, I believe he was expelled but it has not impaired his usefulness in the least. He still talks prohibition and the cause does not seem to have suffered by his acts. You see that elderly man with the Prince Albert coat, sitting with his chin resting in the palm of his hand?"

"Yes."

"He is another of our debtors. A great man for writing to the newspapers, and owes us nine dollars."

"Can't you collect it from him?"

"No, we have tried repeatedly, but find there is absolutely no use in suing him, so we were compelled to write it off to bad and doubtful."

By this time the hall had begun to fill up rapidly, and there seemed to be little room for those who wished to secure seats in the front.

"Shall we push up to the front, or shall we remain here. If we wish to get to the front we will have to hurry up or stay where we are."

"What do you say it we go? To tell you the truth I feel like the guest without the wedding garments amongst this crowd of moralists."

"Very well, if you wish to go, let us do so by all means."

Professor Goldwin Smith, I think it is who informs us that the real aristocracy is the aristocracy of the mind, but what has the professor to say of the aristocracy of those who constitute themselves our moral teachers? Are they not to be most highly commended for their zeal and self-sacrifice and are their efforts on behalf of humanity to count for nothing? The professor may be right, and while I acknowledge that my own code of morality extends no higher than to those who pay their debts, yet it must be borne in mind that a man wno constitutes himself a "teacher" or a "fisher of men", and who does not pay his debts is counted greater than that man who, satisfied with things as they are, lives his life quietly and unostentatiously, but who does not think he has a mission to interfere with the privileges of those who does not agree with him.

The people I have mentioned could easily be multiplied probably by hundreds. It is astonishing how men, who being absolutely bailiff proof, will pose as leaders of great moral movements, when one might consistently imagine that they would first pay their debts and then teach morality afterwards. At a public meeting held in the city some little time ago, out of some forty eight men on the platform, only fourteen were indebted to one of the city newspapers, and they were absolutely uncollectible. As our mutual friend Colonel Ingersoll would say: "I can rob Smith if he will trust me. God forgives me, and threatens to punish Smith if he don't. But how is that going to help Smith?"

I have frequently puzzled myself to describe the relative position of the man who holds his property or his bank account in his wife's name. Can she be called his wife, or is she merely his accomplice? Is he her husband or merely her gentleman usher?

I was amused at a little episode in a newspaper office, where it is the custom to write off to Bad and Doubtful every three months such accounts as are deemed uncollectible. A certain gentleman had an advertising account considerably in arrears, and the accountant and manager were discussing the probabilities of its being paid. Suddenly the manager turned to another clerk and asked:

"C—, do you know this man, A— of S.—?"

"No, not personally, but I know that he leads the bible class in St. P. church Sunday school."

"Oh." the manager ejaculated, and then turning to the accountant he added:

"In that case, Mr. W—, you had better write it off to Bad and Doubtful."

A correspondent who perhaps has had some experience with our "moral teachers" writes to the Telegram as follows:

SIR,—No more dishonest action on the part of residents of this city can be imagined than the practice which is too general at present namely, the transfer of property from a husband to a wife. Of course it is really a swindle and is done to bar out creditors from the first payment of their debts. I can name many people in this city who live in style upon our more private streets such as Jarvis, Sherbourne, St. George and others, who are so situated, and who can hold expensive pews in our fashionable cathedral and other churches, observe the lenten season with extraordinary affectation of piety, live in luxury with their families, whilst, with the most flagrant dishonesty, poor, trusting creditors can realize nothing from the husband because of the iniquitous transfer of his property to his wife. Of course, the woman is just as bad as the man, who connives at such actions. Were the names of these people published it would cause a sensation in the religious and social circles in which these well dressed families move. The hard-working, honest people to whom they are indebted and who have given them credit in ignorance of the state of affairs are just laughed at by these debtors when they are asked to pay. Some quick and decisive mode of legal punishment should be at hand in such cases. It is dishonesty of the meanest kind, because the poor creditor is in ignorance of the true state of matters, and it is ten times worse than the act of the miserable wretch who to satisfy hunger, steals a loaf of bread and is punished for the theft by imprisonment in our goal. Every such transfer should be published with the names of the parties in our daily papers, and the publication paid for by the Government, Let those well-dressed imposters be shown up.—*Citizen.*

THE PRESS.

The press of Toronto is a subject that ought to receive at least a work written exclusively upon it, and in this work it is impossible to give more than a hurried review of it. It can be devided into two classes, the secular and religious. In the former are included all the political and literary journals of the city.

The morning papers of Toronto are amongst the ablest and best conducted in America, as well as among the most brilliant in the world.

Their power is very great and they shape to a very large extent the tone of the Provincial journals; they are conducted upon a most excellent system as far as their internal arrangements are concerned, and the men employed upon them are sometimes the persons of ability and experience.

They are the Mail and Empire, the Globe and the World, representing the two political parties, and in addition, with the exception of the World, the same papers publish evening editions, and the Telegram, Star and News are then added to the list. The latter are a noticeable feature of the city, as they all cost but one cent a copy, and contain all the latest news, gossip, and a variety of light and entertaining matter; they are bought chiefly by persons who wish to read them at home after the cares and fatigues of the day are over. The first issues are at

OF TORONTO THE GOOD. 33

twelve o'clock noon, and the latest at half past five or six o'clock. On occasions of more than ordinary interest extras are issued as late as 8 or 9 o'clock. On the day of the execution of Birchall the special edition of the Telegram, published immediately after the execution aggregated the enormous total of forty-seven thousand all of which were sold in the city.

Appropos of the Birchall trial the following from the pen of Mr. E. E. Sheppard, of Saturday Night, which contains a criticism of the press may not be out of place. At present he contributes a page to Saturday Night over the signature of Don, and I give his sketch, suggested by the mention of this case.

" Have you heard that the devil is dead ?" exclaimed an acquaintance of mine in response to an invitation to tell me something new Odd, isn't it, how a senseless rejoinder of this sort sometimes rings in a fellow's ears and rattles around in the empty places of his mind. This saying clung to me all day and as I sit down to work in the evening it is the first thing that suggests itself as a text.

One slips very easily from the above topic to the great loss Birchall will be to the daily newspapers hereabouts. Poor devil, he is gone, and even yet the press is full of him. Even his hangman has been glorified by publicity which is never given to the man or woman who throughout a life of self-denial and good works tries to rescue the fallen and reduce the woes of the wretched. I don't think the value of the devil to the daily newspapers was ever better proven than by the disgraceful exhibition the *Mail* has made of itself in publishing the authobiography of a young reprobate who, if he had anything in his nature of an interesting sort, it was the careless good-nature with which he asserted before all mankind that he cared for neither God nor man. This moral idiot, who squandered his patrimony, ruined those who trusted him, degraded those who associated with him, violated everything held sacred by gentlemen, took the life of a comrade who followed him, lied to the clergyman who prayed with him, and in every possible way tried to prove by his life and his writings that virtue is a delusion, religion a farce, and honor a snare, has been lionized by the newspapers more than any other man who ever died on Canadian soil What he has written his brought a higher price than anything that before was produced in Canada. His photograph has appeared more numerously, sketches —which are evidently those of a libertine—of ballet girls who have nothing to recommend them but the shape of their legs, have been given as works of art, and this monster of perfidy has in this way been placed before every Canadian as a singnlarly gifted and courageous person. The *Mail*, with cant which is utterly loathsome, has pretended that its publication of Birchall's biography was intended to teach a moral lesson. Such cant, such leprous hypocrisy, it is to be hoped, sickened the public even while they read the degraded and degrading maunderings of the convicted murderer. The *Mail*, which is fighting for Protestantism, which is ready to carry a banner in the procession of prohibitionists, which was not unwilling, at a critical moment, to play traitor to the party which had nourished it, had but to reveal this last and most contemptible phase of its character to be thoroughly understood as a fake and the scarlet woman of journalism. It matters little to the majority of people what a newspaper advocates so long as it be thoroughly understood what the declared province of the paper is to be. Those who take and read the *Police Gazette* know what they are subscribing for, but a newspaper which pretends to be pure and lacks no opportunity of being prurient may mislead, must indeed degrade, those who want purity but are seduced into reading pruriency by false pretences.

There are many other newspapers besides the *Mail* that deserve the harshest possible criticism for their conduct in this matter. The *Telegram*, for instance, which boasts of the enormous editions it sold descriptive of the hanging and last moments of Birchall, apologizes by saying that the newspapers only provide what the people want. The demi-monde explain their existence in the same way and claim to be a necessary evil. Nobody associates with them who would not be ashamed to take them to their home and introduce them to mother or sister. Must not a newspaper which feels that it is unfit to be introduced into a family and put into the hands of innocence have much the same contempt for its calling of the woman of the street has for herself as she solicits the passer-by? It is a dreadful apology to offer and yet it is the one made by the *Globe* and the balance of those who have been in the same work and who fight with one another in draping with pretty verbal garments the unclean and demoralizing things they have published. How glad these newspapers must be that the devil isn't dead !

It is not my purpose to write what properly belongs to the newspapers in reference to the woman who posed as a female martyr at the ignominious end of the career of a most unmitigated scoundrel and blackguard, but it should not be forgotten that this Mrs. Birchall did not scruple by false pretences to pose as Lady Somerset, a title to which she knew perfectly well that she had no claim. And her sister Mrs. West Jones also received her share of the newspaper notoriety accorded to this illustrious family, and did not fail to let the newspapers have full particulars of her actions. For instance when she went to the opera house (which was doubtless in excellent taste at such a time), the fact was duly chronicled in the press, hence the murder was not without its advantages as it gave to the two women that delightful sense of notoriety so dear to the female heart.

The life of a newspaper man, both as regards the editorial and business departments is not by any means a bed of roses. First of all you have to deal with correspondents, of which there are some thousands, all of whom have their pet scheme to put before an indulgent public, and all of them are, of course, intended for the benefit of this same public. Some years ago the Saturday Telegram would have column after column of bosh written by correspondents who assured us that if their schemes were carried out, Toronto would go up by leaps and bounds, which at that time was a favourite expression, and it may not be out of place to state that the writers of these articles had about as much idea of municipal matters as a child might be expected to have. I am not aware whether the Telegram has precluded them from their columns or whether they have become disgusted with the lack of success their efforts have called forth, but it is certain that these nonsensical letters are not inserted with that frequency that once held sway.

On one occasion there appeared a letter from one man, who prefaced his remarks with the announcement that he was a poor man, and that the constant ringing of the bells on the Grand Trunk trains kept him from sleeping, and he proceeded to characterize this as an outrage, breathing vengeance. It is quite likely that the company, therefore, changed its entire system of signals in conformity with his request.

Another, who described himself as a working man, held forth on the criminality of some one of the fire stations for not ringing a bell at six o'clock, I think, in the morning, and further stating that he could not afford to lose his time, which he invariably did, when he was not awakened by the chimes of the bell. The idea of relying upon himself to waken, does not appear to have occurred to him.

Sometimes some portentions individual will scrawl (no other word expresses it), a badly spelled and worse written letter to the editor of some paper, and his position, financially, will deter the editor from consigning it to its proper place, the waste paper basket. The compositor and proof reader are made to suffer, while the writer is delighted with his effort. If one or two such letters were published giving the exact spelling a generous public would be relieved from further encroachment by such people. If this trash were written years ago in an age when even royal personages indulged in a phonetic style of orthography which would provoke the laughter of a modern newsboy, the writing and spelling might be excused. The pretender to the Crown of England wrote of his father as *Gems*, and that he should murder the two languages in which he wrote seems a small thing, and the fact that Frederick the Great, the most accomplished of princes, bosom friend of Voltaire, and sworn patron of the literati should have been unable to spell is perhaps, a matter of some surprise, hence I try to remember these things when, in the capacity of proofreader it has fallen to my lot to decipher the hierogliphics sent in for publication, which it would be the bitterest irony to call writing.

Personal mentions are a source of perennial aggravation to newspaper men. Every man, of course, considers himself entitled to have his arrival chronicled in the daily press, and some are even willing to pay for it. I was amused at the disposition made of one ambitious young man, who hurried into the office of one of the morning papers, and handed the clerk a slip of paper with the remark : " My friends will want to know I'm in the city, so you can put that in."

The clerk examined it, and handed it back with the reply:

" We have nothing to do with such matters here, you will require to see Mr...... the city editor, up-stairs."

The guest to the city hustled up-stairs, and the clerk remarked :

" Mr...... the city editor is home, and will not be here until this afternoon, there is no one to take that slip of paper from him, and by the time he gets through with trying to find the city editor he will come to the conclusion that his friends are not so anxious to know that he is here."

" Do you have many such ? "

" Yes ; we are incessantly bored with people of that class. You see in the country towns the papers are glad enough to get such items, and they seem to think that the city papers are the same." As witness the following :

A number of the elite from our vicinity and the Junction section gave a surprise to Mr. and Mrs. Long, of Centre street, Beeton, on Wednesday evening last.—*Beeton World*.

Contrary to expectations Mr. Moncrieff, M.P., for East Lampton, spoke in favour of the remedial bill down at Ottawa on Friday. Therefore, Mr. Moncrieff's name is pants.—*Sarnia Post*.

Moise Letourneau's horse dropped dead on the road as he was coming home with a load of firewood last week. An over-feed of oats is supposed to have caused death.—*Comber Herald*.

We noticed in the locals of last week's paper that the first crow was anxiously looked for. Crows have been around here all winter, so they are no indication of spring.—*Brockville Recorder*.

Andrew Isaac is making very good fence improvements on a lot next to John Day's. Go on Andrew, you are performing a good example to many young men. Success to you.—*Wallaceburg News*.

To the Editor of the Banner.

Dear Sir,—The Leader editor at Schomberg has crawled into his hole and pulled the hole in after him, by refusing to print my letter of last week.

PRO BONO PUBLICO—Aurora Banner.

A wellknown clergyman who made periodical visits to Toronto World, on his way from some meeting in connection with the church to the hotel, would call on a certain newspaper and buttonhole the clerk with the expression :

"Send a reporter down to the Walker House, to see the Rev: Dr. Blowout, and I'll give him the particulars of a meeting of the ...... association, or ...... board."

To anyone of ordinary intelligence it ought to be patent that in an institution like this the clerk in the financial department would have no intercourse with the editorial department. The clerk merely referred him to that Department, stating that he never saw the reporters, and could not, therefore, give them the message.

"I have nothing to do with that," the preacher answered sullenly, "I leave word with you," and he looked menacingly at his auditor, who replied coolly :

"All I can do is to leave a memo. in the editor's box, and if he gets it all right, and if he doesn't, it isn't my fault."

If the city editor failed to get the memorandum there is no doubt the worthy preacher would have written the paper complaining of the clerk in question, his look of ill-concealed anger showed it ; but it is to be remembered that this man is the exception to the rule of those who call to see the editor. If their business is of sufficient importance to require editorial attention, their own intelligence, if they have any, will teach them that the business office of a concern of that kind has something else to do besides acting as medium between the editorial staff and some self-contained as who wants his vanity fed.

Speaking of this preacher brings to mind an incident in which a model Christian showed himself in a most exemplary manner. His daughter had died, and he called at one of the city newspaper offices to insert the notice. It is a recognized law amongst newspapers that no clerk is to write out an advertisement and when requested to do so, the clerk in question refused to break the rule. The would be advertiser flew into a passion, but finding the clerk inflexible, he finally went to the customers' desk, and wrote "sweetly fell asleep in Jesus," &c., at which the clerk laughed irreverently when he read it.

If the theory holds good, that he who places temptation in the way of humanity is guilty equally witn him who sins, than one of the city newspapers has much to answer for when they introdnced a system of free advertising. The temptation to tell a falsehood is so great that few men and no woman can resist it when they get a free advertisement in exchange therefor.

The wife of a well-known clergyman, who receives a very handsome salary, called in the office for the purpose of advertising for a domestic. After some preliminary skirmishing as to who should write the advertisement, and the clerk having come out victorious, the lady threw the advertisement on the counter and stared defiantly at him while he counted the words.

"Twenty-six cents," the clerk exclaimed cheerfully,

"But those go in free," she answered angrily.

"Yes, twenty words one time free, but you have had this advertisement in before."

"I have no such thing."

"Have you never advertised for a domestic before?"

"Yes, but that's months ago."

"Well, that is of no consequence, you know. We only insert one time free, so you will have to pay for this."

"Is the manager in?" she demanded suddenly.

"No," the clerk answered sweet y, "I regret to say that he isn't."

While this little fusilade had been going on, the lady had worked herself into quite a frenzy, and her passion was beyond all control. Her eyes fairly blazed with anger.

"Do you mean to tell me," she demanded, in a rage, "that I am to have the benefit of a free advertisement only once in every six months?"

"It isn't only once in six months, but always. One time free is what we advertise, and I am obliged to observe the rule strictly."

"Then, I suppose," she answered in a tone, meant to be sarcastic, "if I live to be a hundred years old, I can only advertise once in your free columns, according to this."

"That is practically what it amounts to."

She grabbed the inoffensive little piece of paper. and crushing it in her hand, added scathingly, "I'll advertise in the Telegram where it will do some good, if I have to pay," and she swept majestically out of the door.

This is merely a sample of what happens every day, only perhaps this is a little worse than the generality. The clerk had simply done his duty, and his coolness was the result of long experience. He had grown callous in dealing with such people. Charity, we are informed, begins at home, and one would imagine that one of God's apointed might find his valuable time profitably spent in teaching good manners at that shrine where charity begins, and he would, doubtless, receive the heartfelt thanks of a multitude of people even though they were unable to express their thanksgiving personally.

One scheme that was worked successfully for some time was the practice of sending these advertisements by post card, where they escaped the vigilant eye of the teller, but a few repetitions soon settled that matter, and the post card idea received its death blow. The clerk who checks the advertisements passed a post card to the teller on which was writen :

"Good general servant wanted, must be good cook ; no washing, references required ; apply between 10 and 12 a.m., and 3 and 6 p.m., Mrs. Black, ... Crawford street.

"Please insert several times."

"I think," said the checking clerk "that woman has a good nerve, several times, its a wonder she didn't say fifty."

The teller looked at the card in amazement. It was like a revelation to him. Then he deliberately tore it into pieces.

"Do many of these come?" he asked.

"Yes ; quite a few."

"I'll see that no more are inserted," and he kept his word. Post cards and letters of that nature were henceforward carefully culled out and destroyed, and thus by her desire to get too much for nothing, this worthy lady effectually debarred herself and others like her from getting thereafter by stealth what they knew they could not obtain by legitimate means.

Another annoyance is the telephone, which has become a perfect nuisance to newspaper people.

A family living in Rosedale made a regular practice of telephoning advertisements for domestics, until the accountant exasperated beyond all endurance at his inability to collect the account of some thirty-six cents from them effectually cut them off from further using their advertising columns. He had sent them post card after post card, with *final request* in large letters emblazoned thereon, but they were impervious to all demands, and at last their telephone messages were entirely ignored. At length, however, revenge came to the long suffering accountant. One of the females of the family came in to insert the old advertisement in the Weekly edition.

"It's two cents a word," she informed the clerk, sharply, " and there are twelve words here."

The clerk permitted a diabolical smile to pass over his face as he replied :

" Two and a half cents a word in the Weekly, and there are fourteen words here, thirty-five cents."

The money was paid, and the lady produced another advertisement.

" This is for the daily,' she announced, "and it goes in free."

" No," he replied icily, " it doesn't. We have an account against you now for thirty-six cents for advertisements telephoned and we will not put any more in free. This will cost eighteen cents.

The young woman haggled a little, and tried to get the advertisement in free, but it wouldn't work. Finally she said :

" I didn't know that we owe anything, but anyway I'll see about it, and in the meantime you can put this one in," saying which she placed the advertisement on the counter and turned to walk out.

" You need not leave it," the clerk replied, " it won't be inserted unless you pay for it."

Further recrimination was useless, and the young lady was obliged to take the advertisement with her, while the clerk laughed softly to himself. After that however, the family sent the advertisements down by one of the male members thereof, who would throw it on the counter. and burst out of the door, as though he were shot out of a cannon, while the advertisement itself was consigned to the waste paper basket.

Another lady has a mania for having her name appear in the columns of situations wanted—female, as a philanthropist, and her manner of shedding benevolence is of that delightful kind that costs nothing. Ever and anon the clerk who has the misfortune to be placed near the telephone is called up :

" Is that the Mail ?" inquires a languid female voice.

" Yes," the reply is curtly given.

" I want to put in an advertisement. Are you listening ? "

" Yes ; go on."

" Mrs. Cornwallis Windermere No. 3000 Algonquin street, desires to recommend a clever young girl as mother's help or general servant. Have you got it ? "

" Yes; will you pay for this ? "

"Oh, they go in free. Put it in five or six times, please."

And before the clerk has time to collect himself the lady has rung off, and rather than disappoint the girl who is looking for a place the advertisement is inserted. Since that paper discontinued the free advertising, I notice this charitable lady's name never appears as it previously did.

I strongly recommend this style of philanthropy, particularly as it is cheap and effective It lends the idea to a credulous public that you are interested in the poor, and if you have a telephone it is so convenient, and then too, it costs absolutely nothing.

One of our telephone friends was most beautifully come up to one Sunday night. Special services were being held in the Y.M.C.A. rooms, and at the conclusion thereof, one of the prime movers in the affair rang up the newspaper office.

" Hello," he exclaimed, " Is that number ten thousand ? "

" Yes."

" Well, take this advertisement."

" Who is speaking ? "

Now it so happened that the financial office had not yet opened for business on Sunday night, and the Y.M.C.A. delegate had rung up the editorial department. The city editor who was a Scotchman, was at the phone, and was one of those men who will allow no one to ride over them.

" Never you mind who is speaking," Mr. Smart Alex. replied, " You take this advertisement."

" You can go to hell with your advertisement, I won't take any of your d......d nonsense."

The advertisement didn't appear.

One day a young lady from a law office presented two advertisements—one for a boy wanted, and the other for a domestic. As fate would have it, the clerk had seen the advertisement for the domestic in the Telegram the evening before, so he charged full price for both. The young lady looked surprised but paid the amount.

A few minutes later a telephone message came, and the clerk was called to the phone. It might be mentioned that the advertiser was one of those Englishmen who have wood instead of brains.

" I sent an advertisement over a few minutes ago for a servant and one for boy, and you charged me thirty-eight cents, now I want that money refunded."

" All right," the clerk responded, " but the advertisements won't go in."

" Why not ? "

"They must be paid for."

"No; they go in free."

"The advertisement for the boy is two cents a word, and the domestic is one cent a word, altogether it comes to thirty-eight cents."

"You advertise to insert free."

"Yes; under certain conditions, but you do not come under these conditions."

"Well, I'll see about it."

Some time afterwards the collector for subscriptions called for payment, and was refused the reason for refusal being that his advertisements were not inserted, but how it came out I never heard.

Quite frequently we read notices like the following:

DIED

In this city, on the 25th instant, at No. 240 Piccadilly street, Charles Frederic Angustus Dudley Jones, eldest son of the late Alexander Dagmar Leopold Jones, of Her Majesty's 100th regiment of Irish Dragoons, and the nephew of the Right Honourable, the Lord Keeper of Her Majesty's stables aged 45 years.

London, Liverpool, Manchester and New York papers please copy.

If people would for a moment reflect that all the city papers charge fifty cents for inserting a death announcement, and that it is quite likely others outside of the city do likewise, how absurd must it appear to these papers to be called upon to insert a death notice of a person who is a perfect stranger to them, and if it were at all attempted to be done which in a general way it isn't, a man might be kept busy culling over exchanges for this purpose alone. And yet people persist in putting that meaningless phrase at the bottom of their announcements to an extent that is really remarkable, though the practice of inserting these notices is not carried on to any extent if at all, by the papers which are called upon to do so.

The following is a rather crisp, rat trap and business like sort of a notice:

DeBriggs—On Saturday, Dec. 8th, 1894, at his residence, 201 Bathurst street, James DeBriggs in his 72nd year. Gone home.

Funeral on Monday at 2.30 p.m. Friends please accept this intimation.

I particularly admire the way in which the public are informed he has gone home. It is short and to the point.

In addition to this it will also be observed that the modern spirit of ridicule has done away with those gushing names such as Queenie and others equally inane as formerly, simply that fools who would have called their wives or daughters by such names found they were too sweet for this wicked world, and heaven intervened and took them to itself

I once knew a lad whose adoring parents called him Prince, and I have no doubt he feel like cursing them to their faces. He was simply the butt of the whole school, who jeered at his name, and led him the life of a dog. Consult any of the newspapers and see how many children of tender years who bear outrageous names are amongst the death notices, and compare them with the Johns, Georges, Williams etc., who live to ripe old age, and you will be surprised. A laboring grinder in a concern where I once worked called his son Earl. The child died in four days. I clipped the following from different newspaper and ask a discriminating public, how people, presumed to have good common sense, could expect children possessed of such names to live.

Warner—Queen Victoria Lockwood (Queenie Warner), youngest daughter of Mr. and Mrs. Neil Warner, born Montreal, May 24, 1892, died New York, December 14, 1896. Funeral from G.T.R. depot on arrival of Dalaware and Hudson train from New York, Sunday, May 23rd, 8.15 a.m. to St. George's Church, thence to Mount Royal Cemetery.

Li Hung Chang Jones is the fearsome name with which a heartless father has burdened his helpless and unoffending offspring. It is pleaded that the fact that the portion of Merthyr wherein the child was born on Sunday last is locally known as China, lends a certain appropriateness to the selection. But this ingenious plea ought not to be admitted in justification of such an outrage.—Washington Gazette.

The Funeral of "Birdie" Bates took place yesterday afternoon from East Toronto to Norway church. There was a very large attendance of friends and relatives, among them being Ald. Russell, Messrs. Blong, Morton, Mitchell, Johnston and many more. Rev. Chas. Ruttan and G. L. Starr were the officiating clergy.

Chambers—At 108 McCaul street, on the 17th May, Dorathea Beatrice (Queenie), youngest daughter of Rev. A. B. Chambers, aged 10 years.

Funeral on Tuesday, the 19th, at 2.30 p.m.

Davis—On December 14, 1896, at 17 Anderson street, Montreal, of scarlet fever, Emeline (Emmy) Gladys Davis, dearly beloved and eldest daughter of Horace and Lizzie Davis. Funeral private.

  Little Emmy was our darling,
   Pride of all our hearts at home;
  But an angel came and whispered,
   Little Emmy, do come home.

The body of Irminie Savage, who was drowned some six weeks ago from a canoe in the Humber, was found Saturday and buried yesterday.

Quite a large number of friends of Mr. and Mrs. Geo. B. Longley attended the funeral obsequies on Sunday afternoon of their infant daughter, Zenith Gertrude. Interment took place in the cemetery, Rev. J. H. Ratcliffe conducting the religious services.

Elmer Graydon, living near English, Ind., has named his infant son Abraham Lyncoln Ulyssess William McKinley; and a neighbor, John Vaughn, not to be outdone, has named his infant son Thomas Jefferson Andrew Jackson James Monroe William Jennings Bryan. At last accounts both infants were doing as well as could be expected under the circumstances.

These are a very few of the difficulties of the business offices of newspapers. They, like the Government, are always considered fit and proper subjects for plunder, and men and women do not hesitate to " do " them at every opportunity.

The subscription department have difficulties just as exasperating as the advertising only they are not quite so frequent. A city paper once reduced its subscription to $3.50 to clergymen, on the condition that the whole amount should be paid in advance. After the first' year's subscription had run out and it was pretty well run into the first six months of the second, one of those who had taken advantage of the special terms called to pay the subscription, and tendered $1.75 in payment of six months'.

"This must be paid yearly in advance." said the clerk.

"Oh, no."

"How did you pay it before?"

"Six months, of course."

"Are you quite sure?"

"Certainly."

The teller knew perfectly well that the man, clergyman as he was, was selling a deliberate falsehood, and he turned to the subscription clerk to look the matter up. As he had surmised it had been paid for the full year, and he informed the customer that such was the case. The preacher was greatly incensed, naturally, at being caught in a falsehood, and he paid it will a very ill grace; still, it demonstrates that no one is exempt from indulging in a little fabrication when it suits or pays them to do so.

Of the management of these concerns a great deal might be written, but it must be patent to all that where such immense interests are concerned the greatest care must be exercised, and to keep the advertisers out who will not pay their accounts is no small matter, or insignificant undertaking. When the real estate boom was on some time ago the papers were flooded with advertisements of these people, and one firm who ran up a bill of $138.00 were sued, when they entered the plea of infancy, all being under the age of twenty-one years, and the account could not, therefore, be collected. It was rather stern logic, but it was very effective.

The advertising patronage is something very large in all the dailies, and a man requires all the cardinal virtues to make a successful canvasser. He must be persistent without seeming to push the man he is soliciting, and may other qualifications that are too much to mention. There are journals, however, that can almost command the patronage of advertisers, thought it seems to me like a system of blackmail: I once heard of a well known advertiser meeting two newspaper men, when one with whom he did not advertise, chaffed him about it.

"Oh," he exclaimed with an uneasy laugh, "I'm not afraid of you."

The Telegram, which is the leading paper devoted exclusively to city interests. has the largest share of condensed advertisements and which must yield them an enormous revenue. Their advertising announcements of city auction sales is another special feature.

The reporters of the city papers are as a general rule a long suffering class of men, and generally men of ability, but they ere frequently imposed upon in their desire to do justice to the public. A gentleman connected with one of the morning papers made a remark to me that demonstrates their difficulties. A certain man, whose name is prominently before the public as a somewhat ostentatious philanthropist, and as being connected with different charities, never allows an incident, however trivial to pass without sending his office boy to the newspapers with the report. "If" said my friend, "he were to give a blind man ten cents, I suppose he would send his boy around with a local to each of the papers, announcing the fact." In casting ashes upon his head in the way of giving charity, he takes good care that the public shall know what a saintly head he thinks it is, nevertheless.

During the meeting of the Church of England Woman's Auxiliary Mission Board all matters of interest were freely supplied to the reporters, and every effort made to lighten their burdens. On the other hand, the Presbyterian Women's Foreign Mission Society met in the Westminster church, Bloor street, and not only were the press excluded, but the officials actually wished to be paid for furnishing the names of the delegates. The newspaper men promptly refused to comply with this request, and it was only after they stated would not publish them unless copied out and handed over that a copy was furnished one paper, with the understanding that it should be used by all.

It is not always possible, of course, for either the reporter or his contemporary, the accountant to get even with those who try to slight them, but this incident will be a revelation to the committee who were instrumental in bringing a certain singer to the city. The church in question, at the discretion of the accountant was entitled to advertise at the rate of ten cents a line, the regular rate being fifteen. When the first advertisement appeared the accountant submitted it to the manager, and asked what rate he should charge.

"Shall I make it fifteen cents, and then if they think they ought to get it the old rate, I will refer them to you?"

"Well, yes, do that. If they want it at ten cents, we will have to give it them, I suppose, still if they will pay the fifteen we may as well get it."

The accountant sent a polite note asking for two passes. The obliging secretary of the committee said he didn't have any, but that Mr. Somebody Else, who lived the Lord Only knows where, had charge of them, but he thought they were all gone anyway, and it was extremely doubtful if the accountant could get any in any case. After the concerts the account was sent in amounting to $45.00, being at the rate of fifteen cents per line. The secretary called in a great rush, and handed back the bill.

'We only pay ten cents a line." said he.

"That rate only applies to your Christmas, Good Friday and Thanksgiving services." the accountant answered coolly, "when the collections are for charity."

"But we had a lecture a couple of month ago, and you only charged us ten cents."

"Yes, that was my mistake."

The account was paid at fifteen cents a line, and when the same singer came again the same rate was charged. Had the courtesy of two insignificant passes been extended to the applicant, the committee would have been richer by $22.50 than they otherwise were, as the accountant could have referred the secretary to the manager of the paper, and it could have been arranged.

The modern character who rejoices to have himself interviewed is really the most odious that can be brought to the notice of the reporter, and the prayers of the righteous that avail much might be offered on behalf of him who is sacrificed at this alter of penance. I mentioned to you the circumstance of the clergyman who at some hole or corner meeting of a committee of his church desired to have himself interviewed, and always left word at the business office of the paper to have a reporter call to see him, recalls a character in Hawley' Smart's "At Fault," every time I saw him. This was Mr. Totterdell, who was not inaptly described by a detective, when he said with an air of patient resignation : "Now for that wearisome creature Totterdell," and again when Mr. Totterdell had finished, the detective said to himself : " Darned old fool. He told all he knew, and wanted to tell a great deal more that he didn't. What a wasteful creature of time it is."

We all have our crosses to bear, and if some are heavier than others, and the bearers sink beneath them, remember that this has been the fate of humanity from time immemorial, but consider the trials of those reporters who are compelled to listen to such drivel as these people usually give them. Surely the Great Judge on the last day will remember with mercy these great afflictions, even though the reporter in anguish of soul may, like the prophet, of old, cry out : " How long, Oh, Lord, how long ? "

I had a conversation some little time ago with the managing editor of a journal which I may say parenthetically, is not published in Toronto, and in the course of his remarks he dwelt upon the high attainment possible to women in connection with newspaper work, and mentioned the fact with evident pride, that young ladies were acting as his sub-editors, and also as proofreaders. "They do the work," he remarked complacently, referring to the proof-readers "just as well as men."

He was undeniably correct in his assertion for as a matter of fact they do better than men, in some branches. I consider myself competent to speak with a remarkable degree of authority, and I assert that there is no one more competent to throw dirt than a woman, not only because it seems inherent to her nature, but because, as Balzac observes even in their dissimulation there is an element of sincerity. Some eight years ago Grip had on its staff, a cantankerous disappointed old harridan who used to write acidulated dirt which she thought was satire. I never saw her and do not know her name, yet the way she wrote of Prof. Goldwin Smith and Lord Randolph Churchill convinced me that I was correct. No one but a disappointed woman could have framed such language.

I subjoin the following piece of twaddle as being the work of some sweet creature, and ask your consideration of the last sentence :

He knew that his visit besides gratifying a not altogether vulgar desire to see in the flesh one who had so often delighted, solaced and puzzled him, would give pleasure to thousands of readers to whom Mr. Browning (our English mentors insist on the " Mr,") will be a more real entity from his description. *For our own part we are simply filled with envy* at Mr. Fitch's courage and success, though we would prefer not to be scolded, event at a distance.

In connection with ladies in journalism, the Toronto Telegram recently remarked :

Woman, lovely woman, is needed in the newspaper business to gently turn the edge of editorial bitterness and breathe her own kindly spirit into all the utterances of every well-conducted j urnal. Heads form theories that the feet kick holes in. Profession is formed by hope, and practice by the force of our fallen nature. The professions of woman in journalism are in keeping with her high and holy mission, but her practices coincide with instincts that may be lofty or may be low A woman who writes for a morning paper has just given an example of the thoughtful tenderness, the sweet gentility, the lady-like kindness which are said to be characteristic of the newspaper woman. She visited a summer resort not far from Toronto. Not on mere pleasure bent was she. Ah, no ! Her business was Professional with a capital P. The waiter girl displeased Her. The girl may have been tired or overworked, or perhaps she neglected the august visitor to attend the guests who were less obviously superior. A newspaper man would have probably had tact enough to get good service from the waiter. At all events he would not have avanged his wrongs in print, but not so the newspaper woman. That unfortunate waiter girl was pilloried in the woman's column. Her personal appearance was referred to in terms that would be offensive even if the newspaper deity whom she had offended was a Mrs. Langtry. An incident like this, trifling as it may be, is evidence that women can be mean upon provocation that would not stir a man. Individual character determines the quality of woman's influence in journalism, in politics or in anything else. If the individual be noble the influence will be good ; if the individual be otherwise the influence will be ordinary.

Personally, I consider the Evening Telegram the best paper in Canada. Mr. Robertson has been successful in having associated with him a staff of writers and reporters who are able to keep in touch with public sentiment. It was the Telegram that broke up the cedar-block paving ring, and successfully conducted a libel suit for doing so. It was the Telegram that pointed out to the Ontario Government that the late Mr. Badgerow was no fit successor to Mr. Fenton as Crown Attorney. It did so kindly, but effectually, and a man of ability was placed in that position. It pointed out that there should be a City Crown Attorney and a County Crown Attorney for Toronto and York County and this was done. Just before the general elections in Ontario which it was presumed would be held in September, the Telegram pointed out why it would be better to hold them in June, and three days afterwards the House was dissolved and an appeal made in June, the Liberals again returned to power. The Telegram made a forecast of how the new house would stand, and was out in one case only. The Parliamentary correspondent of the Telegram at Ottawa, from 1891 to 1896 was in my estimation, the best corsespondent in the press gallery, barring none. His articles were the most readable published in Canada. I could go on enumerating reasons for my opinion without number, but anyone reading that journal will know that what I say is perfectly true, and patent to anyone.

The Mail and Empire devoted a couple of columns daily to " For and about Women," and I give you the following item clipped from these columns :

When the tall brunette and the little blonde got on the car at the corner of Yonge and Queen streets it was already crowded. A number of men were hanging on to the straps. There was only one seated; a young man, at that, faultlessly dressed even to a silk hat, and wearing on his doll like face an expression born of ennui and satiety. He did not offer either of the girls his seat. The tall brunette bent down and whispered in the ear of the little blonde, "Follow my lead." The little one nodded her head knowingly. Then the tall brunette said in a voice expressive of intense surprise, and just loud enough to be heard all over the car, "Why, there's a man sitting down:"

"Where?" said the little blonde excitedly. "Let me see him."

The tall brunette pointed him out calmly and deliberately.

"Oh," said the little blonde in a disappointed tone, "That's not a man."

"No?" queried the tall brunette.

"No" continued the little blonde with rising inflection, "that's a street car hog."

There was five seconds of deadly silence, during which the little blonde blushed furiously, while the tall brunette set her teeth and gazed out of the window with a dreamy look in her eyes. Then came a roar of laughter from the standing men, and a chorus of giggles from the ladies who were seated. The hog, white and trembling, rose hastily pulled the bell rope, stopped the car and got off. The tall brunette insisted on her companion taking the vacant seat. As the little blonde settled herself she remarked placidly, "He's cured."

"I don't care for pork in any shape," answered the other dreamily.

Isn't the above story just like the wail of some disappointed old maid? Jealous of the "doll-like face" which was, at least, the symbol of youth, and that her own was getting scraggy and lean, and vinegar-like in its expression. As long as the woman journalist confines herself to descriptions of sleeves and flounces and subjects equally inane, she will be all right, but when it comes to a discussion of other subjects, she cannot discuss on their merits—she is sure to show her vindictive nature. In the above story, she proves my assertion. Girls or young ladies who possess the faintest conception of lady like deportment do not make exhibitions of themselves as the tall brunette and little blonde did. However, I think I may say with truth equal to that of the writer of the above story, that I was on the street car she speaks of, only she does not give a correct description of the episode. When the little blonde with a rising inflection, screeched, "that's a street car hog," the crowd roared, but the ladies did not giggle. The idea at once prevailed that these two persons were of light character—no other conclusion could have been reached after hearing their remarks, and observing their conduct, as ladies do not pass such observations. The "hog" did not leave the car either; he simply ignored these persons, but when at the corner of McCaul street a lady carrying a huge basket did enter the car, the hog arose and tendered her his seat. Does not the tenor of the Mail's article suggest that its writer must have had some such experience herself and the seat she had coveted, had been given to a lady? Men have some discretion in these things you know, and any man prefers giving his seat to a young and pretty girl, or a lady, rather to any coarse-minded young person who would make herself conspicuous by her vulgarity and ill-breeding, or one whose acidulated face would stop a clock.

There is one branch of the editorial department, however, that will be appreciated, and that is the lot of the book reviewer. The time was when the editor would conscientiously run through the volume submitted to him, and give a fair criticism of the work, but that is now rendered unnecessary by the publishers who send along with the copy of the work, a eulogy composed by themselves.

Of the many novels published a large number of them are doubtless meritorious, and possess a degree of originality that is sufficient to satisfy any reader who merely wishes to be amused. Writers like Hawley Stuart, Bertha M. Clay, May Agnes Fleming, Miss Braddon, E. Gaboriau, W. E. Norris and some few others can probably boast the largest number of readers, in as much as they write on subjects that are of possible occurrence, and the narratives are natural and not overdrawn, but how such writers as Rev. E. P. Roe, Maxwell Grey Grant Allan and a few others of similar ilk ever secured publishers is a mystery to me, unless the publishers were desirous of circulating school-boy compositions. If you will take any of E. P. Roe's works you will see a painful effort to fill up paper, and the peremptory manner in which he deals out hell to those of his characters he makes opposed to his dishwater heroines or heroes, seems to me more like the desired spite of some acidulated old maid than the possibility of its being a truthful presumption of what might have happened. Besides this particular feature there are the glaring inconsistencies of his characters, and his efforts at portraying fashionable life make me laugh. They are what one might hear in a laundry. His title of Rev. has been the philosopher's stone that has won an audience for his books, and in his case as in many another, the priestly cloak has served a baser purpose than it was ever intended. People of a goody-goody class who are too squeamish to read a novel by the illustrious Gaboriau, find no scruple in reading of a seduction or two or a life of shame by Rev. E. P. Roe, although they lose in elegance of composition by giving him the preference.

A writer who has very successfully disposed of her books, is Augusta J. Evans Wilson, though I am free to confess my ability to understand why, except it be that her readers flatter themselves they can understand the pedantic phrases she uses, which, after all, could be accomplished by anyone who possesses a good dictionary. I should be sorry to suggest that Mrs Wilson was an inmate of an insane asylum, but the only woman I ever heard use the stilted language such as she puts into the mouth of her characters, was an incurable lunatic, who claimed to be a daughter of Queen Victoria.

A young miss is in penitentiary for a crime she never committed, and having just learned of her mother's death, replies to her comforter in the following language:

Invest no hope for my future ; for escape is as impossible for me as for that innocent victim fore-ordained to entangle itself in the ticket on Mount Moriah. He could have fled from the sacrificial fire and from Abraham's uplifted knife, back to dewy-green pastures, poppystarred, back to some cool dell where Syrian oleanders flushed the shade as easily as I can defy these walls, escape my lawful doom ; loosen the chain of fate.

The above may be very flowery, but I think the average reader will agree that if anyone were to address you or me in that style, even though her mother were dead, I think we would come to the logical conclusion that it was not the penitentiary where that person should be, but the asylum. I heard some school boys discussing her works once, and one had, I think, struck the nail squarely on the head, when in a tone of derision he said, "The characters in all *her* books talk like a lot of d...d fools."

I observed an advertisement a while ago calling attention to a new novel by Maxwell Grey, and commenting upon that writer's ability. I never read but one of that illustrious writer's works thank heaven, and while the work itself contained nothing of an original nature that was even fairly meritorious, it seemed to me that the whole concern was a wholesale larceny from George Elliot's "Mill on the Flos," and the balance that might be possibly original was about as bad a conglomeration of trash as could well have been collected.

People of the present day are essentially independent in thought, and usually take a criticism for what it is worth, and there is little stock taken in such writers as Dr. Johnson and men of his ilk. We read of how he seemed to consider himself the mentor of men, who probably knew just as much as he did, and who accepted his snarls and regarded them as the outcome of a giant intellect.

It is well for him that the worthy doctor did not live in this age of grace, as he would have lived many a long day before he would have found a Boswell to put up with his peevish nonsense. It is not likely indeed that he would have had more than one opportunity of reviling men of this age as fools and blockheads, and contradicting them in defiance of all rules of good breeding. Having done that once, the handsome pair of black eyes, or broken mouth he would have received would have taught him a lesson for the rest of his life.

Mrs. Southworth is another whose giant intellect has produced some singular trash. I think it is extremely amusing to read of the true lady and "perfect gentlemen" characters of some of the modern works of fiction. In one of Mrs. Southworth's works she endeavours to describe the character of one of her "true ladies," but gives herself or the young lady away when the latter twitts an enemy with the remark "I leave *that* for the painter's daughter to do," in order to remind the painter's daughter of her humble origin, and there are any number of writers whose inconsistencies are just as glaring. Judging her by her works, I do not think she mingled with either ladies or gentlemen, or she would have been able to give a better delineation of how they conduct themselves, or had a better idea of what is considered good form.

To-day we would scarcely read the works that once held away and were regarded as highest class literature. The sleepy essays of Elia, by Charles Lamb would not pay to publish, the reading public—and it is they who are to be consulted—would hardly condescend to read them, let alone to pay for them, and many others would receive the same reception. No doubt this is very frivolous on the part of the present generation, but it is none the less true. That ideal gentleman whose unimpeachable honour and immaculate integrity are regarded as pleasant creations of a writer's imagination, is now a thing of the past, or it might be called an exploded doctrine of the past, as no one believed that such men exist now, or ever did exist, because, having

no such characters nowadays, we don't believe that past generation-
were any better than we, or if they were, they must have had a woes
fully dull and slow time of it, and history does not give us to understand that they had a particularly unpleasant life as far as it treats
upon the subject.

If I am wrong, and I do not believe that I am, let me point to the
fact that such works as Albert Ross' "Thou shalt not" "Why I'm
Single," etc., are more widely circulated than those "with a moral,"
notwithstanding the fact that his works are two and a half times the
price of these others; as well as to the enormous circulation given to
the Kreutzer Sonata as soon as Postmaster General Wannamaker of
the United States decided to proscribe it, and of all works of fiction
having similar characteristics, then our moral depravity must be very
great, or else, as I believe, our intelligence is so much greater than our
ancestors. The inane Sunday school trash, and all works of heroics
are so wide apart from the truth and from society as we find it, that
anyone reading them comes to the conclusion that the writers are
simply a species of ass, and when works like Balzac's, Ross', Tolstoi's
and others of that class are placed upon the market, they attain a large
circulation simply because of their probability, naturalness and being in
accordance with what we find in every day life.

A copy of a work called Madeline was placed in my hands a short
time ago, and I was introduced to one of those sweet, unsophisticated
maidens, whose sublime innocence is really comical, that is if you have
a keen enjoyment of the absurd. That such a character ever existed,
I do not believe, that she lived in the present generation is absolutely
preposterous. I admit that there are women who have lived possessed
of innocent faces, but the apparent innocence and artlessness generally
are screen for the parched and hollow souls of the woman of the world,
who knows how to look after her interests and tell her woes to the
person where it will do the most good, but in a manner to childlike and
bland that the majority of men are likely to be duped by it. When
innocence like this can be found it is time that the portals of heaven
should open, for the millenium has been reached. It is noticeable, I
think, that characters of this class are falling into decay or disuse. Men
and boys who read novels wish to have something they can understand,
and as this is a character never to be met with, they very properly have
consigned it to unutterable hence.

In my estimation the ablest novel writer in the English language
is Miss M. E. Braddon. The charm of her writing consists to a very
great degree in the fact that she knows what she is writing about. If
she is describing fashionable life, she handles her subject in such a
manner that the reader knows that she is writing from what she knows.
If the other side of the picture is presented, it is drawn with equal
vividness, showing that she has studied it, and knows it. You read of
almost any writer of the Southworth, Roe, and even the pedantic
Augusta J. Evans Wilson class, and you are at once convinced that
these people never knew the usages or characteristics of polite society

or aristocratic society, but lend the idea that their knowledge is something like the negro washerwoman, who tries to emulate the language and manners of the people for whom she has been washing, and whom she has probably seen only a few times, and heard speak the same number of times. Or like the female contributor of a Parisian fashionable journal, who stood on the pavement and watched the ladies step from their carriages to the house of some grand dame who was giving an entertainment, and wrote of them as though she had been one of the guests. The man or woman who has not read Miss Braddon's works has missed a treat that I would be only too glad to have to indulge in again. As a matter of fact I have read her books over three or four times each. It is also true with regard to American detective stories. There does not appear to be one writer of these stories who is competent to give a story or good society. I have purchased the works of nearly all of them, and consider myself as having been done. I could buy them cheaper. In some cases I paid as high as 30 cents for detective stories, and have kicked myself for having been roped in. I could have bought just as good in the Old Cap Collier series for five cents apiece.

THE WEEKLIES.

These are innumerable and comprise every field of labour and financial enterprise, as well as every mercantile pursuit, and some of them one would think, might very consistently ask themselves what they are published for. But it is to be remembered that it is a very simple matter to publish one of these papers. A large office such as Jas. Murray & Co's. publish several of these papers, and consequently it is not the gigiantic undertaking one might first imagine.

THE RELIGIOUS PRESS.

This class of literature is scarcely of sufficient importance to warrant more than a passing remark. Very few of these papers, if any, are edited with more than average ability, and anyone who has seen one has seen them all. They are devoted to news of church openings, written on post cards (as I have seen them), biographical sketches of the deceased subscribers, and editorial notes culled from other papers that are well edited, though I believe they are considered good advertising mediums. The faithful, however are not, it would seem, to be permitted to enjoy the old-time privilege of being glorified by an obituary in one of these paper, at least, as witness the following from the Telegram :

THE OLD TIME OBITUARY.

Occasionally obituaries printed for the Christian Guardian have been clumsily written. The writers who were enumerating the virtues of their religious deeds wandered over wide tracts of thought, and, when almost swamped in words, sometimes came out at the right end with the help of an apt quotation from the poets. The sins of the old time obituary were all sins on the side of the picturesque. The obituaries built under the new rules lose the vivid, fresh earnestness of the old clogies without any compensating gain of sincerity. The idea underlying the old obituary was that the life recalled in its phrases had some deep, spiritual importance. The new style obituary honours the life and mourns the death, of a good Methodist in prose as cold and unenthusiastic as that in which the church paper announces a quarterly meeting or reports a tea meeting. The picturesque, sometimes absurd, but usually earnest, obituary h d to go along with many oddities which were esteemed in the past, but the degeneration of such a quaint feature of religious journalism is worth a passing notice.

Methodists who die and leave no friends to forward the obituary notice to the office of publication within so many days can go down to the grave " unwept, unhonoured and unsung," as far as the Christian Guardian is concerned. A time limit is a novelty on an obituary page. Delay does not impair the value of the lesson which the life and death of a good man can teach, nor can the prompt publication of the obituary notice give value to a life and death which teach no lessons.

THE STOCK EXCHANGE.

There are few people who read the daily papers, who are not familiar with the reports of the stock exchange—an institution that regulates the prices of the securities we hold or would like to hold, and which sends the values thereof up and down at its own sweet will.

Buying and selling stocks on margin is a somewhat mysterious set of phrases to the uninitiated and I would suggest to those who have never dabbled, not to find out by their own experience, as one of those who compose the class of people who think they are going to make money by speculating in stocks, I can testify that you will wish you had taken my advice after a few ventures in this arena of finance. You will find brokers are ready to advise you in a stock in which you think there is money to be made, and the probabilities are that he will have some of the shares himself to dispose of.

In November, 1890, I was interested in Bank of Montreal, which had been borne down to 216, and it was running up again with a bound, having reached 225 bid in the course of a few days. I asked a firm of brokers their opinion.

"The idea prevails that it will go higher; the bears have had their innings, and run it down to '16, now the bulls are having their turn, and they are going to pinch them as much as they can, just as long as any of them are short."

"Do you think it could be purchased at 225?"

"I doubt it; 226 was bid in Montreal last night, and they are promising to run it up to 230. You see there has not been a transaction at all, although the stock has gained ten points within the last three days."

You will observe, therefore, that the stock was not by any means worth the market price, but it was run up by the bulls simply to pinch the shorts, and that as soon as the latter had covered, the stock would have lost its fictitious value.

The shorts are they who agree to furnish you with stock at a certain price in a stated time, they take the chances of its going up or down—if it goes past the price agreed upon, they deliver the stock at this price or pay you the difference between its present worth, and the price you contracted to pay, if on the other hand it declines in value the order is reversed.

To finish my story anent the Bank of Montreal, I gave the order to buy, the broker very considerately informing me that he thought I could get the quantity I wanted—five shares—at 226. The next morning Bank of Montreal made a sudden break in Montreal and in sympathy it declined here as well. By "a master effort" my friend secured me the five shares at 226, which was the only tra·saction at that figure, the other sales being at 225, 224¾, and on the afternoon board it could be bought for 222¾, so you see my assumption that the firm had some some shares themselves was, I think, really quite logical. So it goes. Take the advice of one of the bitten, and eschew all gambling in stocks.

Take my case with the Bank of Montreal:

5 shares at 226	$2260.00
Brokerage	2.50
	$2262.50

On this I must put up a margin of $100.00, to protect the broker against loss, and he borrows from some Loan Company the balance of $2162.50, hypothecating the shares as security for the loan, upon which I am to pay interest at current rates. After holding the stock some three months, I come to the conclusion that there is no probability of its increasing in value and I sell at 224. The transaction is as follows:

5 shares at 224	$2240.00
Brokerage	2.50
	$2237.50
3 months interest on $2162.50 at 6%	32.44
Net proceeds	2205.06
First cost	2262.50
	$ 57.44
Amount deposited on margin	100.00
Amount I received after sale	$ 42.56

So you see for my experience I paid $57.44, which, though not large, was sufficient, or ought to be sufficient to keep me from having my fingers burned again.

Some years ago we had what were called bucket shops, that is no shares were purchased or sold. You put up your margin, and were treated in every respect just the same as though the purchase was bona fide, you paid interest, brokerage, etc., and if the article you were interested in went up you received the difference between the price you bought at and sold at after deducting these little expenses.

I mean to say that you received this money sometimes—if your bucket-shop keeper had it to give you, and this sometimes became a very important question, for if you did not lose by an adverse market you stood to do so by the unreliability of the broker, whom after suing, you found to be utterly worthless and with no chattel to levy upon.

This bucket shop business became such a crying evil that the Hon. J. J. C. Abbott, the late Premier framed an Act which was passed prohibiting them altogether. For a time this had the desired effect, and the country was free from the unmitigated curse, but now a new phase of the old system presents itself, and insted of having the principals here in our own country, we have only the agents, who correspond with headquarters in Chicago or New York, and who are merely commission men.

The Telegram in speaking on the subject says:

ROOT OUT THE EVIL.

Toronto's righteousness is quick to rise in arms against sentimental evils, and yet it ignores the existence of so-called brokers' offices that have made thieves of trusted employees in other cities, and will do the same here. Either Premier Abbott ought to be ashamed of the Act which is unappropriately labelled "a measure for suppression of bucket shops," or County Crown Attorney Curry and the police authorities ought to be ashamed of their failure to use the sword which the Dominion statutes gave them. This whole bucket shop business is bad. A well-conducted poker game is a respectable and cheap method of losing money compared to sport which is dignified with the name of legitimate speculation. There is nothing legitimate about the business. All the needs of the legitimate grain business are served through the Board of Trade. Outside of that the traffic is simply gambling, for the dupes do not buy grain, but drop into the spider's parlour to lose their money on the chance of a jump in the price of wheat or pork. Often as much as $160,000.00 is telegraphed from a single bucket shop in Toronto to one central operator in the grain gambling business at Chicago. More than one million dollars of good Toronto money has been rhrown in upon the wrong side of wheat margins within the last month. Labelling a bucket shop with the title of commission office does not change the nature of business. It is a cold swindle from start to finish. It deprives legitimate investments of the money which they need and turns the heads of silly boys and sillier old men by tempting them with alleged chances of sudden wealth.

Another time I was interested in Bank of Montreal, a second time, and after the market going against me for some time, I, in despair placed a limit of 223¾ to sell at, and after some little time the market began to show signs of advancing. Inadvertently I did not advise the broker to cancel the order to sell at that figure, and notwithstanding the fact that the market was very strong with a decided upward tendency, he *managed* to sell for 223⅝, although the quotation following that was 225, and finally the stock rose to 230. I called his attention to this matter and expressed regret that he had sold, but he replied that if he had not done so he could have been held liable for it if the stock had by any chance gone down below my limit. So far so good. Five months later I was interested in London and Canadian, and I telegraphed an order to sell it at the market price, which was 137 bid and 138¼ asked. But he did not sell. A day or so afterwards he stated that he would sell when he thought it best in my interest to do so. Unfortunately I was in need of money at the time, and I confirmed this gross piece of negligence or design on his part, and I was compelled to sell at a very great sacrifice to myself, but he never stated that he was liable for this negligence on his part. If you will take my advice and be guided by my experience have nothing to do with the stock exchange, or at least that part of it which deals in margins. You will be nipped as sure as your name is what it is, if I am any judge of the matter, and I regret to say that I am.

The stock exchange itself is situated on King street east on the corner of the recent extension of Victoria street, and was incorporated in 1878. There are two meetings daily except Saturday at 12.30 and 3.10. Each broker has a seat and outsiders are not admitted to the

Board, but anyone may communicate with a member by handing his card to the doorkeeper who will at once call out the gentlemen. Persons wishing to become members are required to make their applications at certain times, which is publicly announced, and if anyone can bring and sustain an accusation affecting the integrity of the applicant he is not admitted. Some time ago, I believe, seats were worth $3,500.00 to $4,500.00, but one was sold some little time ago for something like six hundred, I think, demonstrating that the privilege is not so valuable as it used to be.

People desiring to invest their money will find that Toronto as a financial centre has few equals on the American continent. Her banking facilities are large, few communities being more highly favoured in this respect. The history of the loan and investment companies forms an interesting study, and the fidelity and care with which they are managed make them together a standing evidence of the honesty and trutworthiness of Canadian officials. The development and growth of the city and surrounding country are due to the resources which are placed at our command through these financial institutions.

Canadian banks are of a large capital and the different institutions have agencies here and there in the most profitable districts of the country. Out of a total of 38 banks doing business in Canada under Dominion Government charter no less than 14 of these have agencies here, and Toronto is the headquarters of seven. The paid-up capital of the fourteen banks having agencies here amounts to nearly $50,000,000 while the total paid-up capital of the banks doing business in Canada is nearly $70,000,000. The total deposits of all the chartered banks in the Dominion amount to about $220,000,000.

FINANCIAL ENTERPRISES.

"When I think," said Coleridge, "that every morning, in Paris alone, thirty thousand fellows wake up, and rise with the fixed and settled purpose of appropriating other people's money, it is with renewed wonder that every night when I reach home, I find my purse still in my pocket."

And yet it is not those who simply aim to steal your purse who are either the most dishonest or the most formidable. To stand at the corner of some dark street. and rush upon the first person who comes along, demanding "your money or your life" is but a poor business, devoid of all prestige, and long since given up by chivalrous natures. A man must be something more than an idiot to still ply his trade on the high roads, exposed to all sorts of annoyances on the part of the police, when financial enterprises offer such a magnificently fertile field to the activity of imaginative people. And in order to understand the mode of proceeding in this particular field it is sufficient to read the glaring prospectuses of some of the concerns whose histories are given below.

In Canada we are not as expert as our neighbours nor the Parisians to be sure, but we have had our Central Bank case, and it proves that we are making progress, though it may be perhaps a matter of regret that a larger number did not share the spoils. One man was stated to have had one of his cheques in the hands of the teller for seven hundred and fifty thousand dollars, and it was counted as cash. "What sublime confidence," thought, not without a feeling of envy more than one man, who for merely one tenth of that amount would gladly have become a citizen of the United States. Although such large adventures were somewhat rare, in the present instance the magnitude of the amount more than made up for the vulgarity of the act.

In that same Central Bank case, it will be remembered that one firm was given a line of credit largely on account of their possible influence on the stock market, and if this credit were not given the stock of the bank might suffers at the hands of this firm who could possibly "bear" it, and when the names of some of the Bank's debtors were given, business men must have smiled to themselves at the gullibility of the manager who gave them credit. Emulation of these men will be found to be much wiser than to engage in plundering at the point of a pistol. The Criminal Code does not appear to reach such cases, and the man who can "do" you is almost safe from molestation. Who then would be like the ragged little newsboy, modest as his crime is who steals a loaf of bread to keep from starvation, or steals a pair of shoes to keep his feet warm, when so much more brilliant fortunes can be made from engineering financial institutions.

Man's inhumanity to man is not more strikingly exemplified than in the large number of schemes introduced to make money out of the credulous. Given a kind of insurance scheme, and an agent approaches you with the argument that a large number of those who become members are sure to drep out, and that is where the stock insurance companies make their money. Let us take for example the Alliance Bond and Investment Company, an institution whose name would seem to carry the weight with it that strong financial standing should do.

The following somewhat seductive advertisement appeared in a large number of papers in the city, and the city directory :

The Alliance Bond & Investment Co.
OF ONTARIO, LIMITED.
INCORPORATED FEBRUARY 27th, 1890.

Capital, $1,000,000.   Subscribed, $500,000.

General Offices—27 & 29 Wellington St. E., Toronto

PRESIDENT—W. STONE Toronto.
VICE-PRESIDENT—JAMES SWIFT, Kingston ; T. K. HOLMES, M.D., Chatham.
CASHIER—HENRY VIGEON.
SOLICITORS—McPHERSON, CLARK & JARVIS, Toronto.

The Company issue Bonds guaranteed to the face value. These Bonds are for amounts from $100, and can be bought for any numbers of years from five upwards.

These Bonds are payable by instalments, and the investor obtains guaranteed compound interest, at the rate of 4 per cent. per annum, and are especially protected by a sinking fund invested in first-class Real Estate Mortgages.

This Company is empowered by its Charter to act as Administrators, Receivers, Trustees, Assignees, Liquidators and Agents, under appointment by the Court or Individuals. Having special facilities for the winding up of estates, the Assignee branch of its business is solicited.

Being a responsible Financial Company, Creditors can depend on prompt settlements and quick winding up of any estates they may entrust to the Company.

The Alliance Bond and Investment Company, of Ontario, Ltd.
Assignees, Administrators and Financial Agents.

27 & 29 WELLINGTON STREET EAST, TORONTO.

The company in question was a joint stock affair incorporated with a capital stock of $1,000,000, of which it was stated that over $500,000 had been subscribed. A call of five per cent. was issued in the first instance, and a second call had been sent out. The Company occupied magnificent offices in the Bradstreet building at 29 Wellington street east. The walls were ornate with costly engravings and paintings, rich carpets covered the floor, the furniture was superb; in point of fact the two flats occupied by the company were fitted out in Oriental fashion. The business consisted in selling bonds on the instalment plan, a class of investments which has not proved itself to be excessively popular with the people. At the outset the Col. Potter, of New York, was the manager of the concern. In salaries the Board was generous, Potter received $5,000 a year, Mr. Sparling, the superintendent $2,000, and the president, $1,500.

Potter came from New York, and was formerly manager of the Mutual Reserve in that city. He brought letters of introduction and played the Masonic racket for all it was worth. Some were caught, others were warned by the articles in the Telegram and escaped. The feeling was very bitter that New Yorkers would have given letters to Potter thus inducing innocent people to invest. Potter endeavoured ty capture Hon. G. M. Gibbon with a salary of $9,000 a year, but he was warned by the Telegram and kept out.

The Boston News Bureau has been showing up these bond com-companies in the United States and has this to say of them:

Everybody knows that an insidious form of gambling has been creeping into the wage earning community the last two months under the guise of so-called " investment bond " companies, based largely upon the principle of Mrs. Howe's bank, which could continue to pay large returns so long as deposits increased—in fact security is exactly as in Mrs. Howe's bank, and Mrs. Howe went to prison—not the deposit of the depositer but the deposit of the next depositor. But it has not been generally understood that this form of " enterprise " is rapidly increasing and is beginning to affect the ordinary channels of investment.

The schemes of the investment companies vary in details, but all have these features in common—a promise to pay a round sum of money in return for immediate payment, and regular periodical assessments. The bonds or certificates, often in engraved form, with gold seals are to be paid in numerical order, beginning with the first issued, and each bond is said to mature and become payable, when all bearing lower numbers have been cancelled or paid and "there is sufficient money in the treasury." Any failure on the part of a bondholder to pay the assessment when due forfeits to the company all previous payments.

Thirty-five of the sixty-five investment companies whose prospectuses the News Bureau obtained issue straight $100 bonds, three issue $500 pieces, three issue $1000 pieces, two issue $50 bonds, three issue $35, $75 and $200 respectively, and seventeen give their customers a variety ranging from $25 to $2,000. The average cost for the first payment, including one month's assessment is about $7, and if $500,000 is a fair estimate of business done so far the face of the liabilities assumed already is about $18,620,000. That is to say before the last man who has invested in these schemes to-day shall realize his hopes the class of people who fancy their "investments" will have to contribute over and above all expenses over $18,000,000. Should this $18,000,000 ever be contributed the face of the liabilities then outstanding will be $2,268,000,000, or more money than there is in the United States. If 20 per cent. of the money, and that is the usually stated estimate for expenses, sticks to the fingers of the projectors as it passes throught their hands, they will be rich beyond the dreams of avarice.

The recent prominence given to the Dominion Building and Loan Association by reason of the pending dispute between the directors and shareholders of the concern, has attracted a good deal of attention to its method of doing business. The Society is constructed on the eight-year endowment principle and one correspondent who encloses a literal copy of the membership agreement writes: "By this document it appears that the shareholder is promised six per cent..., on his $50 for eight years, which amounts to $24. At the end of the eight years he is to receive $100, making $134 received in all. That is to say he is promised his own $50 back with an addition of $74, which amounts to a return on the investment and all but 18½ per cent. per annum in addition. If the sum returned were $75 instead of $74, the return would be exactly 18½ per cent. Now why does the Dominion Building and Loan Association sell for $50 an article which if offered to any one of a dozen of our large financial institutions would be snapped up at even a higher price than $81.15? Why does the Dominion Building and Loan offer to pay or have to pay so much for accommodation or for funds for investments which comes to the same thing. And what upon earth or under it is the nature of the financial business that can afford to pay the enormous sum of $124 for the loan of $50 or for the use of $50 for eight years? Is there any financial business going which can pay 13 per cent. per annum, as well as directors' fees, salaries, office rent, printing and all other expenses?

The Telegram was the first journal in Canada to call public attention to the dangerous character of the gambling insurance devised in the State of Indiana, under the name of assessment endowments. An attempt is being made to legalize this kind of insurance by the Dominion Parliament. The same paper also exposed the plans and methods of the Sexennial League, and the Septennial Benevolent Society with its plans and methods was dealt with in an equally plan and faithful manner. The character of the society and its peculiar operations were brought to the attention of the public.

It is nearly ten years ago since a Mr. George L. Clarkson came to town. He chose the west end as his place of residence and joined the West End Y.M.C.A. To the members of that organization he introduced himself as the Toronto Agent of the Dominion Life Assurance Company, of Waterloo, Ont. Mr. Clarkson was undoubtedly the agent of the company, but it is equally certain that Manager Hilliard did not know what sort of man he had to deal with. Mr. Clarkson claimed that his company had struck a scheme whereby a man could be insured for three years at as small a premium as that given by any other company, and could at the end of three years have all his premiums returned to him with interest at the rate of four per cent. per annum. This was too good for the young west enders to let pass, and many of them took out policies. Singularly, none of them seem to have read the documents, which contained no promise regarding the return of the premiums at the expiration of the three year term, and Mr. Clarkson accordingly pocketed big commissions, amounting, it is said, to nearly $10,000. The Dominion Life people at the head office in Waterloo, congratulated themselves on having secured such a pushing agent, not knowing of course, the means which were used in order to get risks. It happened, however, that one of the young men of the Western Y.M.C.A., who had been taken in, told a friend of his, the agent of another company, how Clarkson's company was giving such advantageous terms. The insurance man laughed at the idea saying no one could live and run a business on such a basis. This roused the suspicions of some of the insured ones, and Manager Hilliard was written to. He was out of town and did not return to Waterloo for some time. When he came back he promptly wrote a letter in which he, as manager of the company, declined to acknowledge any such agreement. Mr. Clarkson was interviewed by several of the men to whom he had made promises, and insisted that everything was all right. In the meantime Clarkson had got a Mr. Jenner to deposit $400 as security in a partnership scheme, and then skipped out. His presence in Toronto would now give pleasure to a number of confiding men whose good money has gone to the States with him.

In the examination conducted by Mr. Imilius Irwing, Q.C., as to the methods of the Lion Provident Life and Live Stock Insurance Association, the manager admitted that there were judgments against him for $1,500 in the sheriff's hands, and that there were about 11,000 claims in addition which had been disputed on various grounds, but principally because the premium notes had not been paid on the day when they fell due. The receipt of the money on the day following did not suffice. Mr. Jones admitted that he did not bring the clause referring to the latter to the notice of insurers, but it was on the back of the policy. They accepted payments a day or more after they were due, although the policy was voided by the delay in payment, without informing those who paid the notes of the fact. The manager said he took 80 per cent. of the receipts for himself.

BUSINESS IN TORONTO.

The legitimate business in Toronto is greater than that of any other place in Canada except in Montreal. The city being the centre of Ontario commerce, offers the greatest advantages of any other in Canada to persons engaged in trade. Merchants at a distance buy whatever they can here, as they like to visit the place, and can thus combine business with pleasure. Hundreds of people, or indeed thousands annually visit Toronto, and while here expend large amounts in purchases, besides they are apt to find the best article in the market, as it is but natural that the chief centre of wealth should draw to it the best talent in the arts and trades.

Merchants from all parts of the province like the liberal and enterprising spirit which characterises the dealings of Toronto wholesale men. They can buy here on better terms than elsewhere, and their relations with the merchants are generally satisfactory and pleasant. Everything gives way to business. Private neighbourhoods are constantly being encroached upon for the purpose of business; which is steadily advancing towards the extremities of the city, north, east and west.

But while the visiting merchant sees only the smooth and finished side of the picture, it is none the less true that there is a dark side to it also. He should see the struggles of the employees in the houses he visits to keep themselves in clothing, and the necessaries of life, and to submit to the overbearing manner and petty tyranny of some one who has had the good fortune to get into a position of trust. I was once commissioned to get some laces for a lady friend of mine residing on the other side, and I presented myself at the wholesale warehouse, which had, by the way just the evening before, advertised for a warehousemen. I stood to one side while a young man, who had been waiting a few minutes before me, should be attended to first. A physically impotent looking Englishman wearing a skull cap, and possessing a figure as thin as Cassius, bounced out of the office, and the young man begain :

"I saw an advertisement in the Telegram last......"

He got no further, the Englishman gave a kind of a yell, and answered :

,' Filled !" them bounced back into his hole again.

I decided that my lady friend could get her laces at another place, and I quitely passed out of the door. I confess to a feeling of fiendish glee when a while afterwards I heard that the house in question had gone under most dissastrously. I asked myself if this could be wondered at. In this connection I might mention a circumstance that happened some time ago when the East York campaign was in progress. One of the speakers pointed out the number of young men in the United States, and attributed it to the false political economy of the Government of the day. I have no wish to enter into any controversy on the subject politically, but I would like to suggest one reason for this. Let any young man enter any business house in the United States, and the probabilities are that he will be received and dismissed with courtesy; if there is no vacancy he will be told so in a gentlemanly manner, and is never insulted, besides he has lost no self-respect by making the request. I never saw a similar case to the one I have mentioned and I confess my disgust at the reception given to the young man who was an applicant.

There are, it is a matter of regret to say so, business houses where a man's promotion depends upon his ability to speak evil of his fellow workmen, or in other word to play the sneak. I know a house in the city, where one man has done this so persistently that he is regarded as dangerous by the other clerks, and he is never the recipient of any of the confidences that are indulged in amongst fellow employees in any concern. He is nevertheless a favourite with the chief clerk, who does everything in his power to promote him. First of all the sneak tells the chief clerk the other clerks' shortcomings, and the chief clerk in turn tells the manager or proprietor, so that both are held in high esteem as being interested in the welfare of the company. Could anything be more despicable than this? It is doubtless within the memory of Torontonians how a young bank clerk had been so harrassed by the Inspector that he was driven to tender his resignation, and when after going to Chicago and being unsuccessful, he was driven to suicide. When men reach that pitch that they are incessant faultfinders I think there must be something radically wrong with their minds, morbidity or something of that kind, some such disease as impelled the shocking and debased morality characteristic of the exiled Somerset.

A little story is told of a business house in the city which is worth repeating. In some way they are concerned in advertising. One of the customers of the concern, having been behind in his account, and having a contract rate for inserting his advertisement at reduced rates, was refused any further accommodation until the acccount was paid. He declined to pay for some time, and at length the company placed it in the hands of their solicitor for collection. On the back of the contract there is a proviso that if the customer fails or the space is not all used up, he can be charged full transient rates. This does not apply to a man who does not pay his account, as it would seem clear to the least intelligent, but the chief clerk of the concern decided to have the account made out in that way, and sued it. The debtor fought it out and subpœnæd the accountant who had made out the account in the manner ordered by the chief clerk, and in serving him he handed him a dollar bill. The matter never went into court, however, as the solicitor on being given the statement of the case, held that the company would certainly be non-suited, and the debtor having in the meantime paid into the hands of the division court the sum he really owned. Finding this to be the case, the chief clerk in entering the cheque from the solicitor to be placed to the credit of the account said :

" I'm going to enter that credit of F......'s now, and if you'll give me that dollar, I'll put that with the other that I have received."

" But I spent that money last night, I went to the Grand Opera House, and I have nothing but a ten dollar bill."

" Oh, well, I'll get that changed, if you will give it to me."

The accountant gave the ten dollar bill, and the clerk took it, and placed it to the credit of the account they had used. Is that not a magnificent piece of business? If it would serve any good purpose I would tell you the name of the concern, but if you knew it it would surprise you.

A friend of mine, being out of employment, wrote to a firm, one of the principals of which is one of the trustees of one of the leading Pres-. byterian churches in the city, and asked for employment. He called a few days after posting the letter, and interviewed the firm. A proposition was made to him that he should work for $8 per week, with an increase at the end of three months to $9, and the next six months to $10. He was asked also to write his biography for the benefit of the firm, stating whether he smoked, drank or chewed, &c., and he was also requested to get down at eight o'clock in the morning, or rather he stated his ability to do so. This was just half an hour earlier than any of the other clerks, but he did not mind that so much. The member of the firm after reading his letter, wrote the terms on the margin, and my friend signed his acceptance of them. Then the tiger showed his claws. Heretofore he had been as smooth as velvet, but when the agreement was signed, he commenced :

" Of course, you know, we have no sick benefits here, and if a man misses a day he loses it, it is the same for holidays, we do not pretend to be liberal in our dealings with our employees, we exact so much, and we expect it."

He enumerated a long list of other matter that were too numerous to be remembered, and it is just sufficient for me to say that my friend remained there just four days, and that satisfied him for all time to come. He happened to mention his experience to a young lady friend when she exclaimed : "Don't have anything to do with that man. He is called the sneak of our church."

Owing to the prominence given to advertising lately, shopping by mail has become quite a thing of the present. But unless a very fine quality of goods is required you will find it for more satisfactory to buy your goods from our own dealer, if my experience counts for anything, and I think it does.

A certain store that advertises pretty freely advertised a brand of black cashmere sox at 35c. per pair, or three pairs for $1. I was paying a local dealer 40c. per pair, or for more than two pairs at the rate of 37½. It was a gain of 10 per cent, so I ordered three pairs. They were considerably coarser than what I was getting at home, and I sent ten cents more for the next finer brand, and they were not any better than I was getting at home, nor quite so fine. I ordered some cuffs, and they were very good, and I ordered again, and received some trash that were worth about fifteen cents a pair, and believe I could have obtained them for that at the house where I usually dealt at home. Take my advice and keep your money at home, dont buy by mail, you will rue it if you do.

The true Parisian is always represented as having several means of existence at his or her fingers' ends. It should be the same with the young man or boy in Toronto who is without home or without resources. This applies to the professions as well as to the trades. Advertisements frequently appear where the young man must be a drug clerk, a telegraph operator and a bookkeeper and goodness knows what else. I think the following is really good denoting the requirements for a certain position :

> Wanted a boy who can write shorthand and the caligraph quickly, and make himself generally usaful. Apply to box 443 Telegram.

I suppose the boy who applied for that position, and could fill it would be offered the princely salary of $3 or $4 per week, with every chance of its being less.

Here is another:

> Youth about 18. to assist in office, one who has bicycle and is willing to learn and anxious for advancement. Enclose copy of testimonials to Box 283 Telegram.

I would like to hear whether this youth got $3.00 a week or $2.50, but the following is absolutely princely :

> Young lady as bookkeeper and cashier, wages $2.50 to $3 per week. Box 444 Telegram.

After paying her board out of the above it may consistently be asked : Was the young lady expected to prostitute herself to obtain money for her clothes ?

> WANTED—Hustler to sell ordered clothing at a price, one who is expert at measuring and can sell factory cotton for tweed ; good salary to right man. Apply references and where last employed. Box 142 Telegram.

SUNDAY IN THE CITY.

In Toronto, like all cities of any pretensions, Sunday is a day of rest, but practically it is the very reverse. The morning is usually devoted to church going, and the churches are pretty well filled, for as I mentioned there is a halo of respectability surrounding him who goes to church, which nothing else can give. But those who are impervious to the refining influences of church attendance, if it be summer time, hie themselves down to their boat houses, and prepare for the afternoon sail ; or others again go to the island, there to remain during the day.

Some afternoons in the spring time, the Queen's Own Rifles have a regular parade to some one of the churches, and if the weather is fine, and it usually is, the streets are thronged with the youth and beauty of both sexes. The following is an account from one of the city papers anent a recent church attendance :

> The Queen's Own Rifles mustered 657 strong for church parade. Leaving the drill shed at 3.30 the regiment under command of Lieut. Col. Hamilton and Majors Delamere and Sankey, and headed by the regimental band and bugle corps, marched in half companies by way of

OF TORONTO THE GOOD. 63

Jarvis, Carleton, College and McCaul streets to New Richmond street Methodist church. On its arrival the regiment occupied the seats on the ground floor, which had been reserved for them. Every inch of the remaining space was occupied by the general public, and as usual on such occasions, hundreds had to be refused admission. During the service Mr. Wilson expressed himself in favour of church parades. He did not believe they were inspired of the devil. He thought that much good would come of the fashion.

Like all other amusements, or perhaps I should say attractions, the church parade has its enemies. I give some of the opinions of clergymen who ventilate their views at the meetings of their associations:

After devotional services Rev. Mr. Stark, a retired minister, introduced a resolution condemning the Sunday parades of our volunteers, especially with the reference to the Kilties' parade. The resolution led to quite a spirited debate, some of the brethren being very severe upon the soldier parades. Rev. Mr Parsons said that "the people wanted to play the devil once a month; we pose as strict Sabbatarians, but all these military services were merely chasing the devil around the stump." It was generally felt by the members of the Association that the ministers had this matter largely in their own hands. The opinion was that if the soldiers would only march directly to church instead of taking a circuitous route it might not be so bad. Another said that the very minister who was so opposed to Sabbath desecration was the first to preach to the Kilties. The resolution was withdrawn.

The same subject appeared to provide a bone of contention for the Baptist Ministerial association. At its meeting the subject was thoroughly considered in a free talk.

Rev. Joshua Denovan, a patriarchial representative of the Scottish race, thought it incumbent upon him to vindicate, if possible, his fellow nationalists. If any objection were taken to the parade of the Kilties, the same objection, in his opinion, applied to the parade of the O.O.R. He deprecated, in conclusion, ostentatious demonstrations of any kind on Sunday. Rev. James Grant said that the action of the Queen's Own Rifles in playing the popular air, "Ta ra-ra-boom de ay" on the Sabbath was shameful. He thought it was a great pity that the Lord's day should be thus secularized. The consensus of opinion as by the ideas expressed by those who took part in the impromptu debate evidenced was that parades of any kind on the Sabbath were out of order.

It will be observed in one of the quotations referred to that our mutual friend Rev. Dr. Parsons speaks of chasing the devil around the stump. There are I grieve to say a majority of people who have not the intelligence to see the affinity in connection with church parades and the hazardous diversion of chasing the devil around the stump, so I give the distinguished divine's remarks as delivered to an ignorant public, and commend them as indicative of the Reverend gentlemen's sapiency. Appropos of the term "distinguished divine," I think that is the correct phrase in the case, and is applicable in all cases of referring to the clergy, at least it is the style adopted by the press.

In the afternoon, the park and gardens are open in the summer and those who are intellectually inclined will find a rich treat in store for them if they go to the park. The Salvation army holds forth in all its glory and beauty, distinguished by sacred words adapted to the tunes of different waltzes, bar-room songs, and any class you can think of, while the partakers therein are ever and anon, moved by the spirit to give vent to their holiness and happiness, by yelling, " Glory be to God," "Praise be to God," and various other expressions too numerous to recollect.

A new by-law prevents speaking in the park, and to the majority it is a welcome boom. Some time ago the park used to be filled with men who believed themselves, like Joan of Arc, to be divinely inspired, and held forth in great style.

A dirty, greasy-looking individual used to expound the true Protestant faith, and the corresponding errors of the Church of Rome in accordance with the views of Maria Monk, and others of that ilk, but this tyrannical by-law deprived him of this privilege, and he is quite disconsolate thereat.

It was proposed to employ a band to play in the Queen's park every Sunday afternoon, but this idea was voted down in council, though I confess I see no possible objection to it, except that it would be a welcome diversion to the working-man, but it would be also a source of attraction to children who otherwise are penned up in a stifling Sunday school, having dry as dust texts sweltered into their little bodies, which they must bear in the same manner as the children of Israel bore their trials at the hands of the Egyptians.

At night the streets are crowded with people of both sexes, especially Yonge and Queen, and the promenade is kept up until nearly eleven when the streets become entirely deserted.

By a recent decision sacred concerts at the Island or in the city or elsewhere are as lawful on the Sabbath as on a work day. Chief Justice Armour and Mr. Justice Street having so held and as a result quashed Magistrate Denison's conviction of Band-master John Bayley of the Q.O.R., for playing sacred music at Hanlan's Point on a Sunday afternoon in August last. Magistrate Denison held he was guilty of a violation of the Lord's Day Act, that he was pursuing "his wordly calling" unlawfully and fined him $1 and costs. But with all due deference Mr. Bayley differed as did the counsel, in their interpretation of the "act to prevent the profanation of the Lord's day" from that of the Court street judiciary, and obtained a reserved case, which was argued with the above result in the Divisional Court to-day. The argument was brief, the court at the outset favouring the appeal against the conviction, and holding the act was no more intended to apply to a bandmaster than to an organist in a church. The Appeal allowed with costs. B. B. Osler, Q.C., appeared for Mr. Bayley, and Mr. Moss, Q.C., for the Crown. The concerts were free and were provided by the Toronto Ferry Co.

And now, horror for horrors! the populace of Toronto have decided by a good substantial vote that they desire street cars on Sunday and they have them.

THE DETECTIVES.

The detectives are under the supervision of Inspector Stark, and are men of experience, intelligence and energy. They are well skilled in the art of ferreting out crimes, and generally succeed in the objects which engage their attention. They are distinct from the police force, though they are subject to the order of the Commissioners. It requires an unusual amount of intelligence to make a good detective, in addition to which a man must be honest, determined, and brave, and complete master over every feeling of his nature. He must be also capable of great endurance, of great fertility of resource, and possessed of no little ingenuity.

They are always to be found on Court street, where they have separate apartments when not on duty. Strangers coming to the city get drunk over night in places of bad repute and are robbed, and the next morning they come to ask the aid of the police in discovering their property. If their statement of the circumstances is true, they can generally recover the lost articles through the aid of detectives, if they can be recover at all. They are in constant telegraphic communication with other cities, and are receiving or giving intelligence of criminal matters and movements so that if a crime is committed in any city, the police force of the whole continent really is on the alert for the apprehension of the criminal.

The individually of crime is remarkable. Each burglar has a distinct method of conducting his operations, and the experience of the detectives enable them to recognize these marks or characteristics in a moment. Thanks to this experience, which is the result of long and patient study, he is rarely at a loss to name the perpetrator of a crime, if not person a professional. Appearance which have no significance for the mere outsider are pregnant with meaning to him.

If persons seeking the aid of the detectives would tell the truth in their statements the aid rendered them would be much more efficacious and speedy, for as a rule the detective can tell from the nature of the loss whether the statement of the circumstances be true or false. Persons are often indignant that those who have robbed them are not arrested and held for trial. Undoubtedly this would be a very desirable thing but it is not always possible. Frequently no evidence can be obtained against the guilty party, whose arrest would be a useless expense to the city, and the detective in such cases is compelled to content himself with the recovery of the stolen property. The stolen goods thus recovered and restored to their owners is estimated to amount to a very large sum annually.

In many cases the detective is very loth to arrest the culprit. It may be the first offence of some youth, or he may have been forced on by circumstances which an experienced officer can understand and appreciate. In such cases he leans to the side of mercy, and his advice to the party against whom the offence has been committed is not to resort to the law, but to try the offender again. In this way they have saved many a soul from the ruin which an exposure and punishment would have caused, and have brought back many an erring one to the paths of virtue and integrity.

While Toronto very consistently congratulates herself upon her immunity from the dark crimes such as have occurred in New York, Chicago and London, and other large cities, there is a special dispensation of Providence she has perhaps not taken into consideration and congratulated herself upon, and that is her immunity from that crowning affliction—a detective story.

I do not refer to those literary masterpieces of absorbing interest and unrivalled delineation of character written by Emile Gaboriau, whose works are unquestionably a credit to the literature of any country, and in whose novels not the first trace of inconsistency nor any wearisome unnatural conversations can be found, but to that rubbish which has been flooded over the country written by detectives, ex-detectives and would be detectives, that has been described by the publishers thereof in their circulars to a confiding public and an indulgent press as "thrilling," but which possess neither literary merit nor the possibility of reality.

Do you suppose a child could give a written description of the mysteries of astronomy? The proposition is absurd upon its face, because a child knows nothing at all about it, and its intellect would be incapable of grasping the subject. Then it is just as reasonable to expect from the pen of an underbred policeman a correct delineation of character, and an account of the manners and customs of well-bred people as to expect a child to explain the system that has puzzled the ablest scientists of the universe.

I am not in any respect exaggerating the picture. Some time ago a firm of publishers sent me some of this trash to review. They were like the laboured efforts of a junior schoolboy to fill up paper, and anyone reading the accounts given of fashionable life would exclaim at once, "the writer is not a parvenu but a would be parvenu." Imagine a gentleman of good-breeding calling his daughter "Miss Emma" to one of his friends, or speaking of his house as "the mansion."

Again take the denouements of these novels, and their very tameness is absurd, and altogether weak and inconsistent. As an example a New York belle is married, and her father a millionaire, is giving her a most magnificent present. On the night of the mariage, the bride is kidnapped, and until a certain sum is paid, one hundred thousand dollars, the bride will be held as a hostage. The distracted father puts the detectives on the track, and to his herror finds that the villain who kidnapped his daughter is an old-time acquaintance, who happens to know of an incident in the old gentleman's early life, which he holds over him like the sword of Damascus. To be discovered he knows would be social ostracism, and he is about crazy, not knowing which way to turn, and almost deciding to give up the hundred thousand dollars. After wading through wearisome prosaics, the reader necessarily expects to be rewarded for his Job-like patience by some terrible tragedy in which the old man has taken part.

Vain expectation. When everything comes out all right, the villain dead ; the agonized husband his wife restored to him, and the righteous triumph of the good over the bad, the reader is coldly informed that the father had committed seduction in his early manhood, and endured the agonies of Gethsemane in fear that he might be discovered and be socially ruined.

To anyone acquainted with our national character, the absurdity of this conclusion is at once apparent. He might just as well have said the old man had drunk a glass of beer, and feared social ostracism, which would have been just as reasonable as to express the idea that he did. Such an act in a man's life is no more consequence socially, than a change of diet would be. The great wonder to me is that publishers can be such fools as to publish such dishwater. Imagine for one moment the difference between the writings of the courtly Frenchman whose plots are marvels of depth of thought and study, and whose language is grace and elegance itself, and those of the others who surfeit their compositions with italics and exclamation points in such profusion as to make a compositor frantic with rage, and yet it is simply the childish propensity of the school boy who has learned a new trick which he thinks clever, and is incessantly practising it; besides unlimited interjections such as "there came a time when Sephronia remembered those words of Samantha's" in almost every chapter. I have read the prosaic trash of the Pinkerton's; the conglomerations of an ex-detective a Mr. Lynch, and Anna Catharine Green's water brained productions which lack the elements of satisfactory explanations of her extravagant plots, and I am pleased to congratulate Toronto on her escape from having such bosh added to its already over-burdened soul.

When the work's written by Mr. Lynch were sent to the newspaper upon which I was employed, the publishers informed us that this particular work " had made him famous." It may have done so, but that only proves how cheaply fame may be bought.

I laugh when I read the high sounding names they give their characters, the Lois Clarendons, Irene Chesterfields, Ethel Delafields and such like, but if their delineations of the characters of the people demonstrate anything it proves that Mary Ellen Jones would be the proper name for the majority.

HOTELS.

There are quite a number of people both married and single who prefer to board than keep house. Of these a large number board at the hotels, and the others in boardiug houses.

The principal hotels of the city are the Queen's, Rossin, Walker, Arlington, Palmer, Metropole, and a large number of minor hotels of less importance, some of which are really good, but do not make special efforts to meet the travelling public that those first mentioned do. The transient custom of these hotels is very large, but the permanent boarders of these establishments are also very profitable. The rates are somewhat high, and the majority pay their proprietors well. There are two classes known in the city, those which are conducted on the American plan, and those known as the European plan. The former provide their guests with lodgings and full board at so much per day or week, while the others furnish merely the room and attendance, and are either without the means of supplying meals to their guests, or charge for each article of food separately. The European plan has almost gone out of date, and in fact can hardly be said to exist at all, proving conclusively the popularity of the American style.

The proprietors of hotels are very active in their efforts to exclude improper characters from their houses, but with all their vigilance, do not succeed in doing so. One is never certain as to the respectability of his neighbours at the table and it is well never to be in a hurry to form acquaintanceships at such places. Gamblers and those of that ilk abound at such places, and the proprietor cannot put them out until they commit some overt act, inasmuch as he might possibly get himself into trouble, as he is required by law to give accommodation to anyone who will pay for it. As soon, however, as his attention is called to any improper conduct on their part, they are turned into the street, no matter at what hour of the day or night and left to shift for themselves.

Appropos of this law requiring that the proprietors of hotels shall accommodate any guest who is prepared to pay therefor, Messrs McGaw and Winnet of the Queen's, had a somewhat unpleasant experience with a coloured man hailing, I think, from Chatham, and who, I believe, they declined to accommodate on account of the lack of room. The irate guest got into quite a rage, and threatened suit for damages through Messrs. Blake, Lash and Cassels, but the matter was never threshed out and I do not know how it was settled.

All hotels are the legitimate prey of swindlers, and the devices used are as varied as are the kinds of the operators. It is not a very difficult matter for a man who has sufficient assurance to get a meal without paying for it. He can manage to get in the dining room, if he knows the lay of the house, and by pure nonchalance pass muster, though he runs the risk, nevertheless, of being detected.

At one time there existed a mania for stealing or exchanging clothing in some of the best hotels, though the practice can better be carried out now in those of more modest pretensions, inasmuch as the best hotels employ a man or boy to take charge of the hats and coats of the guests as they enter the dining room, but even with the very best surveillance things are often cribbed. For instance a man may quite easily slip a fur cap in his overcoat pocket, and if the man who is in charge happens to be engaged in assisting some one else, the thief's chances of detection are very meagre, but these thefts do not happen very frequently, and generally only during some very busy time, such as when the exhibition is on, and the hotels are thonged with strangers. It is customary, I believe, or else the law requires that the landlord shall make good any loss of this nature.

It is a most difficult matter for a hotel to get along without being occasionally swindled, but as a rule the amounts out of which they are defrauded are not large. A man may go to a hotel and stay a week or ten days, and settle his account, and he is then presumed to be pretty good pay. He remains perhaps a month longer, and then suddenly leaves, leaving behind him perhaps a hand bag worth a couple of dollars and some old clothing of perhaps one half that value to take up his residence in some other place to repeat the same game.

A somewhat peculiar incident happened some years ago, in which a young fellow of nineteen or twenty figured, and demonstrates that one can never trust to appearances. He was an innocent looking boy, rather good looking, and an American. On his arrival in the city he took up his abode at one of the numerous boarding houses on King street west, and proceeded to look for a position. Not being successful, he left this house and took up his quarters at one of the leading hotels, remaining there some days. In the meantime he had made the acquanitance of a gentleman engaged in mercantile pursuits in the city who was endeavouring to get him a position. At length the manager of the hotel came to the conclusion that all was not as it should be, and he requested a settlement. The young man stated that Mr...... (his friend), had some money belonging to him in the Ontario Bank, and that he would settle his account as soon as this friend had drawn the money out. In the meantime the manager called the friend up by telephone.

" Is that Mr. Blank ? " he asked.

" Yes."

" Well, this is Mr. Jones of the ......House. Do you know a young man by name of ......? "

"Yes, I know him casually, but nothing more. He has been trying to get a position in the city here, and I have been doing what I can to help him, but that is practically all I know of him."

"Well, have you any money belonging to him?"

"No, I have not."

" He says that you have some hundred dollars in the Ontario Bank belonging to him."

" That is not so. I have no account there as a matter of fact, and I certainly have no money belonging to him."

" He says that you have, but if he comes in to see you this morning, don't say that I have spoken to you, will you ? "

" No, certainly not."

A few minutes later the manager called on the gentleman to whom he had been telephoning, and the above conversation was confirmed, but the young man in question never put in an appearance from that time at either the hotel or the office where his friend worked.

That is one incident in many where the hotels are swindled, and were the rooms of some of the hotels where they keep this old truck examined, some funny things would doubtless be brought to light.

In the management of these concerns it is not necessary to speak more than to state that where a specialty is made of keeping permanent boarders a few of the ideas expressed by those who take up their residence in such places may not be out of place. A common cause of complaint in one place where I resided was the fact that the places of the permanent boarders were incessantly taken by transient people, and then quite frequently by a most disgusting crowd into the bargain.

One man, a tailor, and been in the habit of going to a hotel on Yonge street for dinner, and his diet consisted of the coarsest kind of food, such as corned beef and cabbage, and beer the latter of which in time produced its usual effect, and in exact ratio as his wits became clouded, did his ill-breeding demonstrate itself. He would use his napkin in a place of a handkerchief, cough and spit on the floor, and his mouth would make a noise not like one pig, but like two or three. I can not understand how a man with an ordinary degree of intelligence can sit day after day and see people properly conduct themselves at the table and not take pattern.

At the same house, a German, whom I took to be an insurance agent was just about as bad—or more so. His place at the table was always filthy after he had left it; his food would be scattered all over the table and chair, and no one would sit there after him, and certainly they can scarcely be blamed.

You may sit at a table at a hotel after day, and the characters you meet there are really innumerable, and now here is a better opportunity to judge human nature.

At one hotel where I was a guest a middle aged man, or perhaps an elderly man would suit the bill better, as he was somewhere in the neighbourhood of sixty. It was just about the time when it was intended to convert Weston into a town. It seems that some of the wealthier men of the place did not want this conversion, and had given their opinions at a public meeting. Our friend, who was in favour of the scheme, seemed to have spread himself at this meeting. The guests at the table were not in any respect interested in the matter, but he seemed to think they were his legitimate prey to be talked to, and he gave himself that pleasure. He spoke to no one in particular, but loud enough to be heard all over the table.

"As I stated yesterday," he remarked complacently, "at the two meetings where I spoke, money was never yet know to buy brains."

This was intended to apply to one of the wealthy man who had the audacity to oppose him. Besides it gave the impression that his own intellect was above criticism.

"When these people buck against me," he added, "they may just as well know at once who they are bucking against. I say now as I said this afternoon, that brains is a natural gift, and any man can make money. I had the whole audience with me."

The illustrious gentleman glanced around the festive board and not having received that applause he considered himself entitled to, arose and left the table.

"Who may that be?" inquired one the gentleman who had been an amused listener to the conversation of the distinguished speaker.

"I do not know what his name is," someone replied.

"I had an idea from his manner that he might have been the Son of God."

Men seem to think the hotel table is the proper place to air themselves, but to the man of good taste it will appear at once as indicative of bad breeding for anyone to tell his own business and its achievements before people who are perfect strangers to him. On the following morning when Mr. Winbag came to the table he did not receive that cordial reception he considered himself entitled to from his manner the previous evening. He sat down to the table without ever receiving the time of day.

"Well," he exclaimed cheerfully. "How is the weather this morning?"

As no one seemed to answer him, he turned to the last comer, and demanded in the style of a cross-examiner :

"Is it cold out?"

"Not particularly," the gentleman answered curtly, as if to end the conversation.

"Is it as cold out as it was yesterday morning?" he asked persistently.

"I don't carry a thermometer," the other replied coolly, "but if you wish to know the weather so minutely, you might take a walk around the block and find out for yourself."

"And you might learn to answer politely," was the angry rejoinder.

"When a gentleman asks me a question, I usually answer him to the best of my ability," the other retorted, "but I don't propose to allow any windbag like you to gratify his curiosity by me, so I gave you the answer you deserve."

The table was not annoyed by him again.

We have all met the American woman or lady (there are no women in America) who, though she is a guest at a hotel which is not first class, still regards herself in a measure as the mentor of the creatures at the table. Being only the wife of a mechanic she appears to think the Canadians are somewhat of a benighted race, and the women do not know their own worth. You can judge all these characteristics by her face and its expression ; the vulgar insolence which she thinks is independence ; the manner of reaching over the table for what she wants, shows that she is "a lady," although some gentlemen consider it ill-bred, and then the manner she assumes when she snaps off a grape at a time from the dish instead of taking a bunch as a low bred Canadian would do.

Another gentleman sits at the table and sucks his teeth, by some this is considered ill-bred. But to him it demonstrates his opulent manners and familiarity with the code of good breding.

You will find men and women too, by the hundreds who have as much idea of table etiquette as an Indian. My friend Hawley Smart hits them off perfectly. "They are" he says, "not above harpooning anything they fancy with their own forks and utterly ignore salt spoons while their knives are in that hand, plunging the blade in freely when wanting that condiment." He might have added with equal truth that a large proportion do not seem to know what their forks are for, vegetables, everything, being shovelled in with their knives.

These are a few of the characteristics of the people one meets with at the hotel table, and they could be enumerated by the hundred.

RESTAURANTS AND BOARDING HOUSES.

RESTAURANTS.

Of this class of eating houses you will find the city is beautifully supplied, and as your means are limited or unlimited so you can choose a particular restaurant. McConkey's and Harry Webb's head the list of popular and fashionable restaurants, and everything is got up in first class style and cleanliness, but they are, comparatively speaking, expensive, and it is not every one who can afford to indulge in such luxury.

Nearly all the down-town restaurants do a good business during lunch time. So many men and boys who live in the extreme ends of the city prefer to go to a restaurant for a sandwich and a cup of coffee, if nothing more, than to eat a cold lunch and remain in a cheerless warehouse during noon hour. There are some restaurants where boarders are taken, and those can usually count on having their seats reserved for them, which is quite an advantage especially during the busy season.

An amusing incident occurred in a well-known Yonge street restaurant by which a conceited ass was beautifully come up to. He had a great habit of planting himself at a table intended only for boarders, and as he finished each course, and was waiting for another be would spraad out his arms and take up almost the whole side of the table. This continued for some time, when exasperated beyond measure, his left hand neighbour ordered soup, which, as fate would have it, was thick and greasy. He toyed with it for some time until the proper time came, when he adroitly pushed it to one side. In a moment down came the elbow of the sinning one into the thick and gresy mess.

" Excuse—G...d d...n the luck, my coat is ruined."

The young man made haste to apologise, and graciously handed him a napkin, but the old man did not again take up the entire side of the table that day.

It is absolutely surprising how little men know of table etiquette when brought into contact which their fellow men. Men who are considered models in business life, seem to forget that in a restaurant there is an unwritten law requiring the observance of certain rules, to demonstrate that they are men and not pigs, by the observance of which men are judged of their bringing up.

A close observer of human nature who has spent considerable time in the different restaurants in the city gives his experience.

" I came here," he observed, " from King street east where I used to put up, but it got to be so extremely disgusting there that I had to move. I never drink tea or coffee but usually milk. The dose I got on several occasions so turned my stomach that I never asked again, you could absolutely smell the onions, as though the goblet had never been washed, so I had to quit there.

" My next place was nearer the heart of the city, but after being there a short time I came to the conclusion that I must be very hard to please, for I was disgusted in no time. Just at this season of the year you know, there is an influx of veterinary students , all fresh from the farm, and who all know more than the professors themselves. I had the misfortune to be placed at a table where a crowd of Americans were congregated, and at every meal the same subjects were discussed ; dogs, horses and cows were all dissected at the table and the dissection criticised, until at length I was obliged to move to another table, these discussions of such scientific subjects were beyond my limited comprehension, and appreciation, therefore, I asked to be removed. I do not in any way impugn the right of free discussion, nor do I say anything of the question of good breeding, for all Americans are gentlemen, and it was unquestionably my beclouded intellect and not the lack of good manners on their part which was the cause of my inability to sympathise with their discussions.

"I had a fairly good time at the table where I was next seated, and the girl was a gem, but I had the misfortune to change my dinner hour, and a man whom I had never seen before was placed next to me. He was a man with a black heard, and was disposed to be most cheerful under any and all circumstances, and it is perhaps, superfluous to say he was an extremely religious man. During all the dinner hour he discussed church matters with his right hand man, and it was astonishing how animated the conversation would become. At length he commenced on me, but my taciturnity did not seem in the leastwise to give him any embarrassment; he rushed ahead like a torrent, and realizing that I was unable to check him, I permitted him to talk until he got tired, and I resorted to reading a newspaper. When the Exhibition with its myriads of people came my place was given to some transient guests until at least I was compelled to seek another place.

"Waitresses seem to think you are their natural enemies, and they yours, and I used to sit sometimes a quarter of an hour in the morning without the girl ever coming near me, and than I did not get what I wanted; if I asked for boiled eggs, I either got them so hard that I could not eat them, or they were so soft that they were disgusting; and you might as well spare yourself the trouble of complaining, for all the good it would do you, so now I take my meals at a first class house on the European plan, and if I don't like it I simply go and try some other place."

The swindler, as usual, has his experience with the restaurant, and frequently gets the start of them in ways that are peculiar and laughable. Two will go to a place together, and order what they want, and as soon as they are nearly through the waitress gives them a ticket with the amount of their bill on it, each being separate; one will get through before the other, and they make it a point to sit apart, so that he who gets through first approaches his companion and begins a conversation until the other gets nearly through when number one decides to try something on the bill that he did not notice before; he receives another ticket, and the two start out together, when one ticket is presented and only a part of the bill is paid, so the fellow gets a good supper for the price of the small dish he took a fancy to as he was getting ready to go out. Other times a man will stand and talk to a friend after he has got his check, and hang around until the cashier has forgotten to keep an eye on him, and he quietly steps out.

BOARDING HOUSES.

Any stranger in the city who is looking for a boarding house has only to consult the condensed advertisements of the Telegram to find a long list of places to call on, but that he will be suited is quite another question. There is, it seems to me, a good opening for a really good boarding house in a central locality, and circumstances prove the philosophy of my opinion.

Some years ago a lady kept a boarding house on Adelaide street, and it was always crowded ; the reason was very simple, everything was scrupulously clean, the attention was good, and only those who conducted themselves as gentlemen were allowed to live there. It is now the custom, almost universal for the young men, to rent a room in some suitable locality, and then take their meals somewhere else.

Boarding houses, like hotels, have their peculiar characteristics. In some of the former, there is no desire apparently to please. If you like pie hot, you are almost certain to get it cold, or the apple sauce is full of enormous lumps that almost turn your stomach, and the characters you meet in some of them are sources of never failing amusement.

My experience has been a somewhat varied one, and the people I have met and their peculiarities would all fill a volume. At one table where I sat was a man who used to come to dinner only. He was engaged in some business in the city, and lived away up in the east end. He frequently spoke of his Sunday school class, and after ordering his dessert he would use his fork for a tooth-pick, which of course he had a perfect right to do, even though it might be considered somewhat ill-bred. I observed him on several occasions, and finally one day I stared him out of contenance, and I suppose he saw that it was not exactly the thing to do, and he stopped it.

We have all met the men who opens his mouth to its full width while chewing his food, and smacks his lips every time they come together, and who, in eating pie, grabs a piece from the plate, and bites it in the same way as he does bread, ignoring the fact that pie according to the usages of good society is to be eaten with a fork, yet this specimen of humanity is to be found in every boarding house, though one would think that once seeing how respectable people eat they would take pattern.

There is perhaps no place in the world where a man's ill-breeding shows itself in such glaring prominence as at the table of a boarding house. A man sits next to you who eats his soup like a pig at a trough, another will hawk, and finally spit on the floor, while a third, not to be outdone fills his food with pepper and begins to sneeze, using his napkin for a handkerchief, and some of these men really consider themselves well-bred.

I cannot understand how it is that when a boarding house once secures a class of men, they never make any effort to keep them, and yet it would certainly pay to do so ; if a young man gets a house that suits him he is certain to stay there, but after a while the board and the attendance become so bad that he needs be a saint if he can put up with it. To make money is the aim of almost every one's life, but the shortsightedness of the boarding house keeper is like the shortsightedness of the storekeeper who cheats his customers and imagines they will come back.

To the wayfaring man who desires a rational amount to eat and is not a gourmond, I suggest that he decide to pay a fair compensation to a hotel that sets a decent table, and he will find it will relieve him of much vexation of spirit.

The following seductive advertisement canght my eye, and I decided to give it a trial:

BOARDERS—Table boarders can be suitably accommodated at .. Queen corner of King. Dining room on 1st floor; large, well-lighted and elegantly furnished. Every attention given, same as in first class hotel. Delicacies of the season always provided.—Terms moderate.

For breakfast we had thick, lumpy porridge first, and four days out of seven we had liver and bacon. Liver and bacon are not bad, but this liver and bacon bore a striking resemblance to fried gristle and leather. I have never tasted the latter, but I imagine there would not be much difference. The liver looked as though it had been dried in the sun for a week or so, and then cooked for an hour or two; while the bacon I should judge had been sissling for three hours at the least. It would almost break like clay when you touched it.

"Livernbacon" said the waitress to me one morning.

"I had liver and bacon yesterday morning, didnt' I?" I asked, meekly.

"Yes."

"Very well." I said "I will have the same this morning, if it isn't in use."

I put two little pieces in some paper, intending to get them photographed, but they were mislaid, and I cannot, therefore, give you that pleasure.

We usually had toast, dry, thin hard stuff that looked and tasted as though it had been baked, while there was a square slab of streaky looking stuff the lively imagination of the landlady dignified by the name of butter, and it was invariably bad. If we protested that the butter was bad, we were assured that it was impossible to get any better, —a statement I am prepared to believe, if she had added at the price she was willing to pay.

Sometimes we had steak, and such stuff—what I got I think must have done service for four or five before it came to me. It was usually thick with pepper and chopped with a knife during the process of cooking—I never saw anything like it before. Something was put before one gentleman one morning which the waitress called steak, but which he sent back with the remark that it was cold roasted beef cooked over.

For lunch, we had things that are indescribable, sometimes we had soup. For instance if we had had peas for dinner the night before, we would have a thick, slimey, greasy liquid, cold pea soup, if we had beans a previous evening, it would be bean soup; consequently I never ate any. The left over mashed potatoes from the previous evening's dinner were sometimes fried and sometimes worked over into croquettes and were always served cold. I never stayed to catch any. But where the landlady shone was in her manipulation of cake. Little cakes that are sold at ten cents a dozen, were divided up into beautifully cut little quarters or sometimes into six, and spread over the dish to make them look almost countless. I always drank two cups of tea to fill up on, although it invariably tasted like boiled hay. There are people, of course, who prefer their tea boiled two hours instead of one, but this lady boiled hers for three, apparently, on the principle that everyone might be suited. Dinner was served at six, and the vegetables were always cold, on Wednesday nights we had a composition of the week's remains called beefsteak and kidney pie. Now, I don't consider myself as being in any respect hard to please, as I stayed in that house nearly two years, and only left when the landlady desired to wait upon me herself. The line had to be drawn somewhere and I drew it at that. She had indigestion, and I used to bear her all over the house belching up the wind off her stomach and she cleaned her finger nails in the dining room, I couldn't stand that, and when to it is added the additional charm that she used to listen at the doors, I decided after we had a row about her waiting on me, that I would leave, and I did so.

HOLIDAYS IN THE CITY.

Toronto is very careful to observe the holidays of the year, the orthodox English element tending to preserve in all its purity each of the festivals of our fathers or a great national holiday.

ON NEW YEAR'S DAY.

The whole city is stirring by ten o'clock, and the streets are filled with gentlemen on their way to make their annual calls. Private carriages, hacks and other vehicles soon appear filled with persons bent on similar missions. Business is entirely suspended in the city, the day is a legal holiday, and it is faithfully observed by all classes; the cars are crowded and if the weather is fine, everyone is in the highest spirits. Women very rarely appear in the streets in the morning, but in the afternoon King street is crowded. The matinees at the theatres are crowded, especially by young people, and an effort is always made to have a good attraction. Government House is always a scene of great attraction, as all the leading lights in the city pay their respects there. The Roman Catholic Archbishop of Toronto and the Episcopal and other clergy all make New Year's calls.

QUEEN'S BIRTHDAY.

The birthday of our Gracious Queen is always kept throughout the country, and as it comes at a time when the whether is most delightful it is looked forward to for weeks and days before. Excursions to and from every available place are largely patronized, and the city is quite deserted. A large part of the day is devoted to fire-crackers, Roman candles &c., and though the police try to stop them, it is almost impossible to do so; the city resounds with the discharges, and the air is filled with sulphurious vapour.

THE FIRST OF JULY.

Canada's birthday of Confederation is alwas celebrated in a commendable manner, but the extreme heat that usually prevails on that day makes it almost impossible of enjoyment, but like the 24th of May, great preparations are made for it, and excursions are sent out all over, the outgoing steamers being crowded. In the city the lacrosse team usually have a team visit them, and they are well patronized by an enthusiastic audience.

THANKSGIVING DAY.

This day is commemorated by morning services in all the churches, and the rest of the day is given to rest and social enjoyment, and a bountiful dinner. In the afternoon the theatres are thronged with crowds of young and old.

CHRISTMAS DAY.

Every thing gives way to the merry march of the Yuletide monarch. The streets are teeming with preparations for the great Christmas festival, and peace and good will are the universal conditions which animate the human family the whole world over.

One of the gladsome features of the Christmas season, however, undoubtedly is the spirit of kindness and benevolence which becomes universally diffused. This is essentially a season in which the wants and necessities of others are relieved by their more fortunate brethren.

The St. George's society of Toronto make it their special charge to see the more necessitous among those who hail from Merry England.

In connection with the Irish Protestant Benevolent Society, the charity is confined exclusively to the deserving and respectable poor, and the greatest pains are taken to examine into the genuineness of each individual case.

In all the charitable institutions of the city the halls are adorned with Christmas decorations and preparations made on an extensive scale for the celebration.

CITY PARKS.

The Queen's Park is essentially the best in the city, and the Queen street drive is one of its conjunctive attractions. Like all other places in our ancient and beautiful city the children are not permitted as in American cities, to play in the park, but if some crazy jay wishes to shoot off his mouth on some religious question he has full permission to do so except Sunday, and then only such as the Salvation army or some similar organization is permitted to monopolize the Sabbath. This is a very wise by-law, unlike some that the city council passes, as it was, some time ago, Roman Chatholics had to run the risk of being insulted by some half demented fool who thought himself inspired and specially delegated to preach against that church, that prohibits such exhibitions on Sunday.

Some time ago when the proposition was before the council to exchange the block of land between Front, Esplanade, Bay and York streets the Telegram made the following caustic observations :

> Toronto's rulers keep its nose so close to the grindstone that the city has seldom time to look into the future. The problems of the present have always been too big for past concillors. American cities with all the dishonesty that has oppressed them have been more fortunate. The future has not been neglected and the elaborate park systems secured when land was cheap outshine the parks of Toronto the beautiful. The chance of securing a grand and complete system of parks has gone or is going by forever. The acres between the university and Bloor street for which $630,000 has been offered, are almost in the market. The loss of this natural park and plyground, dotted with trees that are the work of a hundred years, would be a misfortune, and civic patriotism ought to sacrifice something to avert a loss that cannot be made good within the lifetime of this generation.

And in connection with the Upper Canada grounds the same journal says :

> Toronto ought to outbid every private tender and secure the use of the old Upper Canada grounds for the city's children during the summer months. It is a small thing, but civic statesmanship could afford to stoop to conquer those convenient acres for the use of boys and girls who have no play ground but the street. Spite of high taxes, the city is rich enough to rent the property from the University trustees. The few hundred dollars which it would cost at most, would be a small price for the boon which such a play ground would be to hundreds of children.

What New York saw in 1851 the Telegram sees to-day for Toronto, and it is certainly to the credit of New York that they have a park which is as free as the air to both rich and poor alike, containing a parade grounds of thirty acres for the manœuvering of large bodies of troops, play grounds, base ball grounds, rides, drives, walks and everything that could be invented for the pleasure of its inhabitants.

During the summer season the council arranges with the different bands to give series of concerts in the parks, and the crowds that attend them outweigh any protestations for or against them, and abundantly testify to their popularity.

Even Montreal' the principal city of the Province of Quebec, which complacent Christians of Ontario regard as being somewhat benighted can boast of resting places for the weary and heavy laden. You cannot take half an hour's walk in that city but you will come to a square of sufficient dimensions to accommodate a large crowd of people, if they desire to sit down and rest. One Sunday evening I walked through some of these parks, and I fervently thanked God that Toronto did not have any such places. Numberless men, actually *smoking* and seeming to enjoy it, their wives with them in some cases and children too, all seeming pleased to be there. They were absolutely enjoying the shade and cool afforded, instead of being at the cemetery weeping and wailing over their grandparents' graves. I never saw anything like it. And if that were not bad enough to see the hardworking, common ruck enjoying themselves in this fashion, even the birds seemed to enjoy it too. The sparrows, bathed themselves to their hearts' content in the fountains. They chirped, dove into the water, splashed it all over, flew out again, and had a glorious time, and it was as I watched them that the prayer of thankfulness went up from my heart that Toronto had no such places. Can you not imagine, dear reader that frenzy, leading to madness that would have taken possession of the senses of the good souls of Toronto had such a frightful desecration of the Sabbath taken place in that saintly city. Those brutes who enjoyed the breath of fresh air with their wives and children and their pipes would soon have been hustled out of a park in Toronto, and as for the birds, I do not know how many of Toronto's policemen would have been required to stand in front of those fountains with two edged swords, keeping the little demons away. Had these things occurred in that city, and had the good people I have referred to been powerless to prevent them, imagine if yon can how many of them goaded into madness would have required places in the asylums already full to overflowing, and then think : Did I not have reason to feel thankful that Toronto did not boast of such places?

THE PUBLIC SCHOOLS.

Toronto stands at the head, and in the front rank of all cities on the continent for the excellence and extent of its system of public schools. The buildings belonging to the public schools are brick, and are amongst the handsomest in the city ; they are commodious in every respect and made equal to the demand upon them. The rooms are large, airy and neat, and the buildings are well warmed and ventilated and every care is taken to render the teachers and pupils as comfortable as possible. The course of study is most thorough, and in the winter months night classes are held and large numbers avail themselves of the opportunity to better their positions ; all these are free. Mr. James L. Hughes is a most thorough inspector, and it is due largely to his excellent management that the system has reached its present thorough efficiency.

The number of students attending the universities is very large, and as is customary with spoiled children, the public are very lenient with them. In this connection the Telegram has an article on the subject of attending the Opera House and says :

Students ought to know enough to stop short of rude interference with the rights of others. It is not to the wild and strange noises with which they decorate the silences of the night that objection is taken. Citizens are anxious that they should have not only liberty but a measure of license. They are allowed to enjoy themselves at the expense of other people's feelings, and public forbearance towards them imposes upon the collegian the duty of respecting the sacred rights of fellow-citizens. There was nothing wildly funny in the uproar at the Grand Opera House. Authors of the disturbance did not act fairly towards Manager Sheppard. His good nature allows them all the latitude they should ask. He owes something to his other patrons, and he could not allow the boorishness of the gallery to interfere with the fulfillment of his obligation to people who go to the theatre to enjoy the performance. Now the students are good Canadians. Individually they are not inconsiderate. The civic by-laws are stretched to the bursting point in order to contribute to their enjoyment. A tax-payer would be jailed for breaches of decorum far less serious than their antics. The public go more than half way to meet the inclinations of the students. They should cover the short remainder of the distance, for it is not manly in them to take from other people the enjoyment which they pay for.

In giving an account of the disturbance in question, the same journal adds :

The students behaved like a lot of blackguards among the gods at the Grand Opera House. They blew horns incessantly during the performance, their uproarious behaviour causing many to leave before the opera was more than half finished. Manager Sheppard went up stairs to remonstrate with the rowdies but his threats to ring down the curtain unless they behaved themselves properly, only met with the discordant tooting of a score of tin horns. After leaving the Grand the students organized a procession outside, and marched on the sidewalk and roadway about 600 strong, shoving and jostling everyone who would not move aside. At the north-west corner of Yonge and Queen streets one of the mob collided with P. C. Dodds, and knocked him down. He collared the offender and clung to him while P. C. Welch called up the patrol waggon. At No. 2 police station the prisoner gave his name as Howard Brown, a veterinary student, who had the appearance of being a farmer's son. After the arrest of Brown, the students continued their wild pranks, among the places and prominent persons being serenaded being Bishop Strachan school, William Mulock and the Moulton Ladies college. At the latter institution the young ladies acted most indiscreetly in encouraging the students. One of them started to sing a song, but some persons pulled her away from the window. Another lighted matches, while a third threw out a pillow, which the gang promptly picked up, and it served as a banner during the balance of the racket. One the following morning Brown was tried before the Magistrate on a charge of disorderly conduct, and was fined $2.

Mr. Sheppard who cannot be said to be anything but generous in his treatment of the students was allowed an early opportunity to interview the Police Commissioners at their regular forthightly meeting. He complained that there was an insufficiency of police at his place of amusement on the occasion of the students' rumpus. Mr. Sheppard was informed that the police duty ceased at the street line, but if he or anybody acting under his authority wanted any disorderly person ejected he could command the whole police force if necessary. The police would remove any individual pointed out or would turn the whole body of students out if requested to do so. The same orders will apply to all other places of amusement, and it is the intention of the Chief Constable to suppress any repetition of the disgraceful conduct in the theatres in the city.

The public schools occupy a considerable space in the correspondence columns of the city papers, and schools are rapidly becoming what religious societies are supposed to do in their world,—become side tracks for the public to shunt their children upon that others may assume the responsibility, or rather take the responsibility, from their shoulders in bringing them up. In view of the kinder-garten of the present time, the time is not far distant when women will be merely what Harriet Beecher Stowe in Uncle Tom's Cabin describes as "breeders." That is to say they will give birth to the child and they will then expect the State to nurse and educate it. A correspondent on one of the newspapers recently complained of the lack of ability on the part of modern young women to cook, and a few days later some sweet creature signing herself "One who is interested in the Girls" heartily agreed with the other correspondent, and suggested that cooking should be taught in the schools. The idea that girls should learn such things at home did uot seem to occur to her giant intellect. She thought perhaps that modern civilization demands so much of a girl's time, that the limited time she spends at home would be inaquate to allow her to learn to cook. The church, Sunday school, ladies' aid society, class-meeting, W.C.T.U., Young peoples' society of Christian Endeavor, Wednesday night prayer meeting, society for the propogation of American dress amongst the Africans, choir practice, etc., are such drains upon a young woman's time that school is really the only place she would have a chance to learn in. I should like just once to sit down to a meal such as two thirds of the present day young women could cook, and it would do me the rest of my lifetime.

Nor are they satisfied with having Sunday schools for religious instruction, but they also desire that something should be done in the same way in the day schools. I attended a public school when I was a boy and for a few moments, I, like fifty or sixty others sanctimoniously turned my eyes heavenward, while that paragon of virtue, who left his position because he could not control his appetite for liquors, read some passages that I never recollect having heard once. That was the law, however, and he complied with it. What more could anyone want? I have no doubt in the fulness of time that women will expect teachers to nurse their brats even.

STREET BOYS.

You can scarcely walk a block without your attention being drawn to one or more of the class called street boys.

Every morning, rain or shine, summer or winter, a perfect swarm of boys make their appearance at the offices of the different newspapers, and boarding the early cars, they have papers to all parts of the city in time to catch the earliest pedestrian or street railway passenger. The World, on account of its condensed form, has a very large sale amongst those who live in the outskirts of the city, as by the time one reaches the city he is master of the news of the day. But the boys who sell the morning papers are comparatively few in number. The newsdealers control a large amount of this trade, and the efforts of the newsboys centre on the evening papers, large numbers of which are sold all over the city. The great stand for the boys is on the corner of Yonge and King streets, and at the railway stations, where in the mornings you hear the cry " Globe, Mail & Empire, World," while in the evening, "Globe, Mail & Empire, News, Telegram and Star" is rattled off as their tongues can utter them. Some little fellows, however, of limited capital confine themselves to the Telegram, and at six o'clock the streets are full of little shavers, yelling " six o'clock Telegram." At the time of the Whitechapel horrors, it was a rare harvest for them, and sometimes when there was no Whitechapel murders on the boards, they called it out anyway. These lads are as a rule bright, intelligent little fellows, who would make good and useful men if they got a chance, but some of them are simply stupid. Some of them have no shoes, no coats, and even their shirts are merely apologies for such, and yet they are rarely, if ever, sick; they can nearly all swim, and enjoy themselves in the summer time, but the cold must necessarily tell upon them in time. Some of the boys live at home, but the majority are wanderers in the streets, selling papers generally, and sometimes forced to beg. In the summer time they can live out all night, but in the winter they are obliged to patronize the cheap lodging houses, the newsboys' home or St. Nicholas home.

Some of the more careful ones have done well, from a financial standpoint. Davy O'Brien, who for years stood at the corner of King and Yonge streets with unfailing regularity, deposited thirty dollars every two weeks in the Home Savings and Loan Company's office, and in addition thereto, he owns a house and lot on Duchess street, the value of which is at least eighteen hundred dollars. Some time ago when the Mail reduced its subscription price to four dollars in the city, the boys were unable to compete against the office, but the company agreed to sell the morning paper at 25c. a month per copy, if they were paid for in advance, this would be a cent a copy. Davy promptly took the matter up and paid for two hundred and fifty copies in advance each month and then sold them to the other newsboys, at a cent and a half a copy. Other boys have records equally good but which have not so bright a side financially. One young chap who used to stand at the corner of Bay and King streets is now in one of the offices learning to be a pressman. He was a reliable, honourable boy, and those with whom he dealt learned this, and when an opportunity presented itself he was rewarded by an appointment to a vacant apprenticeship. Another is now in the mailing department in one of the city papers. He, likewise proved himself worthy of confidence and received this position. Both of those boys are on the way towards making respectable and useful citizens.

In addition to the newsboys proper are also the youths who carry routes for the morning papers. Each paper employs from forty to fifty of these boys, and while the remuneration does not exceed two dollars a week, it is quite an item, inasmuch as the majority of the boys work during the day at some other business or go to school. It requires some enterprise and considerable self sacrifice, as they are required to be up at five o'clock in the morning but their work is finished by seven.

Again there are boys who carry evening papers to subscribers of their own. These are for the most part boys of respectable parentage, and who attend school. They are required to pay for their papers every day, and pay an average of seven cents a dozen, their profit being five cents. Some of these lads make several dollars per week, and have accounts at the savings' banks. They are sure to get along in the world, and their enterprise and pluck demonstrate beyond a doubt their ability to take their places in the battle of life. The boys who carry the morning routes are among the most respectable in the city, and must be of good moral character. One of the boys employed by one morning paper was the son of the pastor of a most prominent city church.

A good many of the regular newsboys sell the newspapers in the early morning and black boots part of the day, taking up the newspapers again in the evening. Their ages run from ten to sixteen years. A few are older, and one or two men follow this avocation in the street. A boy provides himself with a box with a sliding lid, and a rest for the feet of his customer, a box of blacking and a pair of good brushes. All these articles are kept in the box, when not in use, and the owner carries this receptacle by menas of a leather strap fastened to it, which he slings across his shoulder and trudges on with his box on his back. They are generally sharp, shrewd lads with any number of bad habits and little or no principles, and are averse to giving much information with respect to themselves; when asked how much they earn, they give evasive answers, but one dollar is supposed to be the average daily earnings of an industrious boy. The price of a new outfit or kit is perhaps worth a dollar, but second hand outfits can be bought at the junk dealers for much less. Some of the larger boys spend a considerable portion of their earnings for tobacco and drink, and they patronize all the theatres, their criticisms of which are really worth hearing, and their imitations or rather mimics of the different comedians are most creditable and put to shame the baser imitations we are obliged to listen to as being original and which we vociferously encore. The course of life which they pursue leads to miserable results, as when a newsboy gets to be seventeen years of age he finds that his avocation is at an end, it does not produce money enough and he has acquired lazy, listless habits, which totally unfit him for any kind of work. He becomes a vagrant and perhaps worse, and a wanderer all over the country. A boy of seventeen has visited nearly all the large cities of the United States, and the stories they tell of their experiences in Chicago in particular are absolutely revolting. The crime that banished Lord Somerset from London society is committed according to their reports, every night in some of the lodging houses in Chicago.

Like all matters or people who are compelled to reside in the city, the newsboys are, of course, the special care of that august body, the police force, which sought to tag the boys like dogs, and by consulting the chapter on the police force, you will see the opinions of some of the citizens on the subject. At a meeting held in connection with criminal matters, the following report is taken from a city paper:

Sir Daniel Wilson thought the prison was no place to send a boy to. Whipping soundly was the best treatment for boys of all classes who were refractory. The badge system of making newsboys register at police headquarters, Sir Daniel thought, would have been quite successful had not the newspapers given their voices against it. The system of compelling boys to go to school for two hours a day had not been thoroughly successful, because the boys left the respectable lodging houses in order that the police inspectors could not get at them so easily. The badge system must be carried out thoroughly or not at all. Radical were Sir Daniel's ideas as to the treatment of adult criminals. "When a man comes to thirty years of age," he said, " and has been convicted of burglary twice, I think it is ridiculous to look him up for but two years or so, and on the third conviction I would send him to prison indefinitely, for I regard such men as wolves who live to prey on the community."

I call particular attention to the remarks anent the newsboys, and would say for the information of others that when one of the police officers called at a certain office the clerk who sold the papers did his utmost to make himself as offensive as he possibly could, and declared his intention of selling to every boy or girl who asked for papers, whether their age was five or fifty.

"Two members of the police force insulted me one night, and anything that I can possibly do to obstruct them in a constitutional way, I purpose doing," he observed in explanation, and suffice to say he kept his word. Any boy, tagged or untagged got all the papers he wanted in that office at least.

Other legislation has been passed for the benefit of the boys not necessarily newsboys, but as the boys are now almost restricted to looking cross-eyed on the street, and eating their dinners, I give the expressions of Saturday Night on the subject of the restrictive legislation proposed for their benefit:

> Only those who have studied criminal procedure can understand what a roaring farce more than half of it is. Only those who have watched the discussion in Parliament have the taintest conception of the vast amount of a surdity which was eliminated during the discussion. Hanging for sheep stealing was nothing compared with some of the dreadful things proposed to do to people. Then look at the Cigarette Act, which is intended to correct the habits of the young as regards the use of tobacco. Since Dominion day it has been law in this province that all persons under eighteen years of age are prohibited from buying, using, or having tobacco in their possession, and those who sell or give it to them are liable to heavy fines. They should frame a Spanking Act intended to prevent the squalling of babies, the chewing of gum and refusal to take the matutinal bath. Enactments should be provided for the imprisonment of boys who insist on sliding down hill to the detriment of their trousers, and for the making of dreadful examples of girls who let their stocking sag around their ankles. By proper attention to these domestic details the responsibility of parents may be greatly decreased. All they will have to do shall be to provide nourishment and raiment for their offspring, the policeman will do the rest. What a delightful vista is opened for the coming parent when the Kodak theory of parental responsibility is perfected. They will bring the child into the world, the police magistrate will do the rest.

This is given to demonstrate the absurdity of half of the restrictive legislation passed, and the absurdity of making children, or anyone else for that ma ter, good or virtuous by Act of Parliament, and Saturday Night adds:

> The perfection of public schools has endowed the state with the right of even compulsory education. So far we could not quarrel with the idea of government. Unfortunately so many parents were unable to educate their children or even contribute to their education in a technical sense, that to prevent illiteracy the state was forced to invest itself with proper powers. Following in the wake of this, Sunday schools, imitating the Catholic example, relegated the religious education of the child to what may be called professional teachers. The mother, no longer feeling called upon to tell the sweet story of Christ's sacrifice to the child at her knee, had more time to devote to the designing of new gowns for herself and offspring. The father, relieved of his teaching duties, could spend more time at the club or in that odd mixture of secular and religious work designed to benefit the heathen and extend the tenets of his denomination. There is a general outcry for more religious teaching in the schools. Even the careless parent is observing that the proxy system has not yet been perfected, that neglect in providing parental precept and example is having its effect. Of course, parents are not impressed with the idea that they ought to do some of this sort of thing themselves. They feel that the schoolteacher ought to do it, that there is too much long division and too little divinity taught in the schools. The policeman having become the guardian of childish habits with respect to liquor and tobacco, the nursery business should be extended to the Fire Brigade, who could no doubt be profitably employed in their spare moments in washing the knees of the school children and giving dirty little boys their bath before going to bed I think the whole business would be laughable if it were not an innovation of that outrageous and fool idea that good boys and good girls and good men and good women are to be made by statute.

I wish to point out to those people who so ready to clap a boy or young man into gaol for committing some offence against society that society itself might exert some influence to reclaim these people. I have in my mind one particular case, which is but an example of hundreds. A young chap of eighteen, who had spent three years in the Reformatory, met me one night and asked me for some money. I gave it to him, and he told me part of his history, which I have since followed through the newspapers. He has been in the Central once or twice, and is in prison to-day, I believe. On several occasions I have given him money, and the economical use he would make of it convinces me that he would have been honest if he could. I have seen him wait around day after day where work was going on, in the hope of being employed. He once walked a distance of forty miles to get employment, and was unsuccessful. Would it not have been better to have some place where such people could go and stay when out of employment, than to run them in as vagrants? Might not a large share of missionery money—spent in foreign lands—be better employed in feeding and lodging the outcast? I was much struck by the explanations of a parcel of Toronto women of some scheme to which they contributed their money. It was to provide for East India Widows! It made me laugh when I read it. East India widows, Chinese and other Asiatic races having Canadian money spent for their benefit and to teach them a religion they do not want, while boys in Canada who steal because they are starving, are filling our prisons. Singular it is not? I may possibly be mistaken in regard to the objects of this particular missionary society being the assistance of India widows, but it was something just as ridiculous, if that were not it.

The same hysterical asses that live to-day appear to have lived in the times of the immortal Dickens, and I submit an example of his satirical references to foreign missionaries, being from Bleak House:

> Joe is brought in. He is not one of Mrs. Pardiggle's Tockahoopo Indians, he is not one of Mrs. Jellyby's lambs, being wholly unconnected with Boorioboola Gha, he is not softened by distance and unfamiliarity, he is not a genuine foreign grown savage, he is the ordinary home-made article. Dirty, ugly, disagreable to all the senses in body, a common creature of the common streets, only in soul a heathen. Homely filth begrimes him, homely rags are on him, homely parasites devour him, homely sores are in him, native ignorance the growth of English soil and climate sinks his immortal nature lower than the beasts that perish. Stand forth, Joe, in uncompromising colors. From the sole of thy foot to the crown of thy head there is nothing nteresting about thee.

Some time ago Mr. Harry Piper made a practice of taking a cartload of flowers through the Ward for distribution to the ragged children of poverty there. If I had my choice of a record when I stand before God on the last day, I would far rather it should be as a dispenser of such blessings as Mr. Piper's, or contributions to the newsboys' home, than all the glory of assisting missionaries in foreign countries where they are not wanted, but, of course, it is to be remembered that the former get no newspaper mention made of their actions and the latter do.

When I was on the staff of a newspaper published in this city, a lady come into the office to demand a free advertisement for the meeting of her pet missionary society. I took precious good care that she did not get it. That women could go to that newspaper office and with venomous persistency could haggle over the price of an advertisement regarding foreign missions, yet as she swept up the steps of that office she must have passed numerous half starved little newsboys sitting on these same steps who were far better objects for her missionery labors than any foreigners could be, yet I do not doubt, judging from the sneering, venomous-looking mouth and the disposition whose devilishness I had a fair example of that day, that this woman would consider herself contaminated had her skirts touched one of the little fellows she had passed.

THE SOCIAL EVIL.

In writing upon this subject, which is essentially a part of Toronto, I do so in order to lay before my readers many reasons why the crusade against houses of ill-fame commenced some years ago, has not been a success, and never will be a success, in so far as suppressing the social evil is concerned. In suggesting a system of toleration, as I do, I conscientiously believe that houses of ill-fame are absolutely necessary in, not Toronto alone, but every city in America. I reflect public opinion more than any so called public moralist could do simply because I consider myself to be more in touch with the general public than they are. I have tried to prove that suppressing houses of ill-fame is not lessening the evil, it may confine it more amongst respectable people, domestic servants etc., but I think such a state of affairs is far more deplorable than the most open permission of houses would be. Every incident I have given in my work to prove the existence of immorality is absolute truth. It would be an easy matter for me or for anyone else for that matter to give imaginary cases such as I have given here, and declare them to be truth, and I purpose, immediately after this work is completed placing a copy of it in the hands of the Department of the Attorney General of the Province of Ontario, and in that copy I shall number every episode that I have given. Should this Department desire me to do so, I am prepared to go before any judge, Magistrate or Commissioner and submit to examination under oath and I wil give the names and as far as possible the addresses of the parties whose acts I have portrayed. I know the name of every one whose case is mentioned, and can supply sufficient data for an investigation, should they desire confirmation, I am willing to place myself at the disposal of that Department to assist them in determining as to whether I speak the truth or not. Whatever action they desire to take, I shall always be glad to assist them in it.

During the progress of the Convention of the World's Womens Christian T. U., the action of Lady Henry Somerset in signing a petition for the re-enactment of the laws that regulate vice in India, was widely discussed and sweepingly condemned. Lady Henry Somerset states that these women "do not know what the conditions of Indian camp life are," and she might have added with equal truth that they know equally little of the manners and customs that prevail amongst the young of both sexes in this present year of grace, but she was met with the reply that "we know the ten Commandments and are sure they are suited to every condition of human existence—Anglo-Indian camp life included."

My impression is that there was not one woman in the entire assembly who has a son or a brother who is between the ages of fifteen and twenty years, who has the slightest conception of that boy's private character—I am prepared to go still further and I assert it. When Rev. Wilbur P. Crafts spoke of "Lady Henry Somerset's great practical mistake—a mistake into which many ministers of the United States had also fallen," he acknowledged in addition thereto that the question of the extension of licensing is one that is being discussed and ever present, and that it is "assuming alarming proportions." He cited a story of the frightful position of a young girl who had adopted the life of prostitution, which was loudly applauded, but the story came from Paris.

I contend that some system of licensing or inspecting should prevail in every city in America. I do not think it should be necessary for a girl to express her intention of entering a house of ill-fame, to any official, as I believe is done in Paris, but let a competent physician be attached to the Health Department, and have the sole occupation of visiting houses and examining the inmates as frequently as he considers necessary, and when such inmate is suffering from disease let her be taken to a hospital and be properly treated. Licensing in that case would not be necessary, but every keeper of a house should be compelled to have her house registered with the Board of Health, and any not doing so should be punished. In a very short time venereal diseases would be completely stamped out. These houses should not be permitted to sell liquor and when the house is charged with being disorderly, instead of the inmates being punished, the drunken, ill-bred rowdies who do not know enough to conduct themselves as gentlemen anywhere should be the ones to be punished. It is they who are disorderly, never the inmates as far as my experience has shown. In the pages following I have endeavoured to show that social purity is not advanced by suppressing houses of ill-fame, everything I have stated being absolutely true, and my contention is that people who hold positions as social purists are not in a position to give opinions on such matters, for they are not only entirely ignorant of them, but they are illogical. If the raiding or suppression of houses of ill-fame had the effect of stopping the commission of adultery, there would be no reason for making any plea for them, but I know that it does not, and the testimony I give in these pages shows that it does not. I maintain that the ministers Mr. Crafts speaks of as favouring a system of licensing are men who are conversant with the social usages of the present day and know that such places are a necessity. If not licensed let them pay a registration fee entitling them to supervision by the Board of Health. A dozen different means offer themselves by which a system conducive to public health could be operated. And I fail to see that any of the ten Commandments would be violated, if houses were allowed to register at the Health Department, and a physician deputed to make a thorough examination of the inmates of such houses.

In support of my contention that the people representing social purity are illogical, let me say : The Report of one Committee contained the information that they had conserved public morality by having the age of consent raised in certain states in the Union. In the final set of resolutions, enfranchisement is demanded for women. Are not these circumstances somewhat inconsistent ? Women demand the ballot because they consider themselves men's equals mentally. If this be so, why do they require any age of consent at all? I can only deduce that they are not entitled to the ballot as being men's equals, if they require an age of consent. If, however, they are men's equals let us agree for argument's sake, and they demand an age of consent, is not that an acknowledgement of the natural depavity of their own sex? I should be sorry to think this so, but I hold that it is the only logical deduction that can be made. But I have elsewhere tried to show that raising the age of consent does not act as a preventive.

As an evidence that the authorities acknowledge that some system is required, in February 1898, at Montreal, at the conference between Archibishop Bruchesi, Bishop Bond, Judge Desnoyers, Recorder DeMontigny and Mr. E. L. Bond, president of the Citizens' League, it was decided to go before the new City Council, and ask that houses of ill-fame and inmates be examined every week; any found not following certain regulations to be promptly suppressed.

I think the gentlemen above named are quite as competent to deal with social evils as any body of men or women in the world.

Of the houses of the first-class in Toronto those that once had a national reputation as such, are now no more, but their successors have sprung up in different parts of the city. At one time among the most prominent were 248 Front street west, 104 Richmond street west, and one on Albert street, the number of which I have forgotten, besides the house on the corner of Sheppard and Adelaide streets. These places were, I think I can truthfully say, always quiet, and no one, not knowing their character would ever guess it from outside appearances. They were patronized by wealthy men, young and old, from every part of the city and country. Take particularly the case of the house on the corner of Sheppard and Adelaide streets, it was always kept carefully closed, the blinds were drawn and the place was as silent as the tomb. After some years, having this reputation, it finally changed hands, and it is a circumstance worth mentioning that nearly all the boarding houses in that vicinity have since lost caste, and their patronage is of the worst class, while the house itself has undergone repair, and has had a dozen different tenants since is inception to respectability by the owner, who, I have no doubt, has frequently wished he had left it alone. No one appears to stay in it, and it is consequently idle half the time.

In houses of this class the furniture is elegant and tasteful, and the proprietress is usually a middle aged women of good personal appearance, the inmates being generally young women in the prime of life or between twenty and thirty. "My young ladies," I once heard a proprietress call her girls. These girls are carefully chosen for their beauty and charms, and are frequently persons of education and refinement. They are required to observe the utmost decorum in the parlors of the house, until you are fairly well acquainted with them, and then their language is not so polite. Their toilettes are usually extremely acsthetic and voluptuous, and display their charms to the best advantage. They rarely make acquaintances on the street, and indeed have no occasion to do so, and it may be said of some of them that they are women of respectable origin, and are sometimes the wives and daughters of men of good social position. Some have been led astray, some adopt this life to avoid poverty, some have entered from motives of extravagance and vanity, while the great majority have entered from motives of pure licentiousness and at the same time gratify a taste for an easy life. But whatever may be the cause, the effect is patent to all—that some of these places contain women who are fitted to grace the best circles of social life. In entering these houses, women believe they will always be able to keep themselves amongst the best classes of such females. They are soon undeceived, however, they remain in a first class house only so long as their charms continue, and as soon as these begin to wear, they are obliged to leave and their descent is rapid, until they become the inmates of the houses on Centre street and its adjacents, where they sometimes die, or more frequently leave the city to enter some of the dens such as exist on Canal street, Buffalo, or other American cities, where nearly all are habitual drunkards, and are almost putrified with venereal diseases.

The question is frequently asked "where do these girls come from?" and it would be an extremely difficult one to answer. I know of many instances where girls have been employed as domestic servants and seduced by their male friends, which eventually leads them to take up this life to hide their shame in some cases, and in others to be better able to receive the guilty attentions of a lover.

It is a matter for congratulation that Toronto is free apparently from the pervading evil of New York, but there are numerous instances, and I am assured that they are on the increase, where girls have gone astray in the effort to keep themselves on the small salaries paid to them, by yielding merely to a passive sin. These cases are, however, carefully kept from the public, though many young men assert that the evil is so great that if its extent were known it would be like a revelation. I know nothing from actual experience, however. But it is to be remembered, that as Mrs. Besant says, a girl has this advantage over a boy, she can sell herself, where a boy cannot, so that where poverty makes a girl a prostitute, it makes a boy a thief.

I do not consider, that I am in any respect promulgating the evil when I suggest tolerating, licensing or inspecting houses of ill-fame, and I do not hesitate to say that if a majority of men had their way, it would prevail as it does in Paris, and as I believe it does in every European country but England. England, the United States and Canada, however, would, perhaps, consider such a system a frightful outrage, yet England has produced a Somerset and an Oscar Wilde, and by a cable telegram in the Montreal Star of the 12th of April 1897, it is stated that blackmailing operations are carried on on an appalling scale by a gang, the victims being persons of wealth and high standing, whose frightful obliquities are presumed to be the same as Oscar Wilde's. Moreover, I can take you to places in New York and Chicago, where acts of the most appalling bestiality are committed, of so vile a nature that the English language does not supply words to express them, and in comparison with which the inmate of a house of ill-fame might consider herself almost saintly. The record of crime in the Report of Chief of Police of Toronto says : indecent assault, 8 ; rape, 9.

If saintly Canadians run away with the idea that there are no sinners of Oscar Wilde's type in Canada, my regard for truth impels me to undeceive them. Consult some of the bell boys of the large hotels in Canada's leading cities, as I did, and find out what they can tell from their own experiences. A youth of eighteen once informed me that he had blackmailed one of Canada's esteemed judiciary out of a modest sum of money, by catching him in the act of indecently assaulting one of the bell boys connected with a hotel in that city. The judge, with unblushing effrontery had arranged with the boy to meet him outside that night, and the boy had told the blackmailer when and where they were to meet. His honour was highly indignant and threatened every possible punishment, but it would not do. He had to pay the money. This is one case only, but they are countless. Some of Canada's leading citizens could be implicated just as Oscar Wilde was implicated, if some of these bell boys chose to make public what they knew. I know two different merchants in the city of Toronto who have a similar reputation. It was told me by a young man in Toronto some time ago that one of these characters was attending a church social, and upon seeing a boy of probably 16 or 17 go outside followed him and tried to indecently assault him. The boy refused, and the man I believe, threw him down. It cost him his gold watch and chain and all the money he had upon him to keep the boy's mouth shut. My informant also stated that some friends of his, who knew about this man, saw him standing on the street corner one night when they made it up to try him. All the crowd left apparently, except one boy, for home. In ten minutes this man came to the lad and made him an indecent proposal. Both these men are so well known in Toronto that there is scarcely a boy who does not know of their reputation. I have no doubt that, notwithstanding the positions they occupy, both would be punished to the full extent of the law, could the police catch them. But this fact serves to demonstrate how little is actually known to the police of what is taking place almost under their very noses, while these very men and their acts of indecency are the talk of boys all over the city.

Where under heaven people ever learned such appalling things God only knows, and humanity can only conjecture that the people in the places I mention appeal to the degraded tastes of their patrons simply because they are paid for it. The acts in themselves are indescribable. Houses of ill-fame are blots on the morality of a country, not necessarily because adultery is a sin, but because everyone knows of them, and the fact of their being public is what constitutes the sin, because sin, as far as my observation has carried me, is only sin when it is found out. These other places are not usually known to the public, and consequently they thrive, and no effort is made to suppress them, as far as I am aware. In the majority of American cities houses are tolerated, and I do not see that these cities are any the worse for it.

During the sitting of the Lexow Committee in New York, did not one of the police inspectors state that he considered houses of ill-fame an absolute necessity, and say that he would far rather have his son visit such a place than that he should ultimately become the inmate of an insane asylum?

A contention such as the staff inspector makes below is absurd on its face. Men and boys of the highest respectability and some whose social positions would preclude them from even noticing a man in the inspector's position visit houses of ill-fame and meet women on the streets, who would as soon think of committing burglary, larceny, or associating with burglars as they would of committing suicide. The two degrees are not at all comparable.

In the city of Montreal houses are not licensed, but they appear to be tolerated, and as long as the keepers do not sell liquor or their houses do not become a nuisance to the neighbours, they are not molested, and I fail to see that the morals of the people are any worse than those of the people of the city of Toronto. I state that I have never yet been solicited on the streets of Montreal during a twelve months' residence in that city, and I state that I have been solicited on the streets of Toronto if I am in that city only one night. I do not mean to say that women stop me on the street, but every man or boy knows that soliciting can be done without a word being spoken, and that is the way I have been solicited in the city of Toronto.

I think I may truthfully and consistently say that there is in the majority of men and boys an inherent chivalry that impels them to refrain from the seduction of respectable girls, and in preference thereto would visit a house of ill-fame. I also state that in a great many of cases girls are more to blame than boys, and I could give scores of instances where such is the case, so that my contention that licensing houses would not in any respect increase the evil, but really be the salvation of girls who are presumably respectable, but who are not really virtuous. The staff-inspector, I believe, states that he would just as soon license burglars, &c., as license houses of ill-repute, but it may be stated that if the intelligence of the staff-inspector is judged by this remark his opinions need not carry much weight, and at the same time, it is to be remembered that he might very possibly be out of a situation. The following is an opinion expressed by Dr. Sheard at a public meeting:

Our morality department is a standing disgrace to the city. Look at it a whole staff of officials whose principal duty seems to lie in tagging news-boys. Where else do you find such a system? I am informed that the officials of this department spend their time knocking at houses in the ward at all hours, wanting to know who is there, and what they are doing. If the result was satisfactory we might stand the expenditure. But if the result is to scatter throughout the city characters who ought never to be here, we are wasting our money.—Applause.

In giving utterance to these remarks I do not think Dr. Sheard can be accused of having any ulterior motive, such as might possibly be laid to my charge, but his opinion coincides with my contention in so far as the questionable results of raiding are concerned. I do not for one moment believe that there is a prostitute less in Toronto than there ever was. It may be that there are certain houses in the city that were at one time known as disreputable, and are now vacant, but that the inmates have left the city is not likely, the contention of the staff inspector to the contrary, notwithstanding. My intention was called some time ago to the evidence of the aforesaid inspector before the Commissioners reporting on the reformatory and prison systems, in which he is alleged to have said :

<blockquote>
When I was appointed to this work six years ago, I made an unofficial visit to the houses of ill-fame that then existed, accompanied by two other officers. I visited thirty-five houses known to be houses of ill-fame. I found on an average four women in each house, and I found that two-thirds of this number were Americans. I took the name, age, nationality and length of time t hat they were in this kind of life and I compiled a book containing the information. I gave them distinctly to understand that the law for the suppression of vice and houses of ill-fame in Toronto was to be rigourously enforced. I told them that a reasonable time would be given to those who belonged to the other side to go back there, and that if they had not the means to enable them to do so, we would furnish them with tickets to the places they came from. I further told them that if any of them showed a desire to reform I would send them to an institution under the charge of philanthropic ladies who would see that they were provided with all proper facilities for starting a new life. On my second visit I found that half the number had disappeared altogether. I was told by the officers on duty that they went in large numbers with their trunks to the station, and took tickets for the other side. The law has been strictly enforced from that day to this, and the number of houses of ill-fame in Toronto has been reduced to a minimum, the women that are to be found in these houses are very few, and there is more trouble with the class of women who have become completely demoralized and have to be picked up as drunks and for soliciting on the streets.
</blockquote>

So far as this evidence is concerned I have nothing to say in regard to its truthfulness, it being usually polite to say that a man has made a mistake, but I feel constrained to observe that if the women, who, he alleges, left the city, did so, it appears to me that their places have been very rapidly filled up, or else others have joined our shores to make up for them. It may be that certain houses have been closed by placing policemen at their doors, such as I know was done at 104 Richmond, but that other houses have taken their places is equally certain, and the keepers are more careful is the difference. An incident in point will make my meaning clearer. Three girls kept a house on Seaton street for three months, three or four days before their month was up they informed their gentlemen callers that they were going to move to another street, giving the full address, and they kept up this system for nearly a year, at which time I left the city. This I know to be so, I was there. But one thing hapened, worthy of mention. On the very day after they had left Seaton street I am informed that the police raided the house, receiving for their labour an empty tenement.

It seems to me a very singular matter that the staff inspector should make such assertions in the face of the following from the Chief Constable's report :

<blockquote>
The number of houses of ill-fame reported in 1894 was 174 and in 1895, 46. The chief says : " Regularly established houses of prostitution seem less numerous ; the competition from *women living singly* so as not to come within the scope in the law may be one explanation of the cause. Frequenters of houses of ill-fame do not relish the possible visitation of the police, and avoid those places likely to be raided. Solicitation on the street is not rife, though loose women are to be seen on the thoroughfares after nightfall."
</blockquote>

I respectfully submit the following for your consideration and ask an unprejudiced public to judge between my assertion and these of the staff Inspector.:

Fanny Rogers pleaded guilty to a case of illegal liquor selling at her place on King street west, and his Worship remanded her for a week, at the request of her counsel, to consider what sentence he should impose. This is the case, where several lawyers were found in the place when it was raided. One of the police said, that Miss Rogers was induced to plead guilty so as the legal lights in question would not have to be called by the Crown to testify.

I have acknowledged that some of these houses have been closed, but I do not believe that the evil is in any respect reduced, in fact quite the reverse is the case. I wish to call attention to the subjoined heroics which appeared in the Empire, demonstrating the truth of my assertion, and while the actual statements are undeniably correct, the conclusions will doubtless strike the average reader as being so much sentimental rubbish. It is stated that "girls in their innocence and youth" are beguiled into returning to the city in boats belonging to their male friends, and are ruined. I don't believe any such nonsense. If the writer who is probably some school-boy let loose, had said that the great or overwelming majority of girls go over to the island for that very express purpose, he would be correct in ninety cases out of a hundred when girls go unaccompanied by their parents. The case of the school teacher, who was also "ruined" is laid at the door of the young man who seduced her. For my own part, I am constrained to believe that she was an extremely willing victim, and do not, in fact consider it a case of seduction at all, it is simply an act of fornication in which one is guilty equally with the other. This appears to be the only case that has obtained publicity, yet I know of several that happened in the cases of the school teachers, and I cannot agree in good conscience that young men should shoulder all the blame. Could any sensible girl or young woman, and more especially a school teacher, who would be supposed to have more than the average intelligence, expect anything else when they make hap-hazard acquaintances with gentlemen they know nothing at all about? I do not doubt that the parties in question became acquainted in the usual fashion of people who meet on the street, in the parks, or on the island, and one would imagine that this teacher would know better. I have the histories of several school teachers who attended that convention, and know at least five who were guilty of this sin with young men in the city, and I know moreover of a large number of normalite teachers, or pupils, I suppose they are called when attending the normal school, who have been guilty of similar offences with young men who boarded in the houses with them, and with other also. The following, however is the article under discussion, and you can make your own deductions, both as regards the teachers and others who are therein referred to:

Nowadays a man who owns or rents a boathouse on the lake front is liable to have his motives for occupying such a place questioned and especially is this the case if he goes to the trouble of fixing up his aquatic possession to the extent of putting in a few articles of furniture as a sofa, a couple of canvas lounging chairs and furnishings of that sort. If such a thing as a camp bed is to be found within the walls of his boathouse his friends usually eye each other quizically on discovering it. But perhaps the recent revelation of lakeside impropriety and immorality justify the raised eyebrow and the ready innuendo with which the captious friend surveys these things.

Of late there has been much to complain of on the part of the many good people who make the lakeside their home during the summer months. The conduct of certain of their neighbours have been such as to bring discredit on the whole system of boathouse renting and living, and the Empire in setting out to expose a system of immorality as widespread as it is flagrant has met with much opposition from people who are more or less interested in keeping things quiet. One man said: "If you show this practice up you will hurt a good many good men who wont thank you at all. While the immorality is doubtless of wide extent and to be greatly regretted it is to a certain extent an almost necessary evil, or an unpreventable one in a city as large as Toronto. There is not a doubt that the police are fully cognizant of the vice and are doing all in their power to check it."

Many Explanade men were spoken to, and one of them, a gentleman who is a large property owner said: "We would be very glad to get a stop put to the evil, as it often keeps respectable people away who would otherwise be good tenants for boathouses, but the more difficulties we put in the way of these men the more they exercise their ingenuity to thwart us and nullify our efforts to keep the lake front respectable—on the principle, I suppose, that stolen fruit is sweetest."

The boat houses in the vicinity of York street are perhaps the most used for immoral purposes, or rather there are more in that district to which the public finger of scorn is pointed. Originally boat houses were put up with the idea of renting them to people who possessed boats and simply to accommodate boats. Then as there are thousands of men in the city who live in boarding houses and who possess a boat, it was thought that a boat house roomy enough to allow of a sofa being set in it, or one having a living room above would rent more easily. The idea was a splendid one, and the boat houses with living rooms were speedily taken. Charmed with the thought of saving big lodging bills during the summer months, dining restaurants or cooking al fresco meals themselves, many young men in receipt of goodly salaries as a rule jumped at the chance there offered them of becoming lakeside residents, and possessing an apartment where they could enjoy the cool of the evening. It goes without saying that many of the renters of these houses were actuated by baser motives. It was only intended that these houses would be occupied in summer, and for that reason they are as a rule rather airy. The furnishing of many of these must have cost the occupants many perplexing moments, elegantly papered and luxuriously finished several of these little lakeside houses are models of easy comfort. As a rule, however, the houses upon whose adornment the owners have spent much money hear the best reputations and anything which transpires in them is never or rarely heard.

The freedom from interference leaves these lakeside lodgers at liberty to invite their friends into their premises and if these friends are women of the lowest class, who can interfere ! Who is to judge if they are immoral ? The police have tried to interfere with notorious cases, but they cannot legally do so even if they assnme the power by reason of the improbability of the evil-doors taking legal redress, and thus making themselves notorious. Time and again have women of the town been warned off the wharf adjoining several of the boat houses, and they are liable to arrest for trespassing any time they are found on a wharf which is enclosed. But there is no power in Canada which can go into a man's private apartment and drag his friends out, be they high or low In the case of one boat company a circular was issued to the tenants when the property was bought asking their co-operation in maintaining the good name of the premises, but this had not been responded to by several of the boat house occupants. Last year one man carried on the practice of bringing in the most notorious prostitutes in the city so openly that his neighbours reported the matter to the police, who visited the boat house—" raided" it in fact—but nothing came of the matter. Almost all of the lodgers are provided with a flask or two of whiskey in case of chills, but no great amount of intoxicating liquor is kept.

The class of people who rent these boat houses are as a rule well-paid clerks. According to their means they furnish their abodes. The majority content themselves with an imitation of camp life. A boat house is cheaper, handier and safer when wanted only for immoral purposes than a room up town. Although many of the women who visit these places are street walkers, the large majority people hear stories about are shop girls who go to the island and there they fall into the hands of some human hound who is looking for some innocent girl to entrap. These innocent girls are badgered into an acquaintance, and their male friends finally prevail upon them to set out for the city in their row boats instead of by the ferry boats, but the confiding girl whose youth and innocence have induced her to accept the invitation of the fellow who looks with lecherous eyes on her does not land where she desires. The boat draws up in front of the boat house where her courtier hangs forth, and she is induced by specious reasons to enter his net The innocent girl has reason to regret this ill-advised step in most cases. She seldom leaves the place without having taken a drink of liquor, and if she refuses that and all the advances of the individual who has been so successful in getting her inside his boat house she leaves the place with a scarlet face, and has to run the gauntlet of curious eyes. ;These meetings are never of a loud character as the prime requisite is quietness. There are no such affairs as night orgies with women present, as the police would quickly interfere. But while there is much to deplore in regard to boat houses, the percentage of disreputable houses is very small, and the overwhelming mass of house owners and occupants are men who have no thought of wrong doing. But when it is stated that there are four houses notorious for immorality within a hundred yards of one part of the esplanade, it can be easily seen that these remarks are not over-drawn. There are other houses about which stories are told but the quarters mentioned are known far and wide.

The foregoing statements are not secrets by any means. For a long time the police have known of the prevalence of the practice referred to, and are not slow in acknowledging their inability to cope with it. "These young men are safe from police interference" said one man, "and they know it well." The only thing the police could do is being done, and that is, the men on duty along the esplanade have instructions to endeavour to stop the practice as much as possible. If a woman is found around a boat house at an unseasonable hour she is interrogated and if she cannot give a satisfactory account of herself she is arrested as a vagrant. But this does not cover the case at all, as the principal frequenters of these places are young women who do not loiter in the vicinity. When women come down to spend the evening or night, they are usually accompanied by the person who keeps the boat house they are bound for, and as a rule the neighbourhood does not become cognizant of the fact till the night wears on. A police officer remarked yesterday that it is usual to see lights burning at all hours of the night in suspected houses, and the thing is so well understood by the force that no notice is taken of them.

A couple of brothers now bearing a very unenviable reputation in consequence of the seduction of a young girl named Sadie Lavelle who died a few days ago on Terauley street, have the identical boat house hired by the man who first brought boat houses into disrepute. These brothers, one of whom ruined Miss Lavelle in his boat house, are cordially detested by their lakeside neighbours, one of whom yesterday said: "Those boys should be shot on sight. They have seduced more girls than any other two men in the city. Boat house owners would uphold you in showing up such people, as they would be pleased to get rid of them."

It is hard to get hold of incidents which show the prevalence of the immorality which is admitted. There is a sort of feemasonry among the culprits which it is next to impossible to break through, but several very damaging stories leaked out. The wife of a well known citizen made a visit to the lake front a few nights since, and while in a boat house with her paramour she had a $55 diamond ring stolen.

A pitiable story is told about the ruin of a young lady teacher by one of the boat house libertines. She was in the city during the N.P.A. convention and was induced to go for a row by her seducer, who landed at his own boat house. She was a bewitching little beauty, and her betrayer was heard to boast of his dastardly act after she had left the city.

This is only a modified form of what really exists. Boat house are the special privilege of young men and boys, and girls and prostitutes are taken there with a frequency that is surprising. An incident in which a lad of sixteen or seventeen who was employed in the Musee, was arrested for taking a girl to a boat house, is doubtless still fresh in the minds of the public, and though he was threatened with all the thunders of the Morality Department, to his everlasting credit be it said he made a most plucky defence, and showed that he did not come within the meaning of the seduction act, although he was informed, after being discharged, that it was in the power of the magistrate to send him to the penitentiary—which I take the liberty of disbelieving.

In addition to the boat houses, over a large number of stores all over the city, there are scores of young men who rent rooms and furnish them for no other purpose. When a friend requires the room it is loaned with perfect good grace, and the occupant feels, as he is, free from interruption. This method of carrying on the evil is on the increase, and its results are for more disastrous than licensed houses of ill-fame would be, for girls of a more respectable social status, frequently those of very respectable parents, in some cases school girls, do not hesitate to go to a room where they are not known and where there is no danger of interference, and young men who would frequent a house of ill-fame, were it not for fear of being brought before the magistrate, have little scruple in bringing a girl to a place of this kind. This is at least significant:

One or two furnished rooms to be sold cheap, immediate possession, public building, central, privileges, low rent. Box 279, News.
A furnished room for sale, in public building, no questions asked. Box 529, Telegram.
WANTED—Nice, warm room, no questions asked. Box 612 Telegram.

In the summer time the parks and the island are favourite resorts for girls and women to meet their lovers and seek for custom. On Centre avenue where the girls used to stand in the door-way to solicit the passers by, boys were always ready and willing to give the alarm on the approach of a policeman, and the doors were closed and bolted until the way was clear again, and the girls would then come out, only to repeat the same thing over and over again, and the numbers who visited these haunts low as they were, were reputed to be legion. Very few young men regard it as sinful to visit a house of ill-repute the only restraint is the fear of the police, and contagious disease, consequently when fate throws in his way a girl who is presumably virtuous, there is really very little danger in a mutual sin. The girl will assuredly keep it a secret from pride and the young man will tell no one but his most intimate friends, who may, perhaps enjoy the same relations as he, and most important of all there is no danger. Hence there must be a premium on such acts.

It is Mr. Monk, in Oliver Twist who says there is one secret a woman will always keep until it is found out—the loss of her own good name, and they have a saying at the Palais de Justice in Paris that to expect a confession from a woman is like attempting to make the devil confess.

Edmund Burke, it was, who said, at the close of his indignant outburst in memory of the fallen queen of France, that "vice itself loses half its evil, by losing all its grossness," but I incline to the doctrine of Collier, who said that the vice which is draped in the garb of virtue or has the varnish of an outward refinement laid over its leprosy is tenfold more infectious and destructive than the shameless wickedness which hides its loathsome front. These are the differences between our times and the times of Charles the II, and when it may be demanded and justly so, perhaps, on what grounds I base my claims to have houses licensed, I state that girls who are supposed to be respectable are made to take the places of those who would be visited were it not for fear of the police, but that the Commandment, "Thou shalt not" is broken any the less, I do not believe, and that the vice that has "the varnish of an outward refinement" is frightfully common, I shall try to prove.

The Reverend Father Décarie, of St. Henri, says that the extent of the nation's immorality cannot in any wise be measured by the numbers of the frequenters of disorderly houses. The many lying-in hospitals and institutions for the reception of illegitimate children tell but a portion of the story, and it is probable that the immorality that produced such results, widespread though it may be, is remarkably limited in comparison with that which escapes detection. In the upper circles of Canadian society, there is, to say the least, an immense amount of indiscretion on the part of wives and mothers of families, and it is becoming noticeable that there are married ladies, and single ladies who are no longer young, who receive a larger share of attention from youthful admirers than their younger and unmarried sisters and friends. Among the lower classes the evil is much more extensive, principally among factory girls and domestic servants. These generally furnish the subject for the procuresses who periodically visit the country from Chicago and elsewhere. The hospital of the Sacré Cœur, at St. Sauveur, near Quebec, which is in charge of nuns, has recently had to be enlarged, though a large five story building. It is a home for foundlings, who are received nightly in a basket placed at the door, where those who bring them, deposit them without fear of discovery, and leave them to the care of the sisters, after ringing a bell to announce the advent of a new arrival. Such is Father Décarie's picture, and a despatch from Toronto to the Montreal Star, dated April 15th, states that the fourth deserted baby found within the preceding two weeks was picked up the previous evening on the door step of Sergeant Vaughan's house, on Classic Avenue. The child which was a boy about three weeks old, was taken to the Infant's Home, making a total of 85 infants placed in that institution thus far that year.

The News stated in a recent issue that "500 babies know not a mother's love. That number of babies abandoned in Toronto every year." And again the same paper said: "Starve babies for $10. Child murder fearfully prevalent in Toronto the Good. Horrible revelations. Mrs. Boultbee speaks of the evils of maternity houses to the Board of Health." So, of course, there is no commission of sin in Toronto, as the foregoing abundantly proves. Of course not.

A young man of my acquaintance who is about 22 years of age, stated that the first time he had ever broken the seventh commandment was through a married woman. She was then about 26 and he was 16. He did not tell me the woman's name, but he pointed her out to me on the street. He was sent to her house on a message, and after inviting him into the house, made the proposition to him, which he indignantly refused, and demanded to be allowed to return home. To this the woman would not consent. She detained him for over an hour and he fell. Are such cases common? Father Décarie says they are.

Some time ago I attended a ball in Toronto which was attended by Toronto's highest social circles. A lady, one of the handsomest in the room, was invariably claimed by some youth for a dance. I mentioned to a friend of mine that I would not care to be the lady's husband, and was told that my mind was evil. Her husband, a wealthy man, has, I may mention, since applied for divorce on the ground of adultery. My mind may be evil, but I know that Results flow from Causes. This was probably one of that numerous class of women one meets with who would probably tell her husband if he expostulated with her that these young men were nice boys.

I do not pretend that to tolerate houses of ill-fame, will in any respect, condone the sin of the man who visits one, or render his responsibility to his maker less, yet I do say in all sincerity that it would be better than the system that prevails to-day.

I have given you actual statements of cases that have happened, and on these I base my contentions, and how absurd it must seem that any man can truthfully state that these things do not exist.

When I suggest the licensing or inspecting of houses of ill-fame, I have to say that we are face to face with a condition and not a theory. If the Scriptures speak the truth, and there is no doubt of that, happily, it will be remembered that though we are specially warned against the women of lewd character, the passage acknowledges their existence, and I give it word for word :

9. In the twilight, in the evening, in the black and dark night :
10. And, behold, there met him a woman *with* the attire of an harlot, and subtil of heart.
11. (She *is* loud and stubborn ; her feet abide not in her house :
12. Now *is she* without, now in the streets, and lieth in wait at every corner.)
13. S ɩ she caught him, and kissed him, *and* with an impudent face said unto him,
14. *I have* peace offerings with me ; this day have I payed my vows.
15. Therefore came I forth to meet thee, diligently to seek thy face, and I have found thee.
16 I have decked my bed with coverings of tapestry, with carved *works*, with fine linen of Egypt.
17. I have perfumed my bed with myrrh, aloes, and cinnamon.
18. Come, let us take our fill of love until the morning ; let us solace ourselves with loves.
19. For the goodman *is* not at home, he is gone a long journey :
20. He hath taken a bag of money with him, *and* will come home at the day appointed.
21. With her much fair speech she caused him to yield, with the flattering of her lips she forced him.
22. He goeth after her straightway, as an ox goeth to the slaughter, or as a fool to the correction of the stocks ;
23. Till a dart strike through his liver ; as a bird hasteth to the snare, and knoweth not that it *is* for his life.
24. ¶ Hearken unto me now therefore, O ye children, and attend to the words of my mouth.
25. Let not thine heart decline to her ways, go not astray in her paths.
26. For she hath cast down many wounded : yea, many strong *men* have been slain by her.
27 Her house *is* the way to hell, going down to the chambers of death.

This was the admonition of the prophet one thousand years before the birth of Christ, and what was in existence then exists to-day, and in a greater degree.

The churches of God, which state that they shall last forever, have, with commendable forethought and fostering care, done their utmost to crush the evil. The sternness of those sublime Christian martyrs who left Old England that they might worship God according to the dictates of their own consciences, and insisted that all others should do the same, and who were always ready to assist at the sacking of some royal mansion occupied by the ungodly, has given way to a free and easy morality that is really comfortable, and in strict terms is absolute Christianity, or at least it passes for such.

It is stated that attending operas, dancing and playing cards is strictly prohibited by the discipline of some of the churches, and that upon joining a church the sacred assurance, if not an oath, is given by the convert that he or she will observe this rule. Upon receiving their "second sight," however, and comforting themselves with the reflection that "I don't think there is any harm in dancing anyway," the rule is forgotten, and the churches themselves conveniently overlook it, hence by their "liberality" there appears to be no amusement too dangerous for them to tamper with in their desire to secure members and adherents. How many members would two thirds of the city churches, other than those of the Roman Catholic faith and the Church of England, have, if they expelled from their communion those who dance, play cards and attend operas? The late Rev. John A Williams, D.D., General Superintendent of the Methodist Church, said to me concerning a church of which he was pastor :

"My feelings have never been so hurt in my career as a Christian minister as at the present time. The wealthy members of my congregation dance, they play cards and attend operas, and they know it is a violation of the discipline, yet if I were to preach against it they would probably leave the church, knowing it cannot exist without them. They are its main support."

The man who would visit a house of ill-fame to feast his eyes on the charms of women has no longer any excuse for doing so. The opera, and in a greater degree the ball room supply the substitute where society charms us with as much nakedness as they dare expose to view, and in the fulness of time, no doubt, greater progress will be made in the divine art of full dress.

Every once in a while some preacher will pour forth the vials of his wrath or pretended wrath, either for effect or possibly in sincerity, against the evils, but the bosom of society does not appear to be in the least disturbed by their pyrotechnics. Indeed, the very reverse appears to be the case. A few years ago aestheticism used to be the craze. Now, to secure popularity a thing must be sensuous. Our musical settings are sensuous, and now we are led to infer that that old tradition of the forbidden fruit was not an apple at all, but really love, and therefore, cohabitation. The Oratorio of Eve indicated and expressed unreservedly what, in the great majority of cases, people were afraid of giving utterance to.

In the observations I make, I have paid particular attention to girls, because it is in the time of life peculiar to them that the greatest danger lies, and also acting on the assumption that girls are more prone to fall than boys. From fourteen to twenty the strongest element in human nature is the passions, and the disgrace that attaches to their gratification, especially to girls, is lifelong.

An incident came to my notice a while ago, which is an apt illustration. Some school boys and girls conceived the idea of a post-office, and it was soon put into successful operation. Unfortunately the teacher discovered the scheme, and confiscated the correspondence. It was a remarkable and bountiful harvest, and the letters that Cleopatra wrote to her lover were as nothing compared to these. There was a sensuous abandon in them that was really startling in emanating from such a source. Some of the proudest people in that place had sons and daughters concerned in it. What blackmail that teacher could levy if he were an evil disposed person. Every boy who took part in it remembers it to this day, as well as the nature of the letters the girls wrote.

I contend, therefore, in all sincerity, that neither men nor boys, inflamed by passion, would be prone to ask a woman or girl of presumably chaste character, to share a sin that society is said never to forgive, if he ran no danger of being arrested for visiting a house of ill-fame. Dr. Napheys, a medical or rather a physiological writer of considerable prominence in speaking on the subject of dancing says that whatever stimulates the emotions leads to an unnatural sexual appetite. Late hours, flashy papers, love stories, talk of beaux, love and marriage, that atmosphere of riper years which is so often and so injudicially thrown around the children in the United States, parties, sensational novels, the drama, the ball-room, and a particular emphasis is laid upon the power of music and dancing to awaken and stimulate the passions.

In diametrical opposition to the precepts deduced from experience by one of the most widely known physicians in the United States, society appears to do precisely the reverse of what he teaches, and all the amusements which he most emphatically condemns society provides for both sexes, from children to any age this side of the grave. Are they, therefore, inviting the substitution of the social evil by making provision for those who require it?

It is not very long ago that one of the many different mutual benefit societies gave an at-home, and following the at-home with a dance. The daughter of a well-known clergyman begged permission to attend the at home, which was graciously granted, the reverend gentleman considerately deciding to remain up until the young lady returned. Ten, eleven, twelve o'clock struck, and he decided that she had gone home with a friend. An hour or two later, he was awakened by his daughter's return, and was informed that the affair was just over. First an at-home and a dance afterwards.

"And did you dance?"

"Yes."

The young lady had not missed a single dance in the course of the evening.

This could be verified by a cloud of witnesses, and I mention it to demonstrate how little men, no matter what their profession may be, know of the longings of young people, and how little influence they really possess, even over their own children.

I may be permitted to observe, I think, that I am not opposed to dancing, but I mention these circumstances merely from a physiological standpoint, and if Christianity can encourage what the churches are pleased to call vices, (Bishop Dumoulin, I think it was, who called progressive euchre progressive deviltry), in their own way, I do not see that I am trespassing the rules of good taste in suggesting the licensing of houses of ill-fame.

It may be, perhaps, that those estimable women who permit their daughters to run the streets may be philosophical in exposing them to corrupting influences, and running their chances of becoming lax in their morals on the same principle as that famous Frenchwoman, who, when being admonished for attempting to procure a girl as mistress for a rich nobleman, answered :

"It's always a pleasure to have one more woman to torment the men. It's girls like those who avenge us honest women."

It was a belief of ancient races, and indeed a current belief among modern nations that it is not given to man to behold the image of another world and live. The Arab who meets a phantom in the desert goes home to die. He knows the hand of doom is upon him. He has seen that which for mortal eyes it is fatal to look upon, and it is thus in some measure with those who are admitted within the dark precincts of murder's dread sanctuary. Not swiftly does the curtain fall which has once been lifted from the hideous horrors of its ghastly temple. The revelations of an utterly wicked soul leave a lasting impress upon the mind which unwillingly becomes the recipient of these awful secrets. So, too, will this apply to the girl or woman of the age, who is inclined to take the first step in the downward path, and while it may be said that the present system of religion is beginning to teach us that for our sins committed upon earth there will be no future punishment such as was believed in past ages less enlightened than we, it might still be borne in mind that men nor boys ever keep secret a sin of this nature, and the girl who once falls may depend upon it that she will be certain to be known by every intimate friend of the one with whom she shares the sin, and this knowledge is likely to be used by those who know it for their own purposes. Boys have told me of girls with whom they had had improper relations, the girls requesting the most sacred promises that they would never mention it, and then keeping the promise by telling me and others as well.

I respectfully invite the disinterested reader to carefully compare my assertions and the incidents I have enumerated as showing the deplorable extent of the nation's immorality, with those of the so-called public moralists of the present day, such as staff Inspector Archibald.

I hold that men like him are not competent to give a reliable opinion on public morality, simply because they know nothing at all about it. I speak from experience and observation, and consequently with a reasonable degree of authority. The fact that houses of ill-fame are raided and the frequenters punished, thereby breaking up the house, is no evidence that prostitution is on the decrease.

Young women of this character are doing just the same as boys and young men have been doing for years—they rent a room or two over some store and by putting in a sewing machine, carry the idea that they are seamstresses. They take men there at night and no one is any the wiser. In the summer time the parks and the suburbs are used for this purpose, while the island is simply an open air place of prostitution, or charnal house. If this were not so why was it necessary to suggest that the tents be completely prohibited there? The island is simply a rendez-vous for prostitutes, and not only that, it is a rendez-vous for "presumably" respectable girls, as I know by experience and what I have seen.

Men like Inspector Archibald parade around with their noses in the air, and declare such things are impossibilities. Would it ever occur to one of these people to follow a boy and girl or "pike" them as the boys call it—who were walking together and finding out the immorality that exists amongst boys and girls? A decided negative is the answer to both questions. I conscientiously assert that there is not one man or woman in a thousand in the United States or Canada who knows his or her son's private character.

One particular example occurs to me in this connection. One evening in a city of Canada, I, in company with two others observed a youth of about 16 dismount from his bycicle, and tossing away the cigarette he had been smoking, commence a conversation with a little girl of about 14 or 15, and tried to entice her into a laneway for an immoral purpose. The young lady did not go, however, answering him: "No, I won't go." He is the son of an ex-president of the Y.M.C.A. of that town, a gentleman who makes it his special business to admonish all boys who smoke cigarettes, and point out to them the frightful penalties attending those who smoke. Would he for one moment believe that his son would be guilty of smoking or what is apparently of less consequence, breaking the seventh commandment? This shows how little parents know of what their own children are doing. At the W.C.T.U. convention held in 1896, the report of the Plan of Work Committee said that the use of tobacco among boys was growing altogether too fast, and they urged the superintendents of the districts to make an effort to form anti-cigarette and tobacco leagues among the school children. This would pledge them to abstain from the uses of narcotics. They asked that members of churches who kept stores and sold tobacco should do away with the sale of it.

Incidentally, and I am quite sure unintentionally, the W.C.T.U. have given me one of my best arguments against themselves and other public moralists, when they state that the use of tobacco amongst boys was growing altogether too fast. It shows first of all that in spite of the Minor's Tobacco Act, boys still smoke. It also proves the apparent contempt that boys hold for the opinions of these women when they inform them in their Temperance Physiology of the frightful effects of smoking. Also that coercive laws do not avail in the suppression of vice.

I was introduced to a set of students a short time ago, some twelve or fourteen who usually chummed together. They were all under twenty years of age, and quite one half were then under treatment for private diseases. One of them laughingly said to me, when I mentioned that a number of them declined to drink any spirituous liquors with me, that usually sixty per cent were suffering from private diseases, and that sometimes it ran up to seventy-five per cent. Would their mothers believe that?

I venture to assert that if this information were given to any of these public moralists, they would not believe it. It would explode all their pet theories and that would never do. They will believe nothing that they don't wish to believe.

During the past ten years I have met many young men up to

twenty-five or twenty-six years of age, and some as young as fifteen. There is not one who has not broken the seventh commandment, and sixty per cent have suffered from venereal diseases—one of them was only seventeen when he contracted it.

In views of these facts would it not be wiser to permit houses of ill-fame subject to inspection?

I contend that it would keep respectable girls freer from corruption, and check the spread of venereal diseases.

One of the Police Commissioners is Judge McDougall—a gentleman of the highest possible integrity, and one in whom the citizens of Toronto have implicit faith and confidence. I would suggest that he obtain the services of a young man of eighteen years of age, of good appearance, and who has seen something of life. Let him be of good moral character.

A boy like this is a very common commodity, as nine tenths of the boys of the present generation would come under this heading, adverse opinions to the contrary notwithstanding. Let him be informed that he is to act as a private detective and for three months he is to keep a reliable diary of every time he breaks the seve th commandment, giving the name of the girl or woman and the particulars. Let him be employed in one of the large Departmental stores if possible, and board at a house where it will cost from four dollars to four dollars and a half a week. For an expenditure of two hundred dollars Judge McDougall could obtain the services of one of the cleverest boy detectives in New York or Chicago. At the end of three months if no one in the city but the Judge and the young detective knew the latter's business he would send in a report that would make the ordinary man's hair stand' but it would also prove beyond question all the evidences I have submitted. I can even foreshadow the list of people he would have on his list.

My foreshadow would be simply a repetition of what has transpired in the city amongst friends of mine, and I suggest this course as a means of demonstrating to an independent man that it would be better to tolerate houses than that such things should be perpetrated, as I know for a certainty that they are.

I wish to state in connection with my remarks about a boarding house, that I selected, hap-hazard—from newspaper advertisements a boarding house which suited me on account of its locality, the street and number I need not mention. There were three or four lady boarders, the landlady and three servants. There was only one of the whole crowd who was respectable and that was one of the ladies who was married, yet even she allowed herself to be kissed by some of the gentlemen boarders. The landlady's son whom I had taken to the theatre several times, told me in a burst of confidence, what I already knew—that all the domestics were not of good character, and that the landlady and two of the boarders were not I discovered without much difficulty. Such cases as these are far more prolific of corruption than houses of ill-fame would be, but to tolerate houses of ill-fame would be considered something frightful, because its appearance is bad. A woman considers that her son has disgraced her if he be seen drunk, though that is no sin, yet committing adultery, which is a violation of one of the ten commandments and a cardinal sin, would probably not cause her a second thought if it were not publicly known.   Similarly, in the United States the hot bed of moral crusades, the W.C.T.U., the Epworth League and other societies like the sands of the sea, without number, and in a lesser degree in Canada, are not druggists waxing fat on the sales to women of opium, chloral, as well as drugs and instruments that enable women to commit *murder* and still the unburn life within them every time the Almighty has put his seal of blessing upon them, and their families had reached a convenient number, or they did not wish to have children?   Why do not these women who are so fearful about boys and about children being on the streets after dark, turn their attention to something of this kind?   I decline to believe that there is any reason other than because such things are not publicly known, and that there is no notoriety connected with it.

One lad of eighteen years informed me that in five years there had not been a domestic in their house with whom he had not had improper relations.

Another of sixteen stated that it was a rare thing for them to have a domestic with whom he did not have improper relations.

One of fifteen stated to me that he had improper relations with a domestic servant who was twice his age, and he showed me the vermin on his body she had communicated to him. A lad of eighteen for whose family the same woman worked after leaving the first place had similar relations with similar results. The same lad of fifteen pointed out to me the domestic who had succeeded the woman of thirty, and he said he had improper relations with her. A girl from a nighboring town took the place of the last girl, and this lad came to me one night stating that his father had caught him *en flagrante delicto*, and had boxed his ears and dismissed the girl. This is the experience of a boy *not yet sixteen* with three successive domestic servants.

Another lad of fourteen, whom I only know by sight, was importuning a young friend of mine to obtain him some powdered cantharides which he wished to give to a youg miss, the daughter of a gentleman in the employ of the Dominion Government. Precocity it is not?

A friend of mine, a clerk in one of one of the city banks, asked me to take a room with him on Wilton Avenue, informing me at the same time the reason he wished it. A young lady whom he had known before he and she had come to Toronto to live, was rooming there, and she had informed him that a double room was vacant.   He stated the advantages of rooming there, one of which was that the young lady's room was precisely opposite the vacant one, the rest you can imagine. The young lady was a stenographer in the city, and the double room was more than my friend cared to indulge in. The favors to be received from the young lady was the inducement he offered me to leave the room I was then occupying to go with him.

A young man of eighteen or nineteen, a handsome and gentlemanly looking fellow boarded in a house on Shuter street where a widow lady was also boarding. He was attending business college at the time, and one night one of his fellow boarders heard a discussion in the widow's room, between them. She was upraiding him for visiting houses of ill-repute, for which, she said there was no occasion when she was there. He afterwards confessed that she had made the first overtures to him by coming to his room one morning. After having left the city some time he received a letter from the widow in which she had expressed the fear that she was enciente, and hoping that if such were the case he would do something for her. Upon my advice he paid no attention to this letter, as I regarded it as blackmail, and as far as I am aware he never heard anything more about it.

A young man of twenty who was boarding in a house where several Normal school students were boarding informed me that he had had improper relations with several of them, as well as with several domestics in the same house. These normalites would be very efficient instructors of the young, would they not?

I consider such circumstances as the foregoing simply appalling, and demonstrating a frightfully low standard of morality, and I think it is far more to the purpose that men and women should endeavour to inculcate morality amongst their children, than sending missionaries to outlandish places where they are not wanted, also that suppressing houses of ill-fame is not reducing the sin one iota.

I could cover page after page of such examples, did I wish, of experiences that have been told me by boys and young men, though I wish to add that they had no idea I intended using their information for this purpose.

I met a young woman some time ago, and in the course of the evening she gave me quite a biography of herself. She had been in the employ of a well known merchant as domestic, and stated without any reservation that the two sons of this merchant, one a lad of seventeen and the other about twenty had had constant improper relations with her. She enumerated boys and young men one after another, not one of whom was over twenty-three years of age, sons of well known men, who had had improper relations with her.

I could enumerate instances of this nature also almost without number, which I have earned from young women, who were prostitutes, but not inmates of houses of ill-fame.

A young lady the daughter of one of the best known men in the city of Toronto, made the proposition that Potiphar's wife made to Joseph to a boy who delivered groceries at her father's house, informing him at the same time that she was alone in the house. He was a remarkably handsome boy, with a bright healthy color in his cheeks and eyes that shone like stars.

On the broad basis of subtle reasoning I ask : Would it not be as well to give a trial to the system of inspecting houses of ill-fame when such deplorable circumstances as I have given you are constantly taking place?

In the course of a ramble over the island on a Saturday night, I came across several couples *en flagrante delecto!* Houses of ill-fame in Toronto? Certainly not. The whole city is an immense house of ill-fame, the roof of which is the blue canopy of heaven during the summer months. Some of these people whom I run across, after having apparently satisfied themselves from my height that I was not a policeman in plain clothes, ignored my existence entirely. One or two however, jumped up and hurried away.

What is the object of suppressing houses of ill-fame anyway? If it is to elevate public morality, I respectfully submit to an independent public the circumstances I have cited, and ask, does it do so? There is not a single boy whose experiences I have given, that has not stated that he would rather visit a house of ill-fame than do what he did. Fear of disease, the police and as a consequence his father's hearing of it, alone would restrain him. In reason, therefore, I contend that if these boys who related their experiences to me told the truth, and I believe every word of it, is it not logical to assume that the great majority of boys could give similar experiences?

Would it be possible for Inspector Archibald or any other public moralist, male or female, to obtain such information from a group of boys? I am quite positive it would not. And yet what I have told you is nothing to what I might tell if space permitted or I felt it were necessary in illustrating my contentions. I could give the experiences of boys and young men, who made no scruples about telling me girls' names with whom they had had improper relations. The list of girls would include some of the daughters of men of highest social and financial positions.

A young friend of mine who, when I first met him, was a lad in knickerbockers, whom I considered one of the handsomest boys in Toronto, informed me that when he first entered a business house in Toronto, he was invited by different girls in the work room to have improper relations with them, and there was hardly one with whom he had not had such. He was then a boy of seventeen. In three years he was a physical wreck, and the last time I saw him (he was then leaving the city) he was suffering from a long standing attack of private disease. Compare these deplorable circumstances with the vain glory of having suppressed a few houses of ill-fame.

A young friend of mine was away to a certain place on his summer holidays, and as is usual in such places, everyone knows everyone else. One evening he took a girl into the woods hard by, and on his way with her he noticed that a lady—married and with a family—was following. He said nothing to his companion but entered the woods with her, the lady following and maintaining a position so that she saw all that happened, which, I may frankly state, was a breach of the seventh commandment. As soon as he left the girl he walked straight to the lady's house, and opened the conversation :

"I suppose you thought you caught me nice, Mrs. Jones, didn't you? Well I saw you..."

"Just you wait, Johnny Smith, if I don't write home to your mother and tell her what you did."

"If you say one word to my mother, Mrs. Jones, I'll go straight to Mr. Jones and tell him you followed me, and what you saw, and I'll tell it all over here too. No *decent* woman would do what you did tonight." Mrs. "Jones" did not write to Mrs. Smith it may be unnecessary to add.

That incident happened when "Johnny Smith" was fifteen years of age. He told it to me when he was eighteen, and I ventured the remark that Mrs. Jones would easily fall if she had not already done so. Some months afterwards he asked me if I recalled the circumstances he had mentioned, and on my replying that I did, he said the deduction that I had made at that time was correct, that scandal was already busy with Mrs. Jones' name, and that she was being quietly dropped by her former friends one by one. That lady has a family of children and her husband is considered worth a hundred thousand dollars easily.

Do not these circumstances clearly and unquestionably demonstrate that the assertions of Rev. Father Decarie are absolute truth, and that he knows what he is talking about? It is perhaps superfluous for me to add that the names of these people were not Smith and Jones, but they answer the purpose.

From my superior standpoint of observation as well as my experience, I have come to the conclusion that the majority of women are fools. A young friend of mine of fifteen mentioned that two girls were in the habit of coming to the varandah of his house to talk to him. He had had improper relations with both of them. His mother rather laughed at him and declared that he would be married before he was eighteen. The idea that her fair haired boy went with those girls or any improper purpose never entered her imagination. The idea of getting married was so far removed from the boy's mind that he never even thought of it. He went with them for a certain purpose only. Tell that to his mother and she would laugh you to scorn, whatever that may mean—I have seen it in novels quite frequently though. A youth of eighteen was visiting me once, and where I boarded was a young miss of sixteen who sometimes waited on the table—the landlady's daughter. My friend had a moderate fortune, and the landlady having discovered this was quite willing to throw her daughter into his society hoping, doubtless, that he might marry her. She had made some inquiries from me about my friend's financial position which led me to this belief, and still further confirmed it by questions about him. His ideas were rather different. He thought from the young lady's actions that she might fall and made his plans to meet her on the street some night, to try it. He would not have thought of marrying the girl, but was quite willing to ruin her, and schemed with that end in view. He was not successful, however, for I spoke my mind so plainly that he abandoned the idea. However, it indicates what his ideas were and what the girl's mother's were, substantiating my idea, previously expressed, that women are largely fools.

In the early part of October, 1896, I was discussing the subject matter of this chapter with a gentleman who had been born and brought up in the Province of Quebec, and he expressed the opinion that the mother of every girl who goes wrong should be made to pay the penalty instead of the boy or man with whom she shares the sin. He also gave me a piece of information that I may as well publish. Some years ago in the parish where he resided quite a number of girls were in the habit of leaving their homes to go into domestic service in Montreal and Quebec. When they would return on a short vacation they were arrayed in garments of such glory and beauty and expensive jewelry that the parish priest became suspicious. He spent nearly a month in Montreal and discovered that these girls and others besides them were employed as domestics by wealthy people at twice the wages such servants usually received, but that in addition to the light domestic service they performed, they were the *mistresses of the sons of these houses*, and were paid such high wages on account of their youth, beauty and willingness to sell their purity. This circumstance, frightful as it is by itself, demonstrates also how much better able a priest is to judge than any theoretical public moralists are, and how extremely little the public know of what is going on in the very centres of civilization and Christianity.

A despatch from Halifax, N. S., on July 12th stated that Inspector Banks and a squad of police raided a millinery establishment in Barrington street on Saturday night, and found a lot of young women and men belonging to good families. The establishment was found to be a resort of the lowest kind. The discovery has created a sensation.

In the traditions of the Rabbins it is written that those are the elect of God who suffer his chastisement in the flesh. For the others, those who on earth drain the goblet of pleasure, and riot in the raptures of sin, for them comes the dread retribution after death. They are plunged in the fire, and driven before the wind, they take the shape of loathsome reptiles, and ascend by infinitesimal degrees through all the grades of creation, until their storm-tossed, wearied, degraded souls re-enter human semblance once more. But even then their old standpoint is not re-gained, their dread penance not yet performed. As men and women they are the lowest and worst of their race, slaves toiling in the desert, dirt to be trampled under the feet of their prosperous brethren and sisters. Inch by inch the wretched soul regains its lost inheritance, cycles must elapse before the awful sentence is fulfilled. But the Christian faith teaches no such horrors. Even for the penitent of the eleventh hour there is promise of pardon. Men and women, boys and girls are reasoning creatures, and they know that while committing a sin they are doing wrong, yet the fate of the repentant dying thief constantly before them impels them to run the risk, with no principle to guide them, and they fall. The pleasure of draining the goblet of pleasure is too strong for resistance, and they succumb, feeling that it is worth the experiment to enjoy the present and leave the future to take care of itself, just as Eve did in the garden of Eden.

Legislatures are incessantly bringing up the question of raising the age of consent, but to the practical man or boy of the world, it would be no hindrance to him if the age were sixty instead of sixteen. In ninety cases out of a hundred there is no seduction committed at all, it is simply fornication, and in the majority of cases the girl makes the first overtures.

This has been the history of the world since the beginning, and what is true of Potiphar's wife and Joseph is true to-day only on a larger scale, because there are more people to-day then there were then, and our social customs make the opportunities greater.

Examine the Criminal statistics of the Dominion of Canada, and how many cases come before judges or magistrates, where boys or men are charged with seducing girls who have not reached the age of consent? I only know of one during the last six months, and I give you the report of the proceedings in court.

"Not guilty, sir," said Jacob Hopkins, when the clerk of the court asked him how he pleaded. He was arraigned on a charge of seducing Mary Eliza Smart, a girl then under 16 years of age, in the township of Gwillimbury in July of last year. Hopkins was very emphatic in his denial. The girl who is pretty, but small for her years, was a domestic in the service of the prisoner's father at the time of the alleged offence. She gave her evidence planly amid tears. Before cross-examination, Judge McDougall said that if the evidence continued in the same way, he would have the present indictment quashed and one for rape substituted.

Continuing her evidence, Mary Smart swore that her baby, born last June, has died. Upon cross-examination by Mr. Rowell, she said her sister married Charles Pegg. He is the young man who was connected with the Lottie Evans Sharon poisoning case, having been tried and acquitted

Jacob Hopkins, the Whitchurch farmer, was acquitted of the charge of seduction made against him by Mary Eliza Smart. Her story was not corroborated, and the judge withdrew the case from the jury, ordering an acquittal.

Is it not the history of almost every case that is brought into Court that the prosecution can never secure a conviction because the defendant does not happen to be the first one who has had improper relations with the girl in the case ? That serves to demonstrate how few there are who are pure, and what little difference it makes as to what the age of consent is.

I may just mention an incident that will show that the age of consent makes no difference, for if any man discovers that his daughter has been seduced, he would prefer remaining quiet about it than instituting proceedings against a boy for doing so, knowing quite well that the exposure is simply ruination for life for the girl. A lady residing in a town not many miles from Toronto discovered that her stable boy had seduced her daughter. She promptly discharged him. The boy was naturally compelled to tell his father the cause of his dismissal, and the father told it to a friend of his one evening while going home from work. This friend told it to his son, and two days afterwards the whole town knew of the girl's disgrace. The mother of that girl, by her action, simply ruined her daughter for life. And it would always be so. Hence raising the age of consent is not in any respect a protection to girls. But if those old women of both sexes, who talk of public morals with about as much sense as a child prattles of its toys, would take the trouble to instill into the minds of their daughters the disgrace that attaches to such a sin, there might be less of it. A proprietress of one of Chicago's most prominent houses of ill-fame stated to Mr. Stead that girls err through not being informed by their mothers, and that uncongenial homes force more girls into trouble than anything else. I would take that woman's word on this subject in the face of any contrary opinion by all the united forces of professional public moralists in the United States and Canada together. She knows. That is the word. She *knows*.

I do not believe there is one boy in a hundred under the age of 18 who knows that there is a law regulating the age of consent, and what is more the age of consent does not deter these boys from seducing any girl who will listen to him. The only deterrent effect raising the age of consent likely to have is to prevent men from seducing girls and that is almost unnecessary, as men very rarely do so. It is boys of their own age who generally accomplish the ruination of a girl, and there is not one case in ten thousand where I have ever heard that the boy was prosecuted. As a matter of fact I have never heard of a case in my life.

Minds form and tongues give utterance to theories which every day lives kick holes into so that there is not a vestige left of the grand illusions built up by people who pose as public moralists. Let me ask any one of those ladies who are so much concerned with respect to the morals of other people's sons : If her son were found to be guilty of improper relations with a domestic in her house, what would she do? Would she heroically make an example of her son ? Would she condone the offence of the servant ? Not by any means. I have never yet known of a mother having done so. She would do as women have done since the world began. She would blame the girl, whether she were to blame or not. It is very nice to theorize what should be done in the case of other people's sons, but when it come to their own it makes all the difference in the world. Yet these people are driven into a frenzy because the law is not stricter in regard to ages of consent and seduction of servants, etc. These very people would be the last to live up to the requirements of the laws in such connections. In giving utterance to her heroic theories, a woman invariably takes the position that a man or boy is the seducer and is wholly to blame, and is, therefore, the only one that should be punished. In practice, however, it invariably turns out that the girl or woman is blamed, and she is the one that is punished if anyone is punished. I never knew a case different in my life.

Some years ago two boys, cousins, committed rape upon a girl who was the sister of one and the cousin of the other. They were arrested tried, convicted and sentenced to two years in the Penitentiary. The result is that those boys when they got out, did not return to the place where the disgrace occurred, but are to-day respectable citizens while the girl is still unmarried, and even to this day she and her family are looked at askance for an act that happened twenty years ago. Was it any benefit to that girl to have those boys punished ? Would it not have been far better to have let the matter drop, than press it to such a conclusion? That girl is disgraced for ever, she will never be married, and simply because her father, a hot headed English ignoramus determined to punish these boys. This case is not in any respect different from the other one in the sense that the girl is the one who bears the disgrace when such things become known. Raising the age of consent will never purify morals as long as civilization is as it is in the present day. And there is no prospect of its changing. No woman in practice would dream of doing that she demands in theory, or what she demands for the sake of hearing herself talk.

It is not quite within the recollection of every resident of Toronto, how a young girl of fifteen, residing in the west end of the city, being unable to conceal her condition any longer, was compelled to acknowledge herself *enciente*, and confessed that her brother, a boy of 17 was responsible for her condition? And that the brother was obliged to leave the city in consequence?

The scarcity of cases in the criminal courts is not in any respect an evidence that no improper relations are not going on. It indicates what I have always contended—that the evil goes on, and as girls will certainly not tell there is absolutely no danger in its commission, unless conception results from these relations.

I clipped the following from a Chicago paper:

Myrtle Bonnet, Columbus. Ohio, the 13 year old daughter of Dr. A. L. Bonnet, who was dismissed from the Mound street public school a few days ago because she was found to be in a delicate condition, was married to Pearl Colt, the 15 year old boy who acknowledged to the responsibility of her condition.

A young lady of my acquaintance once informed me that her father had stated that if he ever found out anything compromising about any young man with his daughter, he would assuredly shoot him. To the young lady herself he had said:

"Jennie, if any young man ever makes any wrong suggestions to you you tell me, and I'll settle him so that he won't do it again."

It was the young lady herself who told this, and told it to two or three others besides myself, with whom she was acquainted. That was the sublimity of innocence was it not?

If my assertions were not true, how is it that so many girls, apparently respectable, are the contempt of boys with whom they are acquainted? It is an axiom that a girl may share a sin with a boy, and that same boy will have a flippant contempt for her and express it to his friends.

This is simply nature according to Dr. Napheys, who says that woman is endowed with a sense of shame, an invincible modesty, her greatest protection and her greatest charm. Let her never forget it for without it she becomes the scorn of her own sex and the *jest of the other*.

But it is to be remembered that Dr. Napheys wrote his book thirty years ago, and since then social usages have been revolutionized. In this age of grace it is scarcely necessary for a boy to exercise himself to meet girls, for girls go to all places where boys are. You have only to pass any place where boys are practising athletics, and the streets are thronged with girls in their teens—a nightly occurrence. My opinion of the bicycle craze has been that girls ride bicycles simply because it gives them opportunities to associate with boys, on the principle of Mohamet, who, as the mountain would not come to him, was forced to go to the mountain. A girl would be considered decidedly immodest did she go on long tramps with boys, but on her bicycle she can at the same time gratify her taste for boys' society and satisfy the demands of propriety, which takes cognizance not so much of what you do, but how you do it, and questions your motives not at all. If I were to claim this opinion in regard to bicycling as exclusively my own, being of the opposite sex, I should, probably be termed evil minded or worse, and told to mind my own business. The Women's Rescue League of Washington, however, goes even farther than I do, and says it is a vulgar, indecent craze, and has helped to swell the ranks of reckless girls who finally drift into the standing away of outcast women of the United States more than any other medium.

Evangelist Chiverea when conducting revival services at Winnipeg held a meeting for women only at which circulars against bicycle riding were distributed which gave offence to many of the women present. As a result the engagement of the evangelist to address a W.C.T.U. meeting was cancelled by the ladies of the society. It shows that men must not interfere in such matter, whether right or wrong.

Public moralists objected to pictures of ballet dancers being posted on the streets of Toronto, because it corrupted public morals, by which they mean, I presume, creating unholy desires on the part of boys and men. I assert that one girl in a bloomer costume will create far greater and more widespread corruption amongst boys than a city full of show bills, so will a well developed girl in short dresses. One member of the W.C.T.U. was against having the show bills, while another asked what business it was of any member of the school board of Toronto whether the teachers wear bloomers or not. One objection was raised by a man, that constituted a sufficient reason why the lady trustee asked what business it was of his anyway. Where is their consistency? Any school boy can tell you every girl in the school who has well developed limbs, and he will discuss the girl with his friends. The pictures of ballet dancers on the walls would scarcely give him a second thought a girl such as I describe will be constantly before his mind. Would these hysterical fools who wish to have such posters suppressed even think of having their daughters' dresses lengthened to proclude the possibility of impure thoughts on the part of boys? Hardly likely. I contend that girls are less modest than boys, as is proven by experience. Go to a photographer and see some of the samples of his work, and you will see girls draped in every possible manner that will show their arms, shoulders and busts. Do they do that for any purpose other than to influence the passions and create unholy desires on the part of men and boys? During my residence in an eastern city a young miss of seventeen or eighteen had her photograph taken draped, showing her bare arms, shoulders and bust, the pictures being on exhibition in the window. If the young person's intention was to exhibit her charms and inflame the passions, and create unholy desires on the part of boys, I may say for the information of herself and the public generally that she was successful. Numberless boys and young men mentioned to me the fact of their having seen the picture, coupled with opinions of her charms, and expressing desires that while they may be inseparable from healthy youth, are scarcely used in polite society. They would discuss this photograph and all it suggested, yet I never knew there were ballet pictures in that city by hearing them spoken of.

If you will take the trouble to discuss the subject with any dressmaker she will give you innumerable experiences with young girls who will struggle with the pertinacity of a gladiator against having their dresses lengthened. Why is it? Do they know the impression it creates in the minds of boys and are determined to cater to their immoral desires? On the other hand let any man go where there are boys in bathing, naked, and almost every one of them will try to hide his nakedness. I speak from my own observation, and consequently know that it is so.

To expect consistency on the part of this class of people, however would be to expect the impossible. A man and his wife, the latter of whom is something of a speaker, are enthusiastic advocates of some system of education having for its subject teaching kindness to dumb brutes; the same people had a couple of boys working for them whom they treated worse than dogs. I boarded in a house once where the young lady was horrified to find me reading a novel on Sunday. "My father or mother would not allow me to do that," she exclaimed proudly. Her saintly father or mother, however, put no bar to her runing all over at nights, and the son of a prominent merchant boasted that he had frequently improper relations with her. An old gentleman of sixty, whose son aged about eighteen, was lying ill, discovered some cigarettes in his son's room. He was perfectly scandalized. His son! smoking! He almost took a fit of apoplexy, and it required quite an ingenious falsehood to convince the old gentleman that the cigarettes did not belong to his son. It is difficult to conjecture what the worthy gentleman would have thought had he known the cause of his son's ill-health. He was simply suffering from an attack of venereal disease. Is it not an historical fact that when Thomas Hughes' stories of Tom Brown were to be published in America, the saintly ladies on this side of the Atlantic were fearful lest the author's references to drinking should have a demoralizing effect upon their sons? Is it not equally true that some few years ago a young lady in writing a novel stated in the preface that she was poor and wished to be rich, and knowing that novels that suggested filth were the most widely read, she wrote her novel accordingly and it was most successful? Talk of consistency! There is scarcely a man or woman on the face of the earth who pretends to lead some movement for the elevation of mankind, who knows what consistency is. I could take you through a whole list of these men and women in the city of Toronto to-day who might easily commence at home and practice some virtue that they are deficient in, and let public questions such as intemperance, etc., alone.

I have listened to boys give their experiences with women older than themselves, who were employed by their parents as governesses or seamstresses and other positions rather higher than the domestic servant, which I saw no reason to doubt. How many men are there in Toronto who have dismissed this class of upper servant on account of their relations with their sons? I could give the names of some quite easily. I was once given the particulars of a case where a young fellow just come from college fell in with a young woman working in his house as a superior class of servant, nursery governess or something of that kind, who was ten or twelve years older than he. He described minutely that woman's actions in his company, which were of such a nature as could have all but sent her to prison. I believe the narrative, because I do not think a boy of seventeen would possess sufficient ingenuity to concoct such a story. And again what is more morbid than a woman who has passed her thirtieth year in celibacy?

I do not think present day moralists know anything of what is going on around them or they might endeavor to turn their attention from such fads on Prohibition and Woman's Enfranchisement and try to devise some means for promulgating social purity of a nature that has not in it the sweets of newspaper notoriety, but would render the commission of the breach of one of God's commandments less frequent than I have endeavored to prove they are at the present time.

With the progress in religion that has been made within the past few years and the agitation for the right of women to vote together with the interest displayed on the part of women to prohibit other women's husbands and brothers from drinking, it is not to be wondered at that young girls consider themselves relieved from the necessity of the formality of an introduction to a boy or young man whose acquaintanceship they desire to make, presuming, doubtless, that this is one of the fundamental principles which women are striving for, and which the evolutionary process under way at the present time will render qnite unnecessary. It is merely requisite for a significant smile to be exchanged in passing, and to look back after passing and the absurdity of an introduction is done away with. Permit me to ask how a boy would know that a girl will become a partner in such a sin if he did not receive some such intimation from the girl herself. I am not as old as Methuselah, yet I can remember when it was considered necessary for those of opposite sexes to be introduced before they considered themselves acquainted.

As demonstrating that I am not alone in my opinions of modern women and their ideas of moral training, I submit the folllowing from the Toronto Empire:

> In the Peterboro' Review appears a long letter from an "Anxious Mother," offering "sincere and hearty thanks to the Town Council for the great measure of moral reform they have enacted, namely, the curfew bell." The "Anxious Mother" goes on to say that "without some legislation of this kind it would be almost impossible in this advanced age for Christian parents to properly bring up their children in the way they should go" That such opinions are

pretty generally entertained there is no denying, but when we come to examine some of the reasons underlying them, the subject gathers interest. The "Anxious Mother" continues: "I am myself the mother of six children, all boys, the youngest six and the eldest under sixteen, so that you will see that my responsibility is great if I am to rightly train "those whom God has given me." As I am a member of the W.C.T.U., the Royal Templars of Temperance, the Epworth League, the Endeavor Society, the Woman's Rights Association, the Society for the Home training of the Young in Africa, etc., I find it impossible to give close attention to my family without neglecting my duties to the societies of which I am a member, and in many of them an office bearer." Who would have thought of Dickens' missionary spirit. Mrs. Jellyby, turning up in Peterboro'?

I do not believe that any woman ever wrote the foregoing, but it certainly demonstrates that the idea is gaining ground that women of the present day are too prone to poke their noses into other people's business in the way of advocating Prohibition and Enfranchisement and such fads as bring them into notoriety, while their children are free to run the streets as they like. It is simply what the times are coming to; women must interest themselves in the business of other people, and ask the law to do the duty they should perform towards their children.

If exception should be taken that I have no right to advocate a system of toleration of houses of ill-fame, or that a work of this kind has no right to contain a chapter on this subject, permit me to point to stories of sensual filth, placed upon the markets by religious associations who made the proud boast of having disposed of circulations of upwards of one hundred thousand copies, and to state moreover that large numbers of persons of alleged respectability did not scruple to attend "lectures" where extracts were read from such receptacles of filth whose aim was to cast aspersion on the Church of Rome. These aspersions were made in a general way, and were not compromising upon anyone, but every statement I have made in this work is undeniably and absolutely true, and any young man who reads this article will know and agree that it is so, yet I do not pretend to be like Dumas' young hero who agreed that it was possible there might be women and girls who were virtuous, but he had never met any.

While I do not wish to be regarded as one of those odious characters, a moral teacher with a mission, a class of people I have always detested, I consider the system I am advocating would be a proper one, and far less prolific of moral destruction than what now prevails. It is true that staff inspector Archibald states that he would not countenance such an order of things. That is nothing. Similarly a correspondent in the Telegram takes strong exception to the report of the Chief of Police in reference to the social evil, and takes high ground in respect to the suppression of houses of ill-fame. These people are about as competent to judge of such matters as a child shut up in an Assyrian museum until twenty years of age would be. How should they know the desires or passions of the human heart, when association with the young of both sexes and a careful study of physiognomy can alone enable one to read the thoughts and comprehend the thousand longings of youth. Yet they constitute themselves arbiter and judge of what should be and what should not be done for their moral welfare, without any knowledge of human passion. Let any young man of ordinary intelligence and perception make intimate friends with half a dozen boys of from sixteen to eighteen years of age, and having won their confidence place no restraint upon their speech. He will learn more in a month than twenty years of theory will teach him. I give you a quotation from one of Gaboriou's works showing one of his characters, and it will explain my meaning :

> She was the seventh daughter of a poor Protestant clergyman in the neighborhood of London, and had spent her youth in waiting like the princesses in fairy tales, the young and handsome hero who would realize her dreams. He never came, but poverty did She had been compelled to accept a place as governess, and had passed many years in silent resignation. In the evening when she was alone in her bed-room she bolted the door, and compensated herself for all the annoyances of the day by throwing herself with avidity into novel reading She fancied that from these nocturnal studies she had acquired a thorough knowledge of the world, of life and of passion, and above all felt that she had stored her mind with all sorts of expedients and was ready to meet any emergency.

That describes your public moralist precisely. Theoretically and in his own mind he knows everything. Practically he knows nothing.

Then the airs these people give themselves in discussing public questions is rather an advance upon the Pharisees of old, who thanked God that they were not as other men. The Social Purity Agitators of London, England, appeared before the licensing Committee of the London County Council, according to the language of the cable letter to the Toronto Globe, and despite the evidence of these people the applications of various music halls for licenses were granted. Each woman who appeared in opposition before the committee said that when she visited the promenades in search of evidence, she herself was the only respectable woman there, a statement that was so sweeping in its character that it did not meet with belief. The men who testified in behalf of the society gave evidence similar to that of the women witnesses. Their apparent self conceit and self righteousness had a bad effect upon a majority of the committee, and, despite their evidence the licenses were granted.

It would seem that in Canada too the evidence of this class of people is considered of so little value that the billiard license fee has been reduced in Welland, Ontario, Canada, from $200 to $75, although a large delegation from the W.C.T.U., and several representatives of the different churches were present to oppose it.

Your public moralist is so remarkably intelligent and knows so much that when their side of the case was presented they were not believed, although the council one year did refuse licenses to the music halls. Or, again, is it not just possible that they considered such places a social necessity, presuming for the sake of argument that they are immoral, on the same grounds as I advocate the toleration of houses of ill-fame. When the law was first passed permitting cities and towns to adopt the ringing of the curfew bell the W.C.T.U. lost no time in airing their views on the subject and advocating its establishment in Toronto. They seemed to have about as much weight with Toronto's council as their contemporaries in London and Welland had had, for they did not get it, the Telegram promptly informing them that Toronto's police force had something else to do besides running in children of tender years who were on the streets after a certain hour.

At the Social Purity Congress held in Baltimore Rev. C. M. Watch, of Brighton, Ontario, read an interesting paper on social purity work in Canada. He eulogised the moral sentiment of the Canadian people, and said if the whole Dominion should speak at the ballot box on the temperance question there would be 100,000 majority in favor of prohibition. He congratulated his people on having no general divorce law. To procure a divorce he explained requires a special act of Parliament, and the result is that only 48 applications have been filed in ten years. Forty of these were granted or about one for every six or seven thousand marriages. The speaker paid a tribute to Mr. John Charlton, member of Parliament, for favoring legislation on social purity questions, and criticised other legislators for indifference to the importance of a proper age of consent law, and to the one standard of morals. The city of Toronto also received Dr. Watch's hearty commendation as being the best governed city in the Dominion. The morality department in charge of Staff-Inspector Archibald, was highly praised, and when the speaker said there was not a known house of ill-fame in that city the congress applauded.

He did not mention, however, that Mr. Charlton has stated from his seat in Parliament that he favored a divorce Court in Canada.

The following is a solicitor's opinion on American divorces :

The Canadian courts recognize the validity of judgments and decrees of American courts if regularly and properly granted by such courts If the decree of divorce was regularly granted by a court of competent jurisdiction in the United States, and for a cause which would be deemed a sufficient ground for the granting of a divorce by the Canadian Parliament, such a decree could be pleaded as a defence in case of a prosecution for bigamy in Canada.

It is quite true, as Mr. Watch states that Canada has no general divorce law, but Canadians who desire divorces get them just as Americans do—in Chicago and other states where they can be obtained— and the non-existence of a divorce law is no bar to divorce being obtained. No less a person than Mrs. George E. Foster, the wife of the ex-Minister of Finance of Canada, obtained a divorce from her first husband in Chicago. She could not have obtained it in Canada, as her first husband is simply a fugitive, but she did so in Chicago. Mrs. E. F. Blackstock, of Toronto, also obtained a divorce from her husband George T. Blackstock of Toronto on the grounds of non-support, in the court of Newport, R.I. What these people have done other Canadians have done, can do and will do. Hence a divorce court is not a necessity in Canada.

The statistical year book gives figures about divorce in Canada. It shows that since Confederation Parliament has had 57 divorces, of which 40 were for Ontario couples, 14 for Quebec, 2 for Manitoba and 1 from the Territories. Divorce courts have been operating in three provinces, with the result that 82 divorces were granted in Nova Scotia, 64 in New Brunswick and 31 in British Columbia.

When he speaks of there not being a known house of ill-fame in Toronto, I respectfully refer him to my work, and ask him to consider the reasons why there are none, assuming for the sake of argument that his assertion is true, which I add is not. His commendation of Toronto is decidedly refreshing, and I submit the following as a criminal docket taken from a Toronto paper about the time he made his statement:

Queen v Joseph B. Blackburn, defiling a child under 14 years of age, true bill.
Queen v. George Brown and Richard Sadler, removing marks from stamps, true bill.
Queen v. J. B. Blackburn, rape, true bill.
Queen v. William Curry, arson, true bill.
Queen v. Harry May, robbery from the person and violence, true bill.
Queen v. Harry May, Fred Chambers, George White and George Badgeley, robbery with violence, true bill.
Queen v. Fred Chambers, rape, true bill.
Queen v. George Badgeley, rape, true bill.
Queen v. Harry May, rape, true bill.
Queen v. Badgely, White, Chambers and May, rape, true bill.
Queen v. William Broom, assault with intent, true bill.
Queen v. Frank Smith, assault with intent, true bill.
Queen v. William Broom and Frank Smith, murder, true bill.
Queen v. W. J. Kramer and Frank Watts, engraving instruments of forgery, true bill.
Queen v. W. J Kramer and Edmund Barber, unlawfully using instruments of forgery, true bill.
Queen v. David Cooper and W. J. Kramer, forgery and uttering, true bill.
Queen v Thomas Smith, John Crawford, W. J. Kramer, forgery and uttering, true bill.
Queen v. W. J. Kramer, possessing instruments of forgery, true bill.
Queen v. John Crawford and William I. Dickson, unlawfully using instruments of forgery, true bill.
Queen v. William I. Dickson, having in possession instruments of forgery, true bill.
Queen v. Frank Watts, having in possession instruments of forgery, true bill.
Queen v. Edmund Barber, having in possession instruments of forgery, true bill.
Queen v. Thomas Smith, uttering, no bill.
Queen v. George White, rape, true bill.

License Inspector Dexter scored a point against a number of illegal liquor sellers. Mrs. Ann Whalen 15 Centre avenue, was fined $50 and costs or three months ; Peter Green, of the Green Bush, York street, the same amount, and Mike McGorry, of 184 York street, $100 and costs or three months ; John Daly, of 156 1-2 York street, was convicted of illegally selling liquor. He also pleaded guilty to having been convicted on a similar charge in March last. In cases of a second offence the Magistrate is precluded from imposing a fine; the penalty being at least four months in prison. So Daly gets the four months. There were two other charges against " Jack," to which he pleaded guilty, also again admitting previous convictions. He got four months on each of these, and the three sentences run consecutively, making one year Daly will have to stay in jail.

A recent issue of the News stated that there were 80 cases of illegal selling of liquor to be tried.

In giving a report on city Mission work the News said that one clergyman declared that Toronto slums were worse than those of Belfast.

Very much to be commended, is it not? If Toronto is a moral city, what under heaven must an immoral city be like?

It is thus with those illusionary theorists who attempt to dictate and advise on subjects which their limited understandings could never grasp. What is your opinion of Mr. Watch's remarks?

I think I may consistently say that any woman or girl, once entered upon a life of shame, however glittering it may be at the outset, her fate is certain, unless she anticipates her final doom by suicide. She can rarely reform if she would. Few will help her back to the paths of right. There is only one means of safety, and that is to avoid the first step. Once place your foot on the downward part, and you are lost forever. It is generally hard to learn the true history of the lost women, for nearly all wish to make their past lot appear better than it usually is, with the melancholy hope of elevating themselves in the estimation of their present acquaintances. It may safely be asserted, however, that the majority of them come from the humbler walks of life. Women of former position and refinement are the exceptions, for society the higher it is will condone and sympathize with the misfortunes of one of its own daughters, while no language is strong enough to express the righteous indignation called forth by the disgrace of her of humble origin. Poverty and a desire to gratify a taste for fine clothes are among the chief causes of pro·titution in this as in all cities, but at the same time, proprietresses of houses of all classes spare no means to draw into their nets all who will listen to them.

The following cases will, perhaps, not be amiss in demonstrating the cogency of my contentions. The first came to my attention after I had completed my previous work on this subject, and the second one I am giving to strengthen my position, and it will prove more effectually than any amount of theorizing, the truthfulness of my assertions:

> The disaster on the Detroit river, near Belle Isle Park, by which a young man and his companion a young woman, lost their lives, has developed, upon the finding of the young woman's body, into a romantic tragedy of thrilling interest. It will be remembered that a Mr. Morris, a hotel keeper from Jackson, Mich, August Reitz and an unknown young woman were boating on the River. They endeavoured to catch a tow line from a passing steamer, were overturned, and Reitz and the girl were drowned. Every effort to discover the identity of the girl proved unvailing. This morning the body of Reitz was discovered near Amherstburg. It was in fearful condition and was buried at once. A few hours later the body of a young woman was found near Wyandotte. It was badly decomposed, but was identified as that of Emma Fox, of 300 Albert street this city, and also as the body of the young woman of the Sunday disaster. In searching for further information the correspondent brought to light, the downfall, disgrace and subsequent death of a Canadian girl who came here some months ago to seek her fortune alone and without friends. Emma Fox, as she was known here, was the daughter of well-to do people named Fulton, living in Middlesex. Tiring of her home in the country, she went to Drumbo, Ont, and later to Toronto, where she was employed in the office of Wyld, Brock & Darling as a typewriter. Her true name was Edith Fulton, but she frequently went by different names. Naturally of a vivacious nature, she rapidly made friends, principally among a fast set of young men in Toronto. One, a clerk, became infatuated with her, and her downfall soon followed. He had influential friends and parents, and when they discovered the intrigue, the girl was compelled to leave Toronto. She came to Detroit, where she secured employment and was prospering until she met Lou Fox, a railroad breakesman. She fell in love with him, and under promise of marriage in the near future, went to live with him at 300 Abbott street. A short time after Fox was killed while coupling cars at Twenty-fifth street, this city. Again thrown on her resources, the young girl fell into fast company, and was frequently seen in the company of different young men. The body exhibited no evidences of foul play, although the mouth was terribly swollen, and one eye hung from its socket, and about half an inch of the scalp was hairless. These injuries very probably were done to the body by the water and objects with which it came in contact in the water. The girl was five feet three inches tall, of good form, and would weigh about 110 pounds. She had long dark brown hair, and was probably between the ages of 18 and 20. She has a grandmother living in Windsor.

The above is taken from a Detroit paper, and will clearly prove that girls who are presumably respectable, but who are not really so, take the place of those who are professionally unchaste.

The second case even more clearly proves my contention.

Some few years ago two young men of about twenty years of age, asked me to accompany them to a house of ill-fame, and I consented to do so, suggesting that we should go to 248 Front street, or as the new number makes it now, 292. It was agreed that we should go on a Wednesday night, the conclusion being arrived at on the Friday evening preceding. On Monday morning one of the young men informed me that he and his friend and some others of their companions were at the house of one of their young lady friends the evening previous where, altogether, there were some ten or twelve of both sexes. During the course of the evening one of them called across the room to his friend :

"George, where is Mr...... going to take us to on Wednesday night?"

The other answered mysteriously :

"Is it 248 Front or Queen East we are going?"

The young ladies listened attentively to this dialogue, and at length one of them exclaimed :

"I know where you are going. If you go there I'll never speak to you again."

On Wednesday at noon I was called to the telephone.

"Is that Mr.......?" came from the other end. It was a girl's voice, and two or three voices were mingling together, with "Is he there?" "What did he say?" &c. &c.

"Yes," I answered.

"Well, this is Harry Smith speaking. Which one are we going to to-night?"

I did not wish to call out the number, so that everyone in the office could hear it, so I replied :

"Oh, tne Grand."

"No, no," she exclaimed impatiently, "you know what I mean. Is it 248 Front, or Queen East?" and then she added in a lower tone of voice, apparently to her companions : "he knows it isn't Harry that is speaking."

After a few more remarks of an irrevelant nature, she rang off, but we did not go to a house of ill-fame that night, nor any other night, and to any one of average understanding it will be clear that young men who associated with young ladies such as these would have no reason to go to such places.

A day or two afterwards I met my friends and they stated that these young ladies on hearing the street numbers, examined the directory, and having found the names of the people living there, made it their business to go and find out all about them.

Young ladies in the humbler walks of life?

Not at all. They were the daughters of well-to-do men in the city, some of them still attending school, and they were members of the Jarvis street Baptist church and the Bond street Congregational. The mother of one of the young ladies in question had died about the time I speak of, and the house became the rendez-vous for the crowd to meet at.

I could give you the names of these people quite easily if I wished to do so, and if it would serve any good purpose, but I have no doubt if they ever read this article they will recall the circumstances, and I took the precaution to obtain the full and explicit information I have volunteered to you.

Can you wonder that such a state of affairs exists?
These girls were permitted absolute liberty of action, out all hours of the day or night, free to roam as they chose, while their saintly mothers were doubtless too much occupied with temperance work and women's enfranchisement to give attention to anything so common place as their daughters, when there is no newspaper notoriety conected with the fulfillment of such duties.

I do not doubt that if the most overwelming evidence were given to the mothers of these girls, they would still any "it is not so." It was Gaboriau who said : "Evidence will crush the most obstinate man, he ceases to struggle, he makes a confession. A woman scoffs at evidence. Show her the sun, and she will close her eyes, and say "it is night." Men plan and combine different systems of defence according to the social position in which they were born. Women have but one system whatever their condition in life. They deny everything and always, and they weep." Prove or them the statements I have made, and they are like those people who answer you : " Impossible, no such thing ever happened to my laundress."

It was the cynical Balzac who said : "There is one thing admirable in women. They never reason about their blameworthy actions. Even in their dissimulation there is an element of sincerity."

It is astonishing, however, that no matter how blind a woman may be, she can always see the defects of her neighbours' daughters. Some time ago a young friend of mine showed me a picture, drawn by a friend of his, and which he thought to be quite a work of art.

" So-and-so did this, it's good isn't it?"

I need not describe the picture more than to say that part of it was a figure of a nude female, and the rest of the picture need not be mentioned. But that it was well sketched, the could be no doubt. That it was grossly indecent, it is unnecessary to add.

A few days later the same young man came to me with a smile on his face and said his mother had taken the picture out of his pocket one night, while he was asleep.

" She asked me, if I had a picture of a girl drawn with a lead pencil, and I answered no, but that I had picked up a piece of paper a few days before, and thought it was an exercise belonging to some of the school children, and put it in my pocket. But I said I had never looked at it."

"It was a dirty, filthy picture," his mother had answered, "and I thought it just about such a thing as Maud...... would be likely to give you."

You see how able this lady was to correctly fathom the depths of immorality that the young lady whose name she mentioned had possibly sunk to. Yet I know that her own daughter was carrying on a surreptitious correspondence with a young man whose morals were at least shady. Singular is it not?

In the course of a recent address the Bishop of Algoma said he had known cases where young girls ranging from 12 to 15 years of age were compelled by their mothers to produce from hiding places in their bedrooms books, circulars and pictures of such a foul character that anyone with the least modesty would blush to acknowledge having seen them.

At a certain skating rink last winter my attention was called to a handsome, well built young man of about twenty. He stood in the centre of the ice, and braced himself strongly as though warding off a collision, his stomach protruding. Presently a young miss of about seventeen, after several vigorous strokes to get up speed, and having succeeded, ran plump into him. This was repeated several times, much to the amusement of the spectators. Shortly afterwards a young lady friend admonished the giddy miss, and asked her is she had no thought of her reputation.

"My reputation," the other answered flippantly, "I don't give a damn for that, I lost *it* years ago."

This flippant young miss is decended from one of the most prominent professional men in Canada, and if I gave her name, I believe it would make the readers' hair stand.

Why is it? God only knows. When the prophet of old said the human heart is deceitful and desperately wicked, he knew whereof he spoke. In some natures the love of or passion for a human being will works marvels which neither the fear of God, nor the hope of heaven, nor yet the promptings of self-respect have the power to accomplish.

Almost any boy or girl of the present age, lamentable as it may be to say so, has far more experience or knowledge than the oldest libertine of a generation ago. I heard the conversation of some boys who had reached the ripe and experienced age of sixteen or seventeen years. the subject under discussion being girls of their acquaintance. One of them had hazarded the information that one miss of his acquaintance had blushed.

"*Blushed!*" repeated one of the others, with unmitigated scorn, "*her* blush. Why, I never saw a girl yet who *could* blush." I mention this as showing the exalted opinions boys of the present day have for girls and women.

Dr. Napheys it is who states that a wise provision of nature ordains that a woman shall be sought. She flees, and man pursues. The folly of modern reformers who would annul this provision is evident. Were it done away with, man, ever prone to yield to woman's solicitation, and then most prone when yielding is most dangerous would fritter away his powers at an early age, and those very impulses which nature has given to perpetuate the race would bring about its destruction. He adds that woman is endowed with a sense of shame, an invincible modesty, which is her greatest protection, and her greatest charm.

"She flees, and man pursues!" cries Dr. Napheys.

Alone in his study he may assume that what *should* be is, but let Dr. Napheys or anyone else visit any place where young people congregate and see if he is correct.

But his book was written in 1867, quite a generation ago.

I had a conversation with a boy who was attending the Collegiate Institute, and in the course of his remarks he told me some curious things. It appears that his class has for one of its texts books, the story of Hiawatha. I believe that is the work, at all events, it is an Indian name. He said that there was not a boy in that class of any age who did not make it his special business to markedly accentuate that particular passage which says, "and women great with child," for the edification of the girls in the class. He stated moreover that every boy in the school with whom he was on terms of intimacy was very well up in scripture. Not Christ's sermon on the Mount, where we are told of our duties in life, but such passages as contain what in any other work would be termed unfit for publication. That lad knew all the story of Potiphar's wife and Joseph, the story of Lot's daughters, all the suggestiveness of Deuteronomy, and could tell the book and chapter where all such passages as suggested filth occurred, yet he could tell nothing of the divine revelation to St. John, nor those admonitions that are intended to keep people in the path of right. I do not pretend to account for this, but I mention it to show you what the tendencies of the times are, and as showing that ordinary literature is rather flat for the youth of the present day. In some correspondence that took place in the Empire some time ago, I saw that in one of the Methodist Sabbath schools they have in their library the glorious Revelations of Maria Monk. So that even the churches are determined to cater to the popular demand for literature that is somewhat shady. Still it indicates the trend of the times.

There is another position from which this case is to be viewed, and that is where medical science is called upon to step in and save from disgrace young women whose indiscretion has led them to seek in criminal means the way out of their difficulties.

In conversation with a newspaper man some time ago, he stated that in the course of the day he had been called upon to make three calls on as many different physicians. Their conversation had turned upon abortions, and the first doctor had stated that he had applications from some twelve or thirteen different girls to have operations performed upon them. The newspaper man on making the second call introduced the subject and was there informed that the same state of affairs had been his experience, and the third was the same way. That they had refused to take any such steps goes without saying.

But another physician gives an entirely different case and I am impelled to give the whole matter just as it was told to me :

" Some time ago, a young lady, whose mother keeps a boarding house not a thousand miles from my house, called me in a great hurry and asked me to go at once to their house, where her sister was lying very sick in the throes of childbirth. I put in my instruments and left the house with her, and then proceeded to the bedroom where the sister was lying. She was in the throes of childbirth, sure enough, and in a short time was delivered of a child, still-born. I had some difficulty in getting the thing out of the house, but I succeeded and swore that

I would never do a thing like that again. But that only proves how easily pledges are made and broken, especially with yourself, for only a short time afterwards the one who had been delivered of the child called on me.

"I hope it isn't a case of the same kind as I had before."

"Well, yes," she answered, "it is, only this time it is my sister."

"In spite of my declaration to the contrary I went, and this case was even worse than the other. The head of the child was off, and she was having a terrible time of it. To make matters worse her mother was in the room, and could not be got rid of. At least I hit upon a scheme and told the old woman that I must have some very strong black tea, and though she tried hard to get the other girl to go and make it, I finally prevailed upon her to go herself, and then I managed the rest. Pretty risky, you'll say, but the peculiar part of it is, or perhaps I should say the least peculiar part of it is, that I never got a cent for either case."

I give you the following clipping from the Telegram, coming immediately upon the arrest of Dr. Andrews, who was recently tried and acquitted of the charges preferred against him. I shall make no comment on this case, more than to draw your attention to the circumstance of the incriminating letters that were found in Dr. Andrews' house after the arrest. If they prove nothing, they at least demonstrate that the fact previously mentioned in this article that the extent of the nation's immorality cannot in any wise be measured by the number of the frequenters of disorderly houses, must be only too true:

> The detective department presented a heartrending spectacle such as is seldom witnessed when a respectable man saw Inspector Stark and related the story of another sensational case, involving seduction and crime, and a mysterious disappearance of the unfortunate victim.
>
> Nellie Lafontaine, belonging to Pefferlaw, Ont., came to Toronto in September of this year and went to live with her brother-in-law, John O'Connell, 40 Gladstone avenue, who is a shoemaker. About a week or ten days ago she was taken to Dr. Andrews' place, 237 Shaw street by her sister and placed in his care, and $50 paid him by Mrs. O'Connell. She was pregnant at the time, and the object was to restore her to her normal condition, the same as the unfortunate Lucy Denning. As soon as O'Connell found out what had been done, he went to Dr. Andrews' house on Wednesday last, and demanded possession of the girl and $50, but could get no satisfaction. He at last threatened Dr. Andrews with police proceedings, and this is the case which is believed to have frightened the Dr. to take his departure, and not the Denning case at all. Miss Lafontaine has not been heard of since the doctor took charge of her, and both her sister and brother-in-law are greatly alarmed about her whereabouts. "We are ready to hear anything now," said Mrs. O'Connell, with tears in her eyes. "My poor sister is gone, but heaven alone knows where. Perhaps she, too, is.... is" then she broke down completely.
>
> Inspector Stark took possession of all the correspondence in the house, which consisted of between 200 or 350 letters, involving beyond doubt a number of criminal operations, performed both on married and single females, all over the country. Some of these letters are couched in the plainest language by educated as well as ignorant women, written confidentially, but confessing to the greatest acts of shame and seduction, and offering to pay large sums of money for advice and successful treatment. Some contain grateful acknowledgement of what the doctor has done for them, and begging him to keep their secrets from the world. Others ask for immediate advice, and suggest secret interviews, when the would be patients would be the least likely observed. Altogether they form a revelation which will form the darkest blot on society at large and shock the community from end to end of the land. The detectives are hard at work following up certain clues that promise to develop highly sensational features in the case.

If people run away with the idea that no abortion is committed in Canada, it only serves to demonstrate how extremely small is their range of experience and observation, as I happen to know.

What does an advertisement like this mean?

TANSY AND PENNYROYAL PILLS.

Never fails. Any stage. Thousands of happy ladies. Safe, sure and absolutely harmless. These pills are positively superior to all others. Many thousands of ladies in this country and Europe have secretly endorsed these pills Beware of dangerous substitutes and imitations. Price 2 by mail, or send stamp for particulars. Sold only by........

In the same way as a solicitor prepares his case for presentation to the courts by his counsel, so have I endeavoured to give you all the particulars in support of my contentions. In mentioning the circumstances of young ladies I have given you simply what I know to be true, and while it is extremely regrettable that it is so, I think it must be admitted that a very serious state of affairs exists. If what I have mentioned to you is truth, how much more could be said by others younger than I, and who have had later experience. That laws will ever succeed in preventing the commission of the 7th Commandment, I do not believe. When young girls, in spite of the teachings of the laws of God run into exposure, how can any human law prevent their falling? As centuries ago Canute sat at the side of the sea, and told the waves to recede, so might the police force and those who make these laws stand at the foot of Niagara with a broom and tell the water to go back. I have placed before you the facts as the king proved to his followers, that to stop the waves was the power of the Almighty only, and he demonstrated to them by practical illustration how base was the flattery they wished to bestow upon him. In presenting my facts and figures, I have endeavoured to demonstrate the impossibility of its suppression, and I think I may say consistently that I have been successful. My information is not in any respect overdrawn. It is what I could prove before any judge. I know the names of every one whose case I have mentioned. That it would serve my good purpose to state them I do not believe, hence I have not done so.

Coming to a discussion of this matter from a standpoint of social ethics, it must be acknowledged that the latter day opportunities presented to the female sex for earning a livelihood, are bound to culminate into a degeneration of the race. I possess no statistics to show the ratio of marriages compared with previous years, but I can state from personal observation that there are fewer marriages amongst people of the middle classes than formerly. While there may be various means of accounting for this, it must occur to the average beholder that the great majority of people in this class cannot afford the luxury of marrying. Men who formerly held positions, or more properly, positions that were formerly held by men are now filled by women, and nowadays it is much more a problem for a man to decide what he is to do with his boys than with his girls. The latter fill positions in offices, stores, and warehouses, and at salaries that men would scarcely look at much less think of attempting to suport a family upon. The result is precisely what so-called social teachers predicted as a result of licensing houses of ill-fame. If licensing houses of ill fame decrease the possibilities of marriage, so also does the emancipation of women. It is possible, of course, that the woman of the future may consider herself entitled by virtue of her ability to earn a livelihood, to ask a man to marry her, but it is in the highest degree unlikely.

Human passion is quite as strong in the man or woman of slender means and curtailed salary as it is in those of more opulent circumstances, consequently if men and women are precluded from marrying on account of purely financial conditions, it is quite probable and experience has proven that it is so, that the gratification of such will not be debarred by such a simple matter as the absence of the marriage tie. It is reasonable to suppose that when women, as they at present do, outnumber men, a large number of them are certain to fall. That this is so I am aware, but it cannot be proven by statistics nor even by the police records, for such cases do not find their way into the police courts, except in very rare instances, and then only occasionally when trouble shows itself. Individually, however, the vast majority of readers will know that it is so, and would have little trouble in tracing circumstances such as I mention to people even of their own acquaintance. This applies, doubtless, more to men than to women, but both will recognize the truthfulness of my assertions. In a recent issue of the Mail and Empire, a correspondent in addressing the editress of the Woman's Kingdom stated that she was unmarried and likely to remain so, and asked if the editress considered it admissible for her to indulge in illicit love? In reply she was told "No," and the editress added that she received large numbers of such letters.

I clipped the following from a city paper, and it explains itself:

BOSTON, Mass., Sept. 27.—A Landladies' Union, the purpose of which is to secure a system of municipal license and medical inspection for houses of prostitution in Boston, was organized yesterday afternoon. The meeting was attended by 23 women, who, before the police closed them out, kept the most "respectable" resorts in the city Resolutions were adopted that this illicit traffic has not been suppressed, but transferred to other localities, and that many girls, formerly protected by the landladies, are now destitute, homeless and sick. A committee to lay the petition of the union before the Board of Police was appointed.

So that I am not alone in suggesting or advocating what I do and it is to be remembered that this class of women are in a position better to understand the conditions they point out as existing than any other class of people.

In concluding this chapter on the Social Evil, I desire to say that to the best of my ability I have presented my case to the public for them to judge whether in the light of the circumstances I have laid before them, it would not be better to give the matter a trial. I ask the careful consideration of every man, woman, boy or girl of my contentions, and a fair criticism and a fair discussion of the system I advocate, more especially from the judiciary of the country, as they are less likely to be jeopardized than the clergy would undoubtedly be, should they agree with me, but I simply ask a careful perusal and those who do not agree with me can at least acknowledge that there is a wide field for parents to guard their children, and householders to guard the safety of those who enter their service. Even if I succeed in impressing upon these people the desirability of looking more carefully after those they employ whose temptations to sin are greatest, I shall feel that my work is not in vain. My advocation of tolerating, licensing or inspecting houses of ill-fame is because I believe them to be an economic necessity. Did not the Police Magistrate of Montreal or the Recorder as he is called, acknowledge to the Commission of Investigation held there some years ago that there were large numbers of houses of ill-fame known to the police of that city, and they were not molested simply because they were regarded as an absolute necessity. I assert moreover, that the present day theorists are entirely behind the times. Boys and girls of tender years are as well aware of the artificial means by which conception can be prevented as old men of a generation ago. I saw a druggist's advertisement a short time ago in a Toronto paper, with this significant black line : **Rubber Goods of ALL KINDS For Sale**. There is not a boy in Toronto, I dare say, who does not know what that means. I would not be surprised that many of the men and women in the city have no idea that it is ambiguous, and may mean one thing or another according to the person reading it. A lad of sixteen, a druggist's apprentice informed me that it was incredible the quantity of "rubber goods" they sold. " We sold more of them than anything else," he laughed.

It may be remarked by those ladies who talk of passing laws restricting this thing and that thing that it is against the law to sell rubber articles such as are advertised. In reply to any such observations, I might say that there is not a boy in the city of Toronto who could not get any such article if he wanted it. The druggist might and very possibly would refuse to sell to him, if he did not know him, but the boy could easily get what he wanted from the druggist's apprentice as I happen to know is done. A young fellow of sixteen once handed me a pasteboard coin, silvered over. When I mentioned to him that I saw nothing in the possession of such a coin, he laughed and told me to tear off the outside layer. I did so, and discovered one of the articles I have endeavored to describe. I have it in my possession yet, and regard it as a valuable piece of evidence. The boy had obtained it from a lad he knew in a drug store. The use of such articles opens the way for the commission of sin by girls of highest respectability, who fear the results that may ensue from breaking the seventh commandment.' When the possibility of conception is placed beyond all chance —when all danger is removed or obviated—the temptation to sin is augmented to such a degree that hundreds run the chance of falling or indeed, they may be said to be innumerable—who from pride and fear would not entertain the idea of sinning at all. Consequently boys and young men, knowing these scruples on the part of young ladies of superior social position, by having these articles in their possession, have their powers of persuasion supplemented a thousand fold.

I have given you the opinion expressed by the Reverend Father Decarie of St. Henri, and I have demonstrated clearly the truthfulness of the assertions he made, unwelcome as they may appear. But this is to be born in mind : A priest is far better informed on such matters than any other class of people, my article abundantly proving that it is so. When I undertook to write this work, I entered every avenue that promised to reward my research. I considered no means too insignificant to follow and I place my experiences before you, asking you to judge as to whether my advocation of licensing or tolerating houses of ill-fame would not reduce the immorality that I am prepared to prove exists. I always go to the sources of information when I want it, and I now submit the result, apologising for the length of the chapter, but with the conscientious reason that it could not be discussed in a less space. When the historic Collier said that the vice that is draped in the garb of virtue or has the varnish of an outward refinement laid over its leprosy is tenfold more infectious and destructive than the shameless wickedness which hides its loathsome front, he knew whereof he spoke. Do not my illustrations demonstrate the truthfulness of my assertions? Have I not also proven the truthfulness of Father Decarie's assertion that the extent of the nation's immorality cannot in any wise be measured by the numbers of the frequenters of disorderly houses? One of the most successful novelists of the present day in one of his works proves the accuracy of Mr. Collier's reasoning, when he says: Had he (his hero) remained in England his morals might easily have survived the onslaughts made upon them As he strolled through the unfamiliar streets of Liverpool he was horrified by the women who accosted him, leering with reddened eyes into his face, and breathing brown stout and gin into his nostrils. The highways seemed to be full of them. He wondered if any man could be found so low as to accept the fearful invitations with which his ears had been dinned. Crossing the channel he reached Paris. Strolling with a new sense of delight along the grand boulevards, upon the quays and through the numerous parks, he found women there too—and what an astounding difference! Soft voiced demoiselles, tastily clad, shot glances at him with their *bonjours*, from which it was not easy to turn away. When he invited one of them, she replied to his interrogations in modest monosyllables that won his Anglo Saxon heart and turned his Anglo Saxon brain. He lived with her for six months.

If I have overstepped the bonds of good taste in placing my facts before you, or have been too plain spoken in my illustrations, I plead justification by the fact that all I have told you is perfect truth, and I also regret the necessity of having had to speak so plainly. Moreover I feel so strongly on the subject I am advocating that it will be productive of good. Besides my language is not any stronger than appears in the generality of novels.

The great inconsistency on the part of so many people lies in the fact that they dread *appearances*. People may feel almost revolted at the idea of houses of ill-fame, yet I have shown that the sin goes on without cessation. Drunkenness, which is not a sin, is looked upon with abhorrence by Pharisees generally who demand the prohibition of the liquor traffic, but they appear to be quite indifferent to the fates of scores of girls who are going to the bad.

For some time past my attention was called to the newspaper reports of sermons by different clergymen, and resolutions by different societies of men and women, from which it would appear that they have been much exercised by the fact that drunken orgies are alleged to have taken place to the bar of the House of Commons, Ottawa, during the first session of Parliament in 1896. At the second session of Parliament in 1896, it was decided to close the bar. The Prime Minister also promising during this session that he would take a plebiscite as to public feeling in regard to Prohibition, and if the people decided in favor of Prohibition, they should have it. The Women's Christian Temperance Union of Ottawa have also prevailed upon the city council to have the curfew bell rung at nine o'clock at night so that all children under a certain age must be off the streets at that hour or be arrested. All of which are regarded by advocates of these particular fads as brilliant diplomatic triumphs. Let us assume for the sake of argument that every member of the House of Commons came into his seat intoxicated is there any divine law that was broken by their so doing? There was not a breach of any of God's Commandments had every man in the house been drunk, but simply and purely because the public could see it if they were drunk, were these people exercised. It *looked* bad. Let us leave the House of Commons for a few moments and step down to Wellington street upon which the Parliament buildings face, and which has received the suggestive title of Whitechapel. We will commence at the west end of the grounds. On the corner in the shade of the trees are four or five boys talking to, or rather blackguarding two girls in short dresses, who seem to enjoy it just as much as the boys, for they laugh just as gleefully as the boys do. At about every hundred yards one or two boys are standing like sentinels in the shadows of the fence pillars. Are they there for any good purpose, or are they not? A girl of some twenty years passes and one boy makes some remark to her commencing:

"Hello L......, ..." the rest of which I could not discern. To which the young lady answers sufficiently audible for anyone to hear: "Go to......, you......" at which the boys laugh.

"Who is the girl?" I ask, and one lad gives me her name, supplementing his information by advising me to have nothing to do with *that* girl, stating that a friend of his had caught an infectious disease from her, very thoughtfully giving the friend's name, with whom, however, I do not happen to be acquainted. At the entrance gate to the west block three little girls come running along peering cautiously over the fence and looking up and down the street. "There they are," one of them exclaimed excitedly, at the same time letting out an ear-splitting trill, and pointing to the other side of the street, where three boys are just crossing to meet them. I am not the only witness of this by-play, for four or five young fellows are seated on the stone fence commanding a view of O'Connor street, and pass some pleasantries to the girls, which, if directed to decent girls, would have been insults. Further on are two women and two men talking to a hackman, stationed in front of the main entrance. The four of them have apparently come to a settlement for they all get into the hack and are driven away. Seated upon the stone wall at the east end of the grounds are some four or five young fellows, not one of whom is more than twenty. Two girls pass them and as they enter the gate leading to the lovers' walk, they make some remark, upon which two boys slide down from their perches and follow them, and in a few minutes two more follow them. Enter the grounds and it is simply a repetition. Standing in the shadow of the trees, just adjacent to the east block I encounter a couple of lads one of whom I know, and raising his finger warningly he commands my silence.

"Sh...... We're watching......... and......... They're with......... and........., over on that bench," pointing to a bench a short distance away.

Both of these lads who are being watched are sons of Civil Servants whom I know. One girl is a merchant's daughter, the other my friend did not know more than her name. Those two lads watched the boys and girls for over an hour, with the patience of Indians, and eventually saw what they expected to see—a breach of the seventh commandment. They told me so afterwards.

I have introduced this Ottawa matter for one or two reasons. Ottawa has been prominently brought before the public on account of the alleged scenes in the House of Commons, and because of having secured that priceless boon—the curfew bell. I desire to demonstrate to you that the immorality that exists in Toronto exists in the same ratio in every other city in Canada and the United States, and that my assertion that the vice that is draped in the garb of virtue or has the varnish of an outward refinement laid over its leprosy is far more destructive and infectious than the shameless wickedness which hides its loathsome front is perfectly true, besides proving that women who pretend to be public moralists are more exercised over what "looks" bad than they are over what is really sinful. I do not hesitate to say that every incident I have given you in the foregoing culminated in a breach of the seventh commandment, as boys and girls and men and women who meet each other there do so for no good purpose. The environments of Parliament hill—the lovers' walk, the canal bank, and the river bank— afford too numerous places of concealment for there to be any question as to what those people were doing around there. And not only Parliament Hill, but Rockliffe Park, the west end park, the suburbs of the city, in fact any place within a twenty minutes' walk from the heart of the city is a safe place of assignation, as every boy or man in Ottawa knows. What, therefore, have these people accomplished in the direction of good morals? I have no doubt that if the mother of any one of these boys heard that her son had been drunk it would send her into hysterics, if she saw him drunk it would probably produce convulsions, but if anyone were to suggest that she should impress upon the mind of her son that it was better and nobler for him to restrain his passions than indulge them, that God will demand an explanation for every breach of His laws, she would probably compassionate the ignorance of such person, and with a pitying smile inform him or her that her son did not even know what adultery meant! What I have stated to you as having taken place on Parliament Hill all occurred within two hours. I made the trip just to give you an idea of what is going on, and the foregoing is the result of my researches. Compare this with the work so-called public moralists are doing, and as also demonstrating that there is no place on the continent of America where there are not prostitutes, and where apparently respectable girls are taking their places. I would like some of these moralists to accompany me some night to Rockliffe Park and some other of the places I have mentioned and see for themselves what is going on. Perhaps, then they might conclude that there are greater evils than intemperance, and that the curfew bell is not going to make any very great difference in public morals.

It may, perhaps, be remarked that I have never done anything to promote public morals, and in reply thereto I simply say I advocate what I do from the independent standpoint of the logician, and ask the public to judge as to whether it would not be better to tolerate houses than have even a portion of what goes on at present amongst so-called respectable girls.

STREET WALKERS.

Under this heading come the enormous number of young women and girls of all conditions of life, some of whom are respectable to all intents and purposes, and others who make no such pretensions. It will be remembered that the staff-inspector made use of the following language in his evidence before the Prison Reform Commission:

The number of prostitutes is greatly reduced We find that there is not half the number arrested for prostitution that there was before- Their houses have been broken up and soliciting is not carried on at all except in the worst part of the city. I don't think there are half as many as there were in 1865, when the population was not more than a quarter of what it is now. As a general thing citizens say that they find it a very rare thing to be solicited in the streets by women. In fact unless you go to certain portions of St. John's Ward, women will not solicit men on the streets at all, and a few years ago it was quite a common thing to be solicited on the most fashionable streets in the city.

Just as the idea strikes you you can accept or reject the above piece of information. To young men it will be somewhat of a revelation, inasmuch as its information will be so original to the youth or young man who has had the slightest amount of experience on the subject.

First of all women and girls are more cautious, and although it is stated that citizens say that they find it a very rare thing to be solicited on the streets by women, it is likewise to be remembered that the class of people who would volunteer any such information to the Inspector, are not the class of people who are honoured by the attentions of prostitutes. In the face of this evidence, I make the assertion that on every street in the city that I have ever been on, I have been solicited, and these streets include Carlton, Jarvis, Sherbourne, St. George, College and Bloor, while on King, Queen and Church it is so notorious that I need not mention them; nor Yonge and York. I mention this circumstance to show that while women have solicited me on these streets, how much more could be told by younger men and boys—particularly boys—considerable of which latter I have seen myself. Is it to be presumed for one moment that these people are likely to give their experience to the police? I also understand that one of the reasons given for this alleged decrease in prostitutes or more properly speaking streets walkers, is owing to the fact that policemen in plain clothes are or have been detailed to patrol the streets, and every woman caught soliciting is promptly arrested. This proposition is so perfectly preposterous that I confess my surprise that anyone of intelligence would advance such argument in support of such a theory, unless, as I think myself, the theory is so far without foundation that it inquires bolstering up with some such nonsense. First of all if any street walkers are arrested by policemen in plain clothes, it demonstrates that they must be pretty thick, when they are obliged to solicit, or either so far forget themselves as to solicit, policemen, who could be recognized by anyone of the least intelligence, no matter what their disguise might be, plain clothed or any other way. It is also stated that after a few arrests by policemen in plain clothes there is a cessation, and the inference is that they are frightened out of the city, but the cold fact remains that the girls, seeing that arrests have been made, refrain from soliciting the plain clothed policemen, who are easily recognized, for they, like Cain, have an unmistakable brand. Now, as these girls are without a doubt amongst the most intelligent and shrewdest people in the world, it is easy to understand why there is a cessation of arrests, when one or two have been effected.

I submit for your consideration a few cases just to show that in spite of the twaddle these people talk there are cases that come before the Magistrate:

Mary Dean, arrested on the instance of her mother, who alleges that she *cannot keep the girl off the streets*, was charged with vagrancy, and remanded until to-morrow.

Mabel Stuart, the girl who was arrested charged with robbing Geo. Verrall, a stranger, of $20, was remanded. It is said Verrall met this damsel on Richmond street, and was escorted to No. 9. He wanted to leave, and the girl pointed a pistol at him, demanding a dollar. Varrell went into the house again, and he says, that while the difficulty was being adjusted, he was "touched" for all his money.

There are three charges for illegal liquor selling against William F. Stewart, who keeps a hotel on Front street. A month ago Magistrate Kingsford suspended this man's license for 60 days on conviction of keeping a disorderly house. An appeal was taken to Osgoode Hall and in the meantime it is said Siewart's lawyers advised him to go on selling. The appeal has not yet been decided, and License Inspector Dexter claims Stewart had no right to open his bar until the 60 days were up. The case will come up again on the 29th.

This is the case where a hotel keeper allowed people to take rooms at his hotel for a short time when they wished of an evening.

Soliciting on the present day is like every other branch of industry in that it is reduced to a science. The fact that citizens state that they are not solicited to the extent they were some years ago may be perfectly correct, and it may be, too, that this is the result of having policemen in plain clothes patrol the streets. But I assert positively that there is absolutely no diminution in the practice of soliciting—the assertions of anyone to the contrary notwithstanding. There is a difference in the system, that is all. You meet a girl on the street and a flash from her eyes will tell you what she is. You look back after passing her, and she does the same. If you desire to follow her, do so and the probabilities are ninety-nine to one that you have a street walker. No actual soliciting has been done, it is true, but what is the difference ? Of course in the case of respectable girls such a course is called flirting, in prostitutes it is called soliciting. I speak from personal observation, and consequently with a greater degree of authority than those illustrious citizens who assert that there is no soliciting done. If policemen in plain clothes are ever solicited, it does not, in my judgment, prove how little soliciting is done, but how much, for the streets must be glutted with prostitutes when they are obliged to solicit instead of pursuing the tactics I have stated obtain at present.

Supposing for argument that there is any cessation of actual street walking and soliciting, there is still another fact that is to be taken into consideration. It is to be remembered that for the past few years during the summer months band concerts have been held in different parks, and that there is an enormous number of prostitutes frequenting these places is beyond question. How much easier, therefore, it is for them to attend a place of this kind, where there is practically no risk, and secure custom, than to walk the streets. Or take the religious street shows, the salvation army parade, and in fact any event that draws a crowd, will furnish a place where prostitutes can be met, and regrettable as it may be young girls and boys find these places their most convenient rendez-vous. These are only circumstances taken from a dozen which might be enumerated. Again by the evolution and perfection of the practice it is really unnecessary for a woman to speak to a man on the streets ; if a man is at all experienced, he will pass a woman or girl, and one glance shot out from the eyes will tell him her character, and if he wishes to make her acquaintance he turns and follows her. Schools girls or others of tender years have with a wonderful precocity taken up the example set by the prostitute and any boy who wished to make the acquaintance of a girl knows perfectly well that it is unnecessary for him to receive an introduction. He merely speaks to her, and that is sufficient, in ninety cases out of a hundred. It is not a particularly pleasing incident to narrate, or a very healthy state of affairs but that is a matter with which I have nothing to do, I give you the information, and you can trace the cause where ever you wish. I am simply giving you my experience and observation and it may be depended upon for reliability.

In the city of Denver in the wild and woolly west, houses of ill-fame are permitted to exist as a social necessity, and as an absolute safeguard to girls and young women. Some years previously it was almost impossible for a respectable woman to appear on the streets after dark without being insulted, until it became necessary to string a few men up, and as a compromise measure to permit houses of ill-fame to exist. If a man desire to visit a place of this character now he is at liberty to do so, and runs no danger of being arrested and disgraced by the publicity, and at the same time the female portion of the city can walk out at night on any of the streets without danger. Let any girl of eighteen or as young as twelve appear on Yonge street after dark and her reputation is assumed to be light, and she will, in the course of her promenade, be spoken to and at, and followed probably by scores of young men and boys who do not believe that young ladies of respectability appear on the streets after dark in the beautiful and saintly city of Toronto, noted for its morality and absence of houses of ill-fame.

One evening immediately after one of the band concerts in Clarence Square a friend of mine and I walked along Front street west. We did not meet a single pair of the opposite sexes, but fully half a dozen. Boys of 16 or 17 years of age, wearing short pants, and girls certainly not older and in short dresses. What were they doing there? Well, when you see boys with their arms around girls' waists as the majority of these were, and in other positions equally suggestive, I do not think it can consistently be contended that their friendship was purely Platonic.

I happen to know who some of these boys were. One of them was the descendant of a well-known United Empire Loyalist, whose family is known all over Canada, another was the son of a lawyer, who though not a prominent man is still well known in Toronto, and the youth himself has been mentioned in the newspapers as a prize winner in one of the city schools, while a third is the son of a prominent King street merchant. The girls I have not the honour of knowing, but presumed them to be misses in the middle walks of life. I do not say that they had committed any act of wrong, but it is a reasonable presumption that boys of assured social position do not usually go with girls so much their inferior socially for any good purpose, and it might also be mentioned that Front street west is not a thoroughfare frequented by respectable people at nights, to any very great extent. Besides there is the inference that the Grand Trunk Yards and the grounds adjacent to the fort afford a retreat availed of by people of loose morality. I never asked these lads what they were doing there, but I repeat that circumstances were strongly against any presumption of innocent promenading, when the hour of the night, the isolation of the place and the somewhat immodest positions they were in, are taken into consideration.

At nights any time after eight o'clock in the summer, and from seven in the winter these girls pass up and down Yonge street and along Queen west until nearly ten o'clock, when the streets begin to get deserted, and to remain upon them would be to make themselves conspicuous. These are the best dressed who promenade these streets just mentioned, while those of inferior appearance may be met with on Richmond street west, King west, Simcoe and Front west, where the police protection is not so likely to interfere with their vocation. The largest number are young women from the ages of eighteen to twenty-four, but it is becoming alarmingly frequent to meet young girls of fourteen and fifteen, though there is this difference between them, one is seeking custom for money, the others are generally seeking the gratification of pure licentiousness, and very rarely receive money as the price of their sin. Some of the girls are pretty and attractive, but the majority, and especially those of the class who frequent Richmond, King and Simcoe streets, are the very reverse.

A great number of the girls have some regular employment at which they work during the day. Their regular earnings are not large, and this means is pursued to increase them. Some, but they are few, sleep all day, and ply their trade at night, and there are very few young men or boys who do not have a place to take a girl to, such as boat houses and the rooms occupied by young men for this purpose. Again the ferries are a source of supply to men in search of female companions. He will find them both going to the island and coming from it, and on the island as well, a considerable number of characters being over there day and night, especially is this the case on Sundays.

I could, were I disposed to do so, give some information that would open the eyes of the staff-inspector as to where some of the girls who are supposed to have left the city, have domiciled themselves.

A friend of mine met a rather pretty girl on a certain street in the city where the usual sign of recognition passed between them, and he turned back and followed her. On being asked where she would take him the girl suggested that they take a coupe, which they did. Two or three days later, he was invited by a friend to dine. A pretty waitress came along and asked him for his order. He looked up in surprise, but his self-possession was equal to the occasion—it was his companion of a few evenings before.

This branch of the evil suggests at once that it comprises the best and worst of the girls and women who engage in it. Girls who are too respectable to be in a house of ill-fame, and some of whom are living with their parents, do not hesitate to do this while the women who do it are usually those on the last road to perdition, or who are fallen so low that no one will have anything to do with them were they in a house of ill fame.

Perhaps it will not be out of place for me to give an illustration of an occurrence that was investigated in the County court and which will demonstrate beyond question the assertions I have made in regard to soliciting, or if it is not actual soliciting, it may easily be classed as such. It will at least show clearly how easily street acquaintances are made, and I do not think any one will deny that girls are in most instances to blame.

About a year and a half ago William A. Morrison, a young lithographer, who will shortly attain his majority, passed a young lady on Church street, named Alice Fenwick. She was a stranger to him, but he addressed her in a friendly manner. She returned his salutation, and they went for a walk that night. And they met again, and passed some hours in each other's company. In the Civil Assizes before Chief

Justice Armour and a jury there was commenced the trial of an action for seduction and assault in which the mother of Miss Fenwick figures as the couplainant, and young Morrison occupied the position of defendant. At the time of the first meeting on Church street Alice Fenwick was employed in the Granite Club in the capacity of housemaid, receiving nine dollars per month for her services. In consequence of Morrison's treatment her health has suffered, and Mrs. Fenwick seeks redress, claiming $2,000 for the seduction and a like amount for the assault to compensate her for the loss she sustained by reason of her daughter's inability to continue her regular employment. The first witness examined for the plaintiff was Mrs. Fenwick, who testified regarding the points of issue as far as she herself was concerned. Then Miss Fenwick was called. She is a slim young woman, 19 years of age, and gave her evidence clearly and intelligently. She described her first meeting with the defendant on Church street, and they walked together as far as Roxborough avenue. As they went along Yonge street, Morrison made indecent proposals to her, which she rejected. They turned along Roxborough avenue, and he attempted to force her into a cottage that seemed to her to be empty. She left him and started to run away, but he followed her. In the struggle she tripped on the root of a tree and fell to the ground. The defendant assaulted her. About a month later she met him again on Wellesley street, when he again made improper advances to her. She resisted and he tore some of her underclothing off by his violent conduct. In cross-examination Miss Fenwick stated that the defendant's assault upon her had not rendered her enciente. Mr. Lount then asked for a non-suit on the grounds that the girl's mother had not suffered any pecuniary loss on account of the assault This view of the case was concurred in and sustained by his Lordship, who dismissed the action without costs.

This decision will, doubtless, be viewed as perfectly reasonable and just. If girls make hap-hazard acquaintances on the street they may be assured that their friendship is not sought after on account of their sublime attractiveness. It also proves that professional street walkers are not really a necessity, but that my theory that ostensibly respectable girls are taking their places, is based upon a solid foundation.

Nor is the practice of soliciting confined exclusively to women about town. I have known children, actually children, solicit men and boys on the streets. One little miss, who was certainly not more than twelve years of age met me on Jarvis street near Carleton one night, and stopped me.

"But," I objected, "where can we go?"

"There is a lane that runs through to Mutual street, where we can go, and no one will see us."

"And how much do you want?" I asked.

"Anything you like. Twenty-five cents."

Twenty-five cents. Great God : and the staff-inspector states that there is no soliciting done except on the lower streets.

I know that little girls do solicit on the streets, not only from actual experience, but from young men and boys who have stated to me that such is the case, and given particulars of such a minute description that to doubt them would be absurd. They will go into lanes in almost any part of the city, in just the same manner as the girl I have mentioned offered to do. Whether the motive be money or sensuality is foreign to the question. I have given you the facts, the motive you can supply.

LODGING HOUSES.

Toronto is, happily, free almost from the cheap lodging houses but they do exist to a limited extent, and seemingly they pay well. One of these disreputable holes was broken up and none too soon, when the famous Speelman was incarcerated in the Penitentiary. They are planned to afford the greatest accommodation in point of numbers with the least in point of comfort. The places are infested with vermin, and the rooms are small, dark and dirty. In some of these houses no sheet or coverlet is afforded, but even with the best of these accommodations the lodger suffers from cold in the winter and bed bugs in the summer. The business of the lodging house commences before ten o'clock and its greatest rush is just after the closing af the theatres ; and among those who are obliged to take refuge in these holes are doubtless those who have seen better days, besides runaway boys, drunken mechanics and broken down mankind generally. Each one sleeps with his clothes on and his hat under his head to keep it from being stolen. In addition to these lodging houses and not to be confounded with them are the numberless places where are apartments to let. There are hundreds of young men in the city who will rent a room from a private family and take their meals at boarding houses, hotels or restaurants. If you are seeking a room insert an advertisement in the Telegram and in two days you will have fully two hundred answers from all parts of the city. It matters not that you specify some particular locality, you will receive answers from a part of the city directly opposite to that to which you are desirous of going. You get some of the daintily-penned and delicately enveloped billets of Jarvis, Carleton, Sherbourne and other fashionable streets to the ill-spelled, pencil scrawled uncovered note of Adelaide, Richmond, Nelson, Bond and other streets of similar character. After laying aside as ineligible about one hundred and fifty letters, you retain about twenty-five or thirty, and devote a morning to inspection and selection. You become acquainted with strange localities and bell-handles, and informatory scraps of paper wafered beside doorways and in windows. You will endure tedious waiting at thresholds, and find that a single application for admission very rarely procures it, and according as your quest be high or low, so well your experience vary. If the former, you may expect to be ushered into spacious and luxuriously furnished parlors, where seated in comfortably padded chairs you may contemplate marble tables on which gorgeously bound volumes are artistically arranged, and mirrors capable of abashing a modest man to utter speechlessness, awaiting the advent of stately dames whose dresses rustle as with conscious opulence. You will enter grand staircases and gorgeous apartments and listen with bland satisfaction to the enumeration of the modern improvements which are contained in these houses, and if money be not an object you will not fare badly nor seek far, nor even be startled at the figure at which they may be enjoyed. But if your aspirations are circumscribed by a shallow purse your researches will produce very different results. You will see servant girls with unkempt hair and uncleanly physionomy, and you will be ushered into sitting rooms where the blinds are drawn and where you can not have a too searching view of the upholstery. You will have interviews with landladies of various appearances, ages and characteristics, landladies dubious and dirty, landladies severe and suspicious, landladies calm and confiding, chatty and conciliatory. You will survey innumerable rooms generally under that peculiarly cheerful aspect attendant upon unmade beds and unemptied wash basins ; and if of sanitary principles examine the windows in order to ascertain whether they be asphyxiative or movable, you will find how apartments may be indifferently ventilated by half windows, and attics constructed so that standing erect within them is only practicable in one spot. How a threadbare carpet, a twelve by six mirror and a disjointed chair may, in the lively imagination of a landlady, be considered furniture. How double, triple and even quadruple beds in single rooms and closets into which you only succeed in effecting an entrance by dint of violent compression between the bed and the wall are esteemed highly eligible accommodations for single gentlemen. How partitions of purely nominal character may in no wise prevent the occupants of adjoining beds from holding converse with one another, or becoming cognizant of neighbouring snores or turnings in beds. You will observe that lavatory arrangements are mostly of an imperfect description, generally comprising a frail and rickety wash stand which has apparently existed for ages in a Niagara of soapsuds, a ewer and basin of limited capacity, and a cottony, web-like towel about as well calculated for its purpose as a similar sized piece of blotting paper would be. In rooms which have not recently been subject to the purifying brush of the white washer you will notice the mortal remains of misquitos and other such like characters, ornamenting the céilings and walls where they have encountered destiny in the shape of slippers or boot soles of former occupants.

. It has frequently been a source of surprise to me that some capitalist did not or does not, build a place containing twenty or twenty-five rooms and furnish them in plain substantial style and there can be no doubt that it would pay a handsome interest on the investment, and it would make a home for scores of young men who are never satisfied with their present occupancy. If built in a céntral locality its success is beyond question. But at the present time, there are hundreds of places where rooms are to let, and there is always some drawback to their success. Sometimes there is no bath, and again there may be a bath and no hot water. People who rent rooms are too frequently afraid they are going to be swindled, and make themselves objectionable. I know an old couple who had rooms, comparatively nice ones, too, but the man made himself objectionable by presenting himself regularly on Saturday night as soon as he heard the lodgers' foot on the stairway, with the result that no man with any spirit would stay there.

A case was told me sometime ago of how one woman got even with a backward lodger. It appears that in the hey-dey of his prosperity he had been in the habit of going with a young lady and making her frequent presents, fans, an opera glass and some other such trifles until be got out of employment, and could not pay his rent, and seemed in no position financially to do so either. At last the old woman hit upon a scheme. She repaired to the young lady's residence, and told her the story of her lover's infamy. She was listened to with profound respect, and the young lady immediately after her departure, proceeded to a pawnbroker's where she disposed of all these trinkets, and paid over the proceeds to the irate old landlady, satisfying her account in full, but she gave the young man his conge, and he shortly afterwards left the city, where he is now doing well.

Some of the incidents connected with lodging houses have their comical side as well as their more serious aspect, and peculiar stories might be told if the walls could only speak.

One woman with whom I was acquainted and whose experience has been somewhat varied tells of a case that happened in her house that demonstrates how the subtle working of the passions leads many a girl astray.

A young lady a dressmaker came to her and asked for a room and though she did not make a practice of letting rooms to females she finally consented.

After being in the house some weeks, the young lady became somewhat irregular in her hours and finally after having been remonstrated with, decided to give up her room. She had arranged to do so in the course of ten days, and was making her arrangements accordingly when a lady friend came to spend two or three nights with her. On the second night the friend was taken ill, and the next day a physician had to be called, but the first occupant of the room left it as she had first intended, leaving her sick friend in the tenancy. The latter then told the landlady that she was married, and that her husband came home every Saturday night, and she expected he would pay all the expenses of the room on his arrival. This turned out as she had predicted; the young man paid the account, and remained in the house until Monday morning, he and his wife occupying the room together, when he departed. This state of affairs continued for about two months and the pair were getting into debt, until they owed something like sixteen dollars, when the landlady began to suspect something was amiss. She came to the conclusion that the pair were not married at all, and that when the gentleman presented himself next, she would deny him admittance. On the following Saturday night he was going up stairs, when the landlady met him.

"You can't go up there," she said decidedly.

" Why not?"

"Because that woman is not your wife, and I'm going to put her out next week."

The young man laughed uneasily, and then said:

"Well, I suppose if you say you won't, you won't. But I want to pay you a portion of the money I promised to you."

"You promised me," she answered "that you would pay it all to-night."

"Yes, so I did, but it is impossible."

This was on Saturday night and on the following Monday, in spite of many lamentations on the part of the young woman she was compelled to leave although she was still unwell. It was now a question as to how the arears of rent were to be paid, as the landlady, Mrs. B... was unacquainted with the firm where the young man was supposed to work. She consulted a directory and found that he was in the employ of a wholesale firm, on whom she immediately called.

"No," the manager informed her, "he was not with them now, but was in the employ of Smith & Jones, who were in the same business."

She called on Smith & Jones and saw her quondam lodger, who promised to pay her so much a week until the account was paid. He carried out the contract for five or six weeks and finally disappeared and a call on the firm revealed the fact that he was out on a six weeks' trip. Mrs. B... then decided to call on his mother, and see what could be done there. After stating her business, the young man's mother replied that the young woman was not her son's wife. "Though," she added, "I would not be surprised if he married her." After a moment of reflection she added:

"It is now nearly two years since my daughter brought her child here, and with that girl as a nurse. When my son came home from college, she followed him about the house like a dog, until I finally caught her coming from his room one night, and then I gave her notice to leave here. She went away and he followed her, apparently completely infatuated, and from being a most excellent young man or rather boy, he became neglectful of his home and everything else. His father has made it a rule to have the house closed at ten o'clock at night, and when that hour arrived he was compelled to sleep out. From bad to worse he appeared to go until finally he was forbidden the house, and at my personal request the firm by which he is employed consented to give him a trial. He has, I believe, given them satisfaction, and so far is doing well but his salary is not enough to keep him and this girl. I will pay you the balance of your account, and you can give me a receipt in full."

The story ends rather abruptly, but the mother who paid her son's indebtedness died some time ago, I saw by one of the city papers, but whether the son ever married the young woman or not I cannot say.

Very frequently apartments are advertised to let, apply to box ... Telegram, yet if the persons inserting them would reflect for a moment they would see how fallacious it is to expect that people who want rooms would go to the trouble of replying to such an advertisement, when there are scores of rooms advertised from desirable localities, where the addresses are given.

Persons seeking rooms frequently complain of being annoyed for a reference. This is not very pleasant, but it is absolutely necessary, as it is not known whether the applicant is a gentleman or a thief, or the woman a saint or a fallen woman, and a landlady naturally desires to keep her house free from improper characters, and to secure as guests those who will pay her promptly and regularly. In spite of all efforts it may be affirmed that there are few boarding houses that have not some time or other contained improper characters. Travellers frequently bring women to houses where they keep them during a short sojourn in the city, and no one ever knows anything more about it.

A lady on Mutual street who taken borders occasionally had an experience of this nature, and considerable difficulty in getting rid of her fair guest. A gentleman claiming to be her husband engaged a room and board for some days, and they lived quite pleasantly though the landlady noticed that the gentleman rarely, if ever, looked her squarely in the face, and she became somewhat suspicious, but when the week was up, he paid their expenses and announced that his wife would remain. The first day after his departure the wife fell into the rather bad habit of sleeping late, and having her meals served in her rooms, but to this such strenuous objection was taken that a conflict ensued, and the woman was told to leave. She deferred doing so, however, until another day, and her husband returned. He paid their bill, and promised to move the next day but that morning was the last they saw of him, though his wife serenely remained as though she were the most welcome guest imaginable. At last the inmate landlady became exasperated, and waiting on the stairs one morning, she told the lady she must go.

"Indeed," the latter replied, "when I get ready."

"No," she rejoined furiously, "to-day."

After breaking into a silvery little laugh, the guest continued :

"Do you know I had just been saying to my husband before he left that I was sure you were drunk the last night he was here, but he laughed at me. I'm sure if he saw you now he would come to the same conclusion as I have."

The landlady was quivering with passion but she said angrily "I'll see you get out to-day."

But the lady didn't.

The next morning the man himself took a hand in and rapping at the lady's door, he called out:

"If you don't get out of here by the time I come home at noon I'll throw your trunks out and you after them."

That had the desired effect. That morning she went out and in a short time a cabman called for the trunks, where no doubt a similar game would be played upon some one else.

POOR OF THE CITY. PAWNBROKERS. GAMBLING HOUSES. DRUNKENNESS. IMPOSTERS. PICK-POCKETS. CROOKS. THIEVES. ASSIGNATION HOUSES.

THE POOR OF THE CITY.

As has been before stated land for building purposes is high and scarce in Toronto, and in consequence, dwellings rent for more than in other Canadian cities. The poorer classes are to be met with in all parts of the city, but Bathurst street, Lombard, and in the heart of the city, in St. John's Ward, are places where they are the most numerous. The majority of them are, beyond a doubt, honest and willing to work, and in times of great commercial activity nearly all can find some means of employment, but in dull seasons, when merchants and manufacturers are forced to discharge their employees, hundreds are then thrown out of employment and the greatest suffering and distress prevail. Besides there are numerous vagrants, drunkards and disreputable persons who would rather steal or beg than work, and whose misery must be very great. It is not to be presumed that all who desire employment can procure it in Toronto; the contrary being really the case because labour and skill of almost any kind are here in excess. For every position of regular labour there are at least five applicants, and a man must be highly recommended to obtain a position. Many and many a young man respectable in appearance, honest and upright, can tell his experience with want, and how almost impossible to obtain work it is, and who is depending upon some more fortunate companions for his room and board, just as they invite him, while boarding house keepers can tell by the score instances of this kind.

PAWNBROKERS.

The sign of the three gilt balls is very common on York street and Queen street west, and where the ancient badge of the pawnbroker is not seen the words, " Exchange office" answer the same purpose. The law recognizes the fact that these people are a necessity in all large communities, and while tolerating them as such it endeavours to interpose a safeguard on behalf of the community by requiring that none but persons of good character and integrity shall exercise the calling. In a great many instances, however, they are with but few exceptions a most rascally set. They are little more than receivers of stolen goods, and the police often trace stolen property to them, notwithstanding the fact that they are compelled to produce a statement every day showing their transactions. Interest at the rate of ten per cent a month is allowed the first month, at least that is what they charge, and after that it is reduced to five, and it is surprising how many persons are compelled by force of circumstances to obtain accommodation from the pawnbrokers. Goods taken to them are received generally, without question, and they advance a fraction of the value of the article which is to be redeemed in one month, that being the time limited upon all pawn tickets, but the price at which the articles are taken is sufficiently low to render it certain that the sale of it will more than cover the advance.

The principal customers of these people are the poor. Persons of former respectability or wealth, widows, and orphans are always sure to carry into their poverty some of the trinkets that were theirs in the heyday of prosperity. Jewelry, clothing ornaments of all kinds and even the wedding ring of the wife and mother come to him one by one, never to be regained by the owners. They are taken at a mere pittance and sold at a profit of several hundred per cent. You may see the poor pass into the doors of these shops every day, and the saddest faces to be seen are those of the women coming away from them. Want leaves its victims no choice, but drives them mercilessly into the hands of the money lenders.

GAMBLING HOUSES.

Games of chance of all kinds are forbidden by laws which describe various severe penalties for the offence, but in spite of this prohibition, there is no country where gambling is more common than in Canada, and no city where it is carried on the a greater extent than in Toronto. But where do these places exist? That is telling. There are some professional gamblers in the city and the favourite game is poker. Gambling for money is not, ostensibly, carried on. The stakes consist of checks or counters provided by the people interested, and the losses are settled by means of these checks or counters representing an understood value. In this manner the letter, if not the spirit of the law, is carried out. Scores of young men in the city spend the entire Sunday afternoon in playing poker. They meet in the room of some friend and play for a certain limit. In another way some young man will have a room where he has a complete gambling outfit, and if several friends desire to have a game they can do so by permitting him to have what is professionally called the "rake-off," and this sometimes amounts to quite an item. I was acquainted with about twenty men in the city who rent a room in which there is a complete outfit. When several of them wish to use the room, they get the key from the gentleman who keeps it, and no one even suspects that there is such a game going on.

DRUNKENNESS.

Drunkenness is very common in Toronto. Thousands of arrests are made annually for drunkenness alone, and disorderly conduct. In addition there are thousands of cases of which the police never hear. The vice is not confined to any one class, it is to be seen in all conditions of life, and in both sexes. Day after day you will see men under the influence of liquor, reeling through the streets or lying under the trees in the parks. The police soon rid the streets of such cases, which are comparatively few during the day. At night the number of intoxicated persons increases, when you will see all classes of drunkards. There goes a young man, handsomely dressed, evidently the son of rich parents, unable to stand by himself, and piloted by a friend whose chief care is to avoid the police. There is a clerk whose habits will soon lose him his situation. The high and the low are represented on the streets. A funny thing in connection with the drunkenness of young men is the desirability and proneness of people to blame some one else for the downfall of their sons. An incident happened a little while ago, demonstrating this point. A young man who lived a most exemplary life, and was on the way to promotion, had the misfortune to meet a young man of wealthy connections in a state of helpless intoxication. He had only a passing acquaintance with the young fool, but like the good Samaritan he undertook to take him home, and finally accomplished that arduous duty. Imagine his surprise the next day when the principal of his firm of employers called him into his private office, and after reading him a lecture on the evils of intemperance, informed him very curtly that another such occurrence as the one of of the previous evening would result in instant dismissal. The young man protested his innocence of any wrong doing on his part, and narrated what had accurred. Fortunately his integrity was so great that he was believed. It seems that the drunken young cub's father had called upon the principal and informed him that his son had been led astray by this clerk. His own son could, of course, do no harm, but the other fellow who helped him home was deserving the highest censure, and discharge from his position is possible.

Bar rooms are in full blast, and will not close until eleven. The better class establishments are quiet and orderly, but the noise and confusion increase as we descend the scale of so-called respectability of these places. The sale of liquors of all kinds is very large, and it is always of doubtful quality. A large number of young men, and old ones too for that matter, make a practice of laying in the supply of the liquors they require on Saturday night for Sunday use, and to treat their friends, and it is found to work satisfactorily.

IMPOSTERS.

Toronto is not large enough to sustain to any great extent many imposters, but those who can obtain a foothold practise all sorts of tricks on the unwary, and are off before one can lay hands on them. If they are caught, they are tried and sent to the Central or the penitentiary. But there are men and women to be found in the city seeking aid for some charitable institution. They carry books and pencils in which the donor is requested to inscribe his name and the amount given. Small favours are thankfully received, and they depert thanking you deeply and sincerely for your contribution. If you are unable to give to-day they will come to-morrow—next week— anytime to suit your convenience. You cannot insult them for like Uriah Heep, they are very humble. In a great many cases they are soliciting money for themselves alone. Besides these one armed or one legged beggars whose missing member sound as your own, is strapped to their bodies so as to be safely out of sight, women wishing to bury their husbands or children, women with borrowed or hired babies, and any other object likely to excite pity, meet you occasionally, and if you give them money it will go for drink, in many cases.

PICKPOCKETS.

Toronto is comparatively free from this species of criminal although not entirely, and it is now reduced to a science, and is followed by many persons as a profession. It requires long practice and great skill, but these when once acquired make their possessors a dangerous member of the community. Women by their lightness of touch and great facility in manipulating their victims make the most dangerous operators. Crowded places of all kinds afford the best opportunities to pickpockets for the exercise of their skill. A gentleman sitting in a crowd discovers that he has lost his money. A well dressed gentleman sits next to him, whose arms are quietly crossed before him, and his fingers encased in kid gloves are entwined in his lap, in plain sight of everyone who could swear that he has not moved them since they first saw him. An officer could tell after a glance at the faultless gentleman that the arms so conspicuously crossed in his lap are false, that his real arms all the time being free to operate under the folds of his coat.

CROOKS.

Some time ago there existed one of the most barefaced swindles ever practised, but this has now almost gone out of existence. It was called the "patent safe" game, and was carried on as follows: A stranger would be accosted by a well-dressed individual, who would immediately begin a careless, friendly conversation. If the overtures of this individual were not repulsed in the first instance, he would soon be joined by his accomplice, who professes to be a stranger to swindler number one. The accomplice has in his possession a small brass ball or sphere, which he says is the model of a patent safe much used by merchants in China and India. He is trying to introduce it in this country, and would like to show the gentleman his model. The brass ball is, to all appearances, solid, but to the initiated is soon made hollow by pressing on a certain inner circle, when the centre of the ball, which is in the shape of a small cone, drops out. The bottom of the cone may be unscrewed, when a little chamber is revealed in which is a long piece of white paper, carefully folded and secreted. The other end of the cone, the top of it, can be unscrewed, and a second chamber is revealed in which is a second piece of paper exactly like the first. Swindler number one takes the ball, examine it, and declares that it must be solid. The accomplice then presses the spring and the centre drops out. He then unscrews one of the chambers, and reveals the paper to the admiring stranger and swindler number one. The accomplice's attention is here called away for a moment, and number one, winking at the stranger abstracts the paper from the chamber, screws the lid on, and replaces the centre in the ball. Handing it back to the accomplice, he wishpers to the stranger that he is about to win some money. He then bets the accomplice a sum which he thinks proportionate to the means of the stranger, that there is no paper in the ball. The bet is promptly taken, but swindler number one finds that he has no money, and asks the stranger to lend him the amount offering to divide the winnings with him. The latter, who has seen the paper abstracted from the ball is sure his new found friend will win, and not being averse to making a little money on the spot, produces the desired amount, and hands it to his friend. The accomplice then opens the second chamber reveals the duplicate piece of paper, and claims the stakes. The stranger loses his money and is taught a useful lesson.

Another swindling game is thimble rigging. The apparatus is three brass thimbles, and a little ball resembling in size and appearance a green pea. The rigger, in the most nonchalant manner imaginable, places the ball apparently under one of the thimbles, in plain view of the spectators and offers to bet any sum that it isn't there. Our friend who is looking on an interested spectator, is astonished at such a proposition, and looks upon the individual making the bet as little better than a fool, for didn't he see the ball placed under the thimble, and must it not be there still. His idea on that point is soon confirmed—a bystander takes up the bet, the thimble is raised and there is the ball. Again it is covered, and once more the bet is offered. Eager to prove his sagacity our friend produces a bill and covers the sharper's money. The thimble is raised and the ball is gone.

THIEVES.

Thieves are not very numerous in Toronto, as the poor creatures who steal a few dollars' worth in open day from stores and stands are not considered by the professional thief as amongst the "fraternity" which embraces housebreakers, pickpockets and burglars. These persons are carefully trained by old hands and are by practice made as perfect as possible in their arts. To be an accomplished burglar requires a very great degree of intelligence, courage, strength and ingenuity, but the lives they lead, stamp their countenances and general bearing with marks, which an experienced officer will recognize at a glance. The sneak thief, the pickpocket and the burglar have certain habits, attitudes and haunts; they act in certain ways when placed in certain positions which reveal their occupations to a practiced eye with almost as much certainty as the form and aspect of a blade of grass reveals its species to the eye of the practiced botanist. A sneak-thief will pass along with that rapid rolling, glance of the eyes which distinguishes the tribe; now he checks himself suddenly in his career, but only for an instant; an unprofessional eye directed towards him would not notice it, but that sudden pause would speak volumes to an experienced detective. He would know that the thief eye had caught sight of some booty easy of access. In an hour after he hears that something is stolen, and he knows who has stolen it, but without proof he is powerless. By a regulation pawn brokers are compelled to give a statement daily of their purchases, and in this way large amounts of stolen property are recovered. A favourite pastime lately has been to steal the lead pipe from new vacant houses, but it is happily being rapidly put a stop to. The magistrate is dealing severely with these thieves and receivers and it is not worth while to indulge in the luxury.

ASSIGNATION HOUSES.

There are no houses of assignation in Toronto in just the same way as there are no houses of ill-fame, but there is hardly a prostitute who meets you on the street who has not some place where she can take you. The rooms are hired from the proprietor or proprietress at so much per hour, the price being generally pretty high, and if refreshments are desired they are furnished at an enormous price. Some of these houses are locoted in respectable neighbourhoods, and in various ways they soon acquire a notoriety amongst persons having use for them. In the majority of them the proprietress resides alone, and her visitors are persons of all classes of society. But of late years this class of house has lost its value; with the large number of rooms occupied by young men, and the open sesame enjoyed by others, together with the boat houses there is really little for them to do, and as a consequence they are falling into the things of the past, but that they still exist is beyond question. I was once in a barber shop, when after having shaved me, the barber remarked mysteriously:

" Do you meet any women in the street?"

" Occasionally," I answered.

"Well, if you want a nice quiet place to go, come here, only keep it q.t."

CHURCHES AND THE CLERGY.

Toronto is essentially a city of churches, and glancing over the city from the Eiffel tower of the Mail building, the many spires form a really edifying sight, and there is scarcely a quarter passes but some church is enlarging itself or planning to build elsewhere, especially is this the case where a church divides against itself as occurred some little time ago when one faction required that a certain preacher should be employed, while another were equally determined that some one else should have the honour. It is, of course, preposterous to say that these rivals or rather differing factions quarrelled as that would imply a breach of Christian discipline. and then, too, we knew that Christians never quarrel; but it is true that one branch of the church left it and built a home for itself in a distant part of the city and under more congenial circumstances.

In addition to the salaries given the Ministers, many of them also receive residences. In this respect the Methodist ministers are favoured

more, proportionately, than others. A number of the
the free use of a parsonage, but also of the furniture it
Anglican clergymen have rectories and a few Pres
have the use of a manse included with the salary.
vilege is limited to the larger and wealthier churche
priest is given his home and living but his salary i
Some of the priests in the city do not receive more tl
simply enough to buy their clothing. A certain pi
and revered, gets very little over $100.co a year fo
The salaries named in connection with the Anglican
represent what the rectors get. They show only th
individual congregation. All rectors in the city,
amounts paid them by the vestries receive endowm(
Toronto Rectory Surplus Fund, and, in some cases,
tation Trust Fund. Otherwise the amounts paid by
to the rectors would seem very small, much smaller c
amounts paid to the curates of said churches. Th
connection with the Anglican churches represent
rectors and curates. The ministers of a few sects, thos
church, the Christians, the Quakers and the Christ:
no stipulated salary being content to receive what
vountarily. The appalling amount of $1,251,457 show
debt of the city and suburbs is. But this is not all.
only the bonded debt and the figures are either c
registry office, the minutes of the churches or from re

It is universally agreed that the morning attend;
fairly and justly represents the backbone of a church. '
a church and are directly interested in its welfare are
rule, who attend the morning service. Judged by
church debt is $68.42 per capita or $21.91 for each :

To the stranger visiting the city it is always a m
contemplate the large number of young people who fre
and it is worthy of note that the attendance is not c
but both are well represented. This applies with p;
to the evening services. This is as it should be. An)
mencing life in the city, and seeking advancement s
or otherwise, will find no habit that will produce s
results as to become a constant attendant at some (
with it a respectability that no other course of acti
abstain from church going is almost sufficient to r
outlaw.

Every reader doubtless remembers what were c
atrocities some little time ago, when missionaries w
to death in that country. In the light of my exper
members and Chinese in this country, I say all hor
for having wiped from the face of the earth the impe
whose presumption led them to that country to inc
they did not want, and which might better be giv

Upon an occasion not long since past, I took a parcel of laundry to a Chinaman, valued at two or three dollars. When I called for it he informed me that he had had a fire and that my clothes were burned, asking me at the same time their value. When I stated six dollars, he tendered me that amount without a word of dissent. I accepted one dollar for my loss, but the principle of the thing was there—he was honest enough to pay me my own valuation.

In the month of August, 1892, a young man who sings in the heavenly choir of one of the prominent Presbyterian churches of this city, addressed me a letter asking me for the loan of fifteen dollars and stating that unless he had it by the 15th of the month his furniture would be sold. I loaned him the money, glad to be of assistance to him, and told him to be in no hurry in paying me. He accepted the latter suggestion to the very letter, for he has not paid me yet. I have asked him for it times without number, and even placed it in the hands of a solicitor, but he never even answered either myself for the lawyer, and I have not received one cent of it to this day. That is one case.

In 1890 a student from some religious school in Woodstock and with whom I had become acquainted the previous summer, called at the office where I was employed and asked for the loan of three dollars, stating that he had remained in Toronto rather longer than he had intended, and would require that amount in addition to what he had, to settle his account at the hotel. A candidate for the ministry, his father a wealthy farmer—I loaned him five dollars without any hesitation, and he promised to pay me the money by return mail. I have not received it to this day.

Here is my experience with the Heathen Chinee and two Canadian "Christians." I hope the public will excuse me for saying so, but I must express my unqualified admiration for the Chinese when they made such short work of those people who went to their country to teach them Christianity.

And it is ever thus. People are ready and even anxious to send the glad tidings to all people, but are very apt to forget the sufferings at home and the need of Christain charity nearer their own homes.

When an appeal was made to assist "bleeding Armenia" indignation meetings were held all over the country protesting against England's inactivity in bringing the Sultan to time. Yet on the day that a long list of contributors to the Armenian fund was published in a Toronto paper, a poor wretch was tried before Colonel Denison for stealing twenty-five cents worth of coal to keep his starving children from being frozen to death.

These are exemples of Christian churches.

In addition to the churches proper, there are scores of young peoples' societies of every possible description, and others too numerous to mention. One of these is called by the sublime and divine title of "The King's Daughters," the king in question, being presumably, the Almighty, inasmuch as there is at present only one rigning king, he of Denmark, and I do not think he is the father of such a numerous family, nor do I think he would feel flattered at having such a multifarious family. I believe the daughters are religiously inclined, but the Empire gives us an instance where even religion seemed to satiate and a deviation was made in favour of the skirt dance:

> Young women who call themselves the King's daughters have been skirtdancing in public at Hamilton. They are now discussing pro and con the question of womanly propriety involved in their conduct. This should have occurred to them before they danced. They hardly know themselves why they did it, or where they found the precedent. Lady Russell has skirt danced on a public stage, but it did not matter so much to her; besides she is not a princess. There is no heavenly authority for the thing. Skirt dancing was originally copied by the stage from Spanish women of elastic modesty. It has been condemned by the Christian churches, but has been adopted in what is called "smart" society, where king's daughters do not, as a general thing, foregather.

This is a delightful occupation, and I am sure will be a cause for congratulation for the public to know that the young ladies can so easily depart from the rugged path of religious practice to the more worldly delights of questionable pleasure.

In connection with these daughters is also a kind of street show, I suppose you might call it, consisting of an old organ or melodeon, and some male and female voices, not specially noted for their accuracy of rendition or sweetness of expression, who congregate on the corner of Richmond and Yonge streets on Sunday evenings, and which are addressed by different people present, in a manner, quite frequently, that would send Her Majesty to a mad house from the manner in which her English is so diabolically murdered. However, if good is accomplished thereby, it is not for me to say anything against it, even though I very much question this result.

The Salvation army, with headquarters on Albert street was commenced in London in 1864. Within the decade following the organization was strong enough to undertake foreign conquest, and its legions began the conquest of America via Canada. They came, as it has proved to stay, and to-day their sanguinary banner waves over barracks in nearly every city and town throughout the Dominion of Canada and the States, not to speak of other quarters of the globe. I visited their headquarters once, and I am only doing justice to the organization in expressing the highest appreciation of their methods for the salvation of souls. A coarse-prize-fighter-looking Englishman with a decided accent was the presiding genius on this occasion, and his language was decidedly refreshing to say the least. In the course of his address he sent people to hell in a manner that was really edifying, though he did not inform his andience when or under what circumstances the Almighty had delegated to him this authority. But that he was divinely inspired could readily be uuderstood from the flippant familiarity with which he spoke of and to God and His Son.

He was followed by a young woman in an immense Persian lamb cap, which gave her the appearance of a female grenadier. Her voice had a decidedly twangy sound, and doubtless after hearing it many a poor sinner wished he were dead. She spoke of the words of Christ where he admonishes the young man "to go and sin no more." The young woman marched up and down the plateform with her arms in front of her at right angles, repeating with exasperating persistency that formula, "go and sin no more," she pronounced as one word as though to rhyme with sycamore. Her address was very edifying. It must have been, for I never heard its like before nor since. At its conclusion some boys were threatened with immediate ejection for misbehaving themselves. Poor boys! The wonder to me was not so much that they whispered during this address, but that they did not go up in a body and strangle the speaker. Had their ear drums not been of a peculiar structure, that rasping voice must have split them. The address itself was not much worse that I have frequently heard from Doctors of Divinity, and she used the same means when suddenly brought to a full stop in a spasmodic flight of oratory, such as " Glory be to God," " Bless His Name," and such like which have such a sonorous roll in the mouth of the charlatan. If any converts were ever made through that woman's agency it must have been a miracle. I think I speak for the majority when I say that after hearing that rasping monotone they were seized with an intense desire to murder the speaker. I have not the slightest doubt, however, that if the young woman were asked the question she would probably answer that she had been " called " by God to preach.

Then one man gave his experience. His language and mode of delivery were certainly original. He paid a tribute to the army for rescuing him from the beggarly elements, and blamed the churches for not having exerted themselves to do this, though he did not mention the particular church that had been derelict in this respect. Then he proceeded to tell of his improvement and if he had ever been worse than he was at that particular time, he must have been pretty bad. He paced up and down in the limited space of four or five feet, like a wild animal in a cage, and his eyes gleamed like a hyena's, while his words were hissed out in something the same manner as a hungry lion might be supposed to emit a succession of growls while guarding a piece of meat from a comrade. It was a succession of snarls. Then God was praised in a " hymn " the chorus of which was " My Savior is a Jolly Good Fellow, My Savior's a Jolly Good Fellow &c., &c.," and I felt that the heavenly host must have been edified by this tribute of familiarity with the Son of God.

Apart, however, from the objectionable style of oratory, I have just given, no one can deny the immense, or indeed, the immeasurable amount of good that has been, and is being, done by the better element of the Salvation Army. By the better element I mean the men and women of judgment and sense to guide them. I do not think the characters I have described could do any good anywhere, but they are not the whole Salvation Army. I have repeatedly heard the ensign in Montreal, whose text was about this : " I do not care what you are. I say nothing against any religion, Baptist, Presbyterian, Catholic, Methodist or anything else, so long as it makes you good." I never heard any man or woman speak like that before, and I never was impressed before as I was then. When I was told of the work that had been done in reforming drunkards and thieves and criminals of all classes, I could readily understand it. That man did not send people to hell off hand as though Christ had commissioned him to do so. He was filled with love and sympathy. A man who was timekeeper on the wharf at $9.00 per week, and who had spent two terms in gaol for stealing, had been rescued by the Salvation Army. Another who had been dismissed from the Grand Trunk for drunkenness is now getting $15.00 per week, and is a respectable citizen. He was rescued by the Army. And such cases I am told are countless. My informant was particular to impress upon my mind that the Salvation Army reached people that the churches could not reach. My own opinion is that they reach people the churches would not wish to reach. I once heard a Methodist D.D., long since passed to his "reward" state that he would not condescend to do this, and would not condescend to do that. I consider that man a disgrace to Christianity as well as a perjurer. But it is just such as he who are responsible for the almost universal agnosticism that prevails to-day. Imagine Christ informing people that he would not condescend to do this or that? Churches might easily follow the example of the Salvation Army, if they are in the field for doing good. Is it any wonder that the City Missionary, Mr. R. Hall, stated that in Toronto more than one hundred thousand people who have reached years of responsibility have not been brought face to face with the gospel, and that the number of those who are indifferent in the matter of religion in increasing? Surely not.

Apropos of the style of singing the churches have imparted unto themselves the following appeared in the Globe:

> We are aware that several books without words have been put upon the market, but the general hymn book such as hymns ancient and modern of the Church of England has not yet made its appearance. When it does come, it is to be sincerely hoped that it will be free from the tunes of objectionable form and character, many of which should be consigned to the region of the burnt cork fraternity. "Tit-willow" and "Robin Adair" are all right in their proper places, but should not be introduced into hymn books and set to sacred words. Tunes of the McGranahan type should be relegated to just where they belong, and that is anywhere but in church. The good and true and pure in style tunes are the only ones that will endure. They are inspiration as much as sacred poetry. None other should be admitted into use. The bookmaking and bookselling for a profit should for once be set firmly aside in the desire to aid the great cause of religion and promote the common good of the great mass of the denomination.

Music in in churches has become, like the oratory, a matter of catching the crowd, and some of the most beautiful lines that have ever been composed are set to music that has been originally produced and properly belongs to the concert hall or New York dance house. "Nearer My God to Thee" is improved upon by singing to the tune of "Robin Adair," while a rollicking prayer meeting piece called "Happy on the Way" is sung to the tune of "Old Roger Ram." The old negro melody "None knew but to love thee" supplies the tune for a favourite prayer meeting selection running something like this "He's the lily of the valley, the bright and morning star, He's the fairest of ten thousand to my soul." During the progress of a prayer meeting or revival one of the favourite "hymns" was a parody on the negro melody "Keep in de middle of de road," the leader of the movement—the illustrious

Jones—remarking that he liked the piece because there was so much gospel in it.

What sublime conception! In the fulness of time we shall no doubt require no music whatever by which the lines are to be sung, the preacher will simply give out the hymn in this fashion: "Hymn 350, Nearer my God to Thee, please sing to the tune of little Anny Rooney."

In the Methodist churches some time ago congregational singing was one of its peculiar attractions and characteristics, but after their copyright ran out a new hymn book was issued, and the lower notes transposed, or new music substituted so that now few members of the congregation presume to assist the choir in their laudable efforts to praise God in the old time fashion. The following taken from the Telegram gives their opinion of what they are pleased to call Musical Pharisees:

Organists and solists do not always add strength or significance to the religious services at which they assist.

A player or singer whose brain or voice is ruled by the prejudices that condemn the music that people love, can do more than a rainstorm to dampen a meeting. Their playing and singing are Greek to the multitude. The tastes of an average congregation may be common, but they are the outcome of sympathies and emotions common to the whole human family, and musicians cannot educate them out of a fondness for tunes that appeal to our deepest experience in the language of the heart. Toronto has many players and singers who to high culture add a true appreciation of the worth and power that may dwell in music stamped as popular. It also ahs its share of musical pharisees who make the organ growl or their voices tremble in the vicinity of high, in efforts to express the artist's thankfulness to the Almighty that he or she is superior to the common herd. Meantime the common herd does not find in music the wings upon which its thoughts can soar heavenward. Its saddened heart is possessed by a simple desire to assassinate the organist whose playing is not an act of worship, but an endeavour to exploit his acquaintance with the old masters. The organist with all his antice and the tastes that separate him from the multitude is preferable to the soprano soloist who at the close of a pathetic heart-searching sermon arises to cloud the preacher's description of the Golden City with "Nearer my God to Thee" screeched out in a steam whistle voice.

I was invited on one of my visits to Toronto to visit a fashionable church and was informed that I would probably see the largest choir consisting of fifty two voices, and the best music that ever fell to my lot to hear. The singers arrayed before me ran, in ages, all the way from seventeen to seventy, and it is to be observed that this was a model choir, notwithstanding the fact, and I speak with all deference, that it occurred to me that it was more like the dumping ground for all the old stagers in the church than that they were there for their musical ability.

One little man, who occupied the seat with some four or five ladies who sang soprano, appeared to be the chosen comedian of the church. He smirked pleasantly to the young ladies as they entered the church, and subsequently made faces at them to demonstrate, I presume, that he had not forgotten them as the services progressed.

One young lady sitting on a front seat in the same choir seemed to be afflicted with tight boots, for she stooped down and gracefully, and without embarrassment removed the guilty shoe, while her countenance shone with a heavenly radiance as her torture was temporarily suspended, so that there can be no doubt that choirs as they are now composed, are not, as has been popularly supposed little lower than the angels.

My friend who had extended me the invitation was prone to be somewhat snappish when I expressed my inability to appreciate the music rendered, and those who rendered it, and yet I was assured that the young lady who removed her shoe made a practice of doing it every Sunday, and the young gentleman who acted the clown was a very superior person indeed. That he had, in fact, left a choir because the leader thereof had committed the unpardonable breach of decorum or Christian discipline, or something of that kind, by singing in a theatre!

I submit the following as representing some of the words rendered :

> Oh, to be nothing, nothing, only to lie at his feet
> A broken and emptied vessel for the master's use made meet,
> Emptied that he might fill me, as forth from his service I go.
> Emptied that so unhindered that life through me might flow.

I do not think anyone could by any possibility compose more trashy or nonsensical sentimental drivel than that, yet the people who sang it are supposed to be " clothed and in their right mind."

What unmitigated rot it must appear to any sensible being when he analyzes the language of some of the hymns sung :

> " I nightly pitch my moving tent "

is nothing but an absolute lie. Another one informs us that

> " In his arms he carries them all day long."

What a pair of arms Christ must have in the lively imagination of some people.

This is fairly good :

> I *can* believe, I *do* believe that Jesus died for me
> A token of His love he gave a pledge of liberty.

I once heard it sung to the tune of some flippant waltz in the following language :

> I can, I will and I do believe, I can I will and I do believe
> That Jesus died for me.
>
> There is life for a look at the crucified one.
> There is life at this moment for thee
> Then look sinner look unto him and be saved
> Unto him who was nailed to the tree.

It cannot be denied, after hearing the above that "life" is offered pretty cheap, though it is a matter of regret that we were not informed where, by looking, we should see.

> I have a Saviour, He's pleading in glory,
> A dear precious Saviour though earth's friends be few
> And now He is watching in tenderness o'er me
> Oh, that my dear Saviour was your Saviour too.
> For you I am praying, for you I am praying
> For you I am praying, I'm praying for you.

I think the above about as fine as piece of Pharisaic twaddle as any impaired imagination could conceive.

> Then be hushed my dark spirit the worst that can come
> Will hasten my journey and hasten me home.

OF TORONTO THE GOOD.   155

In spite of the above sentimental couplet, I do not know of anyone who has ever seemed anxious to hasten home. In fact quite the reverse has always appeared to me to be the case.

> Some say that John the Baptist was nothing but a Jew
> But the bible doth inform us that he was a preacher too.
> He rose, He rose, He rose from the dead
> And the Lord did take my spirit home.

I do not quite understand the drift of the foregoing breakdown, but I suppose it must be all right, as it is sung in some of the churches.

> Come Holy Spirit, Heavenly done, with all thy quickening power
> Come shed abroad thy sacred light on these cold hearts of ours.

The above was sung by a full chours, then a young lady elegantly dressed, moistened her lips and sang:

> See how we grovel, here below, fond of these earthly joys, fond of these earthly joys
> In vain we strive to reach, to reach eternal joys.

I feel constrained to observe that it would essentially require the telescopic eye of the Almighty to see any signs of grovelling on the part of those who sang the foregoing. In fact they seemed to be quite well pleased with themselves.

When in the fullness of time, common sense has become epidemic, and those who have not been vaccinated read such sentimental, senseless drivel as is contained in a large number of the effusions called by courtesy hyms, I think they will understand why church members generally so strongly protest against the cold light of reason being thrown upon so-called Christianity by such master minds as Colonel Ingersoll, Bradlaugh and others, although they claim that Christianity is as firmly fixed as the rocks of Gibralter.

DWELLING IN UNITY.

There is trouble in Centenary Church choir, arising, it is said, over the introduction of some new voices from the Sunday school. An objection was made by some of the members to singing with the younger people, and, as a result, a number, if not all, of the choir members have been requested by the choirmaster, L. H. Parker, to hand in their resignations.—Hamilton Spectator.

In a number of churches the singing is a matter not in any respect second to the preacher, and salaried singers are quite numerous, as indeed they should be. One might suppose that the array of talent would conflict, each supposing that they were the attraction; but as the majority of sensible people know that the preacher is above such petty jealousy, and the choir soloists equally unsophisticated, this element does not, happily, enter into consideration, both being thoroughly conscious of their powers to please. In Ottawa recently when a singer belonging to one of the opera companies was announced to sing in a certain church, and quite a large crowd had gone to hear him, the preacher announced that before taking up the collection those who had come to hear the singing might retire, and the singer did' not render the solo expected of him.

Jealousy on the part of the preacher?

Not at all, though evil disposed persons stated that once when

Mr. Jarvis or Mr. Douglas Bird had been advertised to sing in that church it was crowded to the doors, and many could hardly gain admittance, but to suppose the circumstances had any relation would be absurd, even though these same people considered it a gratuitous insult to them to have such a speech made by a preacher concerning the collection. It is quite true that he was within his rights to speak as he did, but was it the action of a gentleman, let alone a Christian?

Some time ago, quite a controversy took place in the city newspapers concerning the music rendered in Bond street Congregational church, and I thought it was about time someone bestirred himself in that direction, although I only visited the church once. A yourg lady, whose name I do not know, arose and sang "The Better Land," or perhaps I might say with greater truth she attempted to sing it, as having heard it sung by a competent vocalist, I could hardly understand that the young lady in question should be paid for such work, and it remained a mystery to me why a church so wealthy as they were reputed to be, should not have creditable singing.

In his paper on the place of music in the sanctuary, read before the Presbyterian Ministerial association, Rev. Dr. McTavish pointed out that the tendency of the present day was towards transforming the services of praise into a sacred concert. He maintained the music in the place mentioned should only be used for devotion purpose. The paper which was clear and logical throughout, occasioned a large amount of discussion. The was a substantial unanimity of feeling in regard to the position that music kept within proper bounds was indispensable to the proper carrying on of Christian worship. The point that provoked most argument was the question as to how far classical music should be permitted. Rev. John Neil said that as so few people knew how to appreciate this class of music it should be relegated from the service altogether. Rev. D. J. Macdonnell took an entirely different view. The higher class the instrumental and vocal portion of the service could be made the more beneficial to the great mass of the people church-going would become.

Another subject in connection with the churches is the subject of church entertainments. You remember how Paul states that God dwelleth not in temples built with hands? So now in accordance with that view the house dedicated to an all wise and just Providence is used for giving "grand sacred concerts," the Jubilee singers, and different entertainments of a like character. The Rev. Dr. Hall in the course of an address urged strongly that all buildings consecrated to God should not be desecrated by unholy entertainments. By these a moral germ of disease might be introduced and he, for one, would do everything to keep it out. Debt was also a bad thing, and he thought that in many cases with a little extra exertion on the part of the congregation this might be avoided.

The premises were good, but how many churches would agree to such sentimental expression. However, Dean Wade of Woodstock, in the course of an address on the subject does not take the mild and easy manner of Dr. Hall, but strikes out from the shoulder and expresses himself in a fashion not to be mistaken.

He stated that he did not propose to deal with methods for raising money for any man made institution, but for the church of God. He said that the title of his paper would indicate that something counter to apostolic usage and custom in the matter of raising church funds had obtained ; something in direct opposition to all that was scriptural and apostolic, and which was eating the vitality of the church It had been said in defense of the modern method, that while as a rule, good people would be so influenced by the holy ghost as to give of their substance to the cause of God that there were places and circumstances when pressing needs called for the adoption of unscriptural methods. In plain English the poor cause should depend upon weak supports. The weaker the cause the more dependent upon the promises and faithfulness of God. This was what God's people believed. The poorer the congregation, the greater need there was to depend upon the infinite resources of God. There was a time when Christians were taught that with the presence of Christ and congregation when two or three might be assured of all its needs being met, but things had altered. The heavens were impenatrable brass ; the cry of God's elect was lost in space ; we should put our wits to work. We were going to run this church, and we meant to succeed We form a committee, each member of which acts as a spy to ascertain the nakedness of the land. We agreed that the church could not be kept without money, we could not get the money without the crowd How should we get both ? We should get something greatly in demand. What would catch the crowd. What was in demand in every city, town, village and hamlet ? That which would satisfy the claims of the devil, the world and the flesh. We are bound to make the church a success anyhow. This is the committee's set purpose. We will get consecration money if we can, but we will get money, money ! The man of modern methods had this excuse : Modern methods find work for young Christians, and by employing them in a good cause they are kept from evil associations. In other words, that by the church catering for the passion for pleasure there is a guarantee that the young will not seek for such satisfaction in the pomps and vanities of the wicked world, which they have renounced. The only power which can keep the young Christian is that mentioned by Peter : Kept by power of God. Modern methods of raising church funds were both dishonouring to God, and disastrous to the church's best interests All hope of the church fulfilling her mission lies in her being faithful to God and to herself as the bride of Christ. The modern methods are 1. The encouragement of Christians to rob God. 2. The sin of obtaining under false pretences 3. The sin of helping to develop a passion which was one of the greatest hindrances to true religion Dealing with the first method he said that it was evident that God was being robbed, else modern methods would not be adopted to make up the deficiency. Dealing with the second method, he said that people, goodly people, and goody goody people bought tickets for church shows in order that they may support the church. The vendor sells them, and the purchaser buys them under conditions of sale. The thing is a fraud. The church belongs to God. He can provide for his own house. Dealing with the third method, he said that in many places the church is robbing the world of its legitimate means of amusing the world. Now let us give the world and even the devil its due. Theatrical companies need not visit certain towns. Clowns, harlequins and negro minstrels and crack singers are at a discount in many parishes. The church provides for all that is necessary for both saint and sinner. Let me read a portion of an advertisement which appeared in a Brockville paper in November, 1891 ;

"Novel soiree under the anspices of ...... church. Miss Blank, Prescott's sweet canatrice is herself a treat. The Russian tea, attended by all the placid loveliness of the ice clad steppes of Russian Siberia. The lemon queezer adorned by beauty and grace (who will no doubt squeeze you all they can). All will be born to the land of weird and phanton spirits where all will be surrounded by the dark and mystic enchantments of the future. Be prepared for extra charge. One continual strain of music. Before the morning breaks the sweet and gliding music intermingled with reels and graces of ye ancient and modern lassies will be of the past. Doors open at 8 o'clock ; tickets 25 cents, including past or present supper."

Dean Wade had fond in the same paper immediately under the above this notice:

A chicken pie social at the M. E. Church Morristown last week realized about $17, and about 100 people ate pie until they could not talk.

He said that sort of thing was going on all over the country. In an advertisement of a lawn social given at Woodstock last fall this appeared : The refreshments will be all the season's delicacies, and in addition an ambrosial nectar, made from a receipt from which the ancients prepared the feasts for their gods will be served A witty Presbyterian elder had said : And now brethren, let us get up a supper and eat ourselves rich. Buy your food and give it to the church. Then go buy it back again. Then eat it up and your church debt is paid."

The dean read an extract from a handbill which he said was not the handbill of a theatre, but that of a church, where periodical revivals of religion were alleged to take place. The bill read: A star of the first magnitude. A grand high class concert will be given on Friday March 16th, in the Blank church. The remainder of the bill was devoted to eulogiums descriptive of those who were to perform. He said that one of the songs rendered from the pulpit of the church upon that occasion was by a gentleman who kept constantly asserting that somebody grew more like his daddy every day. He continued: "One might hear such tomfoolery one night and the next from the same pulpit the most sacred of subjects treated upon. To-night the banjo, niggers and bones, to-morrow the penitent forms and groans. An infidel might go to the doors any evening and ask as he might at a theatre, what is on to-night, is it a play, a ministrel show, or a revival?"

As might be expected from the above remarks by gentlemen who are not likely to detract from any church what is meritorious, the churches teem with attractions every Sunday. If you will consult the Saturday Telegram, you can scarcely fail to find something to suit you. Like the merchant, or the theatre, the church of God advertises its wares to the wayfarer, and he is lamentably fastidious, who, consulting the bountiful bill of fare placed before him, finds nothing to his taste. I regret I cannot give you the whole bill as it appeared, but I submit the following for your consideration as fair examples:

CARLETON STREET METHODIST CHURCH

REV. JAMES HENDERSON PASTOR.

SABBATH, AUGUST, 21st, 1892.

11 a.m., Rev. Dr. Barrass—Subject, Holiness on the bells of the horses.
7 p.m., Rev. J. E. Lancely, Pastor of St. Paul's Methodist church.

PROGRAMME:

Anthem......................Great is the Lord..................Sydenham.
Solo, Zion....................Rodney......................Mr. Chattoe.
Quartette....................Abide with me..................Torrington.
Solo........................Humbly before thee...Millard—Miss Hortense Jones.
Miss Jones resides at St. Antonio Texas and is a graduate of the Boston Conservatory of Music.

Holiness on the bells of the horses! what rot!
Please don't forget the solo of Miss Jones who is a graduate of the Boston Conservatory of Music.

BOND STREET CONGREGATIONAL CHURCH

REV. JOSEPH WILD, D.D., PASTOR.

Anniversary services, Sunday October 2nd, 1892.
Special Music by the choir.
Morning at 11 o'clock—Subjects—Twelve years' work. Cornet solo, Master Bértie Plant.
Evening at 7 o'clock, subject How long will things continue as they are. Saxaphone solo. Hymn with variations, Mr. Bert Kennedy. The usual anniversary collections will be taken up.

A cornet solo and a saxaphone solo! Quite a band concert.

BERKLEY STREET METHODIST CHURCH.

Rev. W. Galbraith, L.L.B., pastor, will preach a 11 a.m., and 7 p.m. Morning A defective ministry. 7 p m., A great reformation needed. Good music. All welcome. Sunday school and bible class at 2.45.
E. Coatsworth, M.P., superintendent.

BROADWAY TABERNACLE

REV. J. PHILP, M.A., PASTOR.

Sunday October 2, 1892, sermons by the pastor. 11 a.m., A character study. 7 p.m., Success or failure. Lessons for all to learn. Miss Bonsall, the popular and favourite contralto will sing at the evening service. All made welcome.

Miss Bonsall seemed not to have been sufficiently attractive to keep the public always amused, as the following seems to testify:

BROADWAY METHODIST TABERNACLE

LEAGUE SUNDAY. OCT. 6th. 1895.

Sunrise Prayer Meeting, 7 a.m. 8 a.m.
Sermon to Young People, 11 a.m. and 7 p.m., by Rev. Ward B. Pickard, of Hornellsville, N.Y.
Special musical service in the evening by a choir of sixty voices, under the direction of Mr. E. R. Doward.
Organ Recital by Mr. Doward 6.30 to 7 p.m.

Soprano Solo and Chorus ...."Inflammatus"......................Rossini
Tenor Recit.............. ...."Comfort Ye" ... .Handel
Tenor Air................... ..."Every Valley"........ ....Handel
Chorus...................."And the Glory of the Lord". ....Handel
Baritone Solo.................. .."The Palms"....................... Faure
Chorus.........................."Hallelujah"....... ....Handel

Monday Evening, Oct., 7th—Lecture, "The House That Jack Built," 8 p.m. by Rev. Ward B. Pickard. Special Music. Collection.

I consider the above nearly perfect, you have the whole programme presented to you, no opera could do more than that.

BROADWAY METHODIST TABERNACLE.

REV. J. C. SPEER, PASTOR.

S. S. ANNIVERSARY.

SUNDAY, MAY 3rd, 1896.

11 a.m.. and 7 p.m., Rev. John Philp, D.D.
3. p.m , Rev. W. F. Wilson, 7 p.m , Rev. A. B. Chambers.
Offerings of the day are in aid of school.
GRAND CHORUS of 500 voices, assisted by great organ and first-class orchestra will lead the service of song at each service.

MONDAY, MAY 4th, SUNDAY SCHOOL ENTERTAINMENT.

SPLENDID PROGRAMME—Solos, duets, dialogues, recitations, kindergarten, songs and drills choruses, (including " With Sheathed Swords,") orchestral selections, etc., etc.
Doors open at 7.15 p.m. To commence at 8 o'clock.

You still see the marks of progress, which rivals any of Corinne's performances, chorus and orchestra ; songs and drills : One step further —costuming the performers in tights—and the theatre is outdone.

Wilson family of revival workers at Broadway Tabernacle to-night, splendid singing. You are invited, Mrs. Wilson is a sister of the late P. P. Bliss.

Don't forget that Mrs. Wilson is a sister of P. P. Bliss, which in itself ought to be sufficient to attract the multitude.

A while ago some of the female portion of one of the many Methodist churches were given "talents" in order that they might show what they were able to accomplish with them in a given time. A meeting was held and the results announced. Business men who read the reports must have felt astounded at what some of them had been able to do. I venture to assert that there was not a single woman in the crowd whose transactions were strictly honorable. How they increased them God only knows, and it was a wise dispensation that required them not to explain how they realized such marvellous increases, or I think some peculiar and shady transactions would have been brought to light. If Christ be in heaven at the present time, I think his face must wear a puzzled expression many a time and oft when money is paid into His Church to be used for Him, and He knows how it was come by.

If the son of God were to make His second coming and were to be advertised as going to preach, would his sermon or the singing be the attraction?

I regret that I have no circus advertisement at hand just now, or I would give you that also for your comparison.

That prince of satirists, Max O'Rell gives the following as having appeared in some paper in the United States, and he seemed to regard them as something most extraordinary. It may be said as an extenuating circumstance in his favour that he probably has never seen the Saturday Telegram, and consulted its church announcements.

To make sure that he will be believed, he asserts that "he copies them word for word."

MUSICAL EVANGELIST

Solos. Short sermons. The place to be happy and saved. Walk in, ladies and gentlemen, walk in.

The other more seductive still, was worded thus:

No reason for not coming. Free seats. Books supplied to the congregation. The public are requested to leave the books in the seats after use.

Some little controversy has lately taken place in the newspapers respecting Sunday schools, and one Episcopal clergyman has had the effrontery to question their usefulness, bringing out opinions, good, bad and indifferent. Judging from an impartial standpoint, I think Sunday schools are a modern innovation inspired of the devil, but representing nevertheless, the progress of modern civilization, one of the salient features of which is to shunt our responsibility upon somebody else. People send their children to swelter and chafe in a Sunday school to learn what they are too lazy, too indifferent, too sinful themselves, to impart, or practice themselves as a living example to their children. I was about to add that they were also too ignorant, but no one is too ignorant to teach in a Sunday school. I was at a school once where one verse in the lesson started "Howbeit the high priest" and in the course of the review the teacher asked "Now, who was *Howbeit* the high priest!" I attended Sunday school myself, until I was thirteen, and I only say the truth when I tell you that it was simply a species of hell to be cooped up in that place for two hours on a Sunday, and I think that is the experience of ninety out of a hundred children. My surprise is that the majority of children are not infidels, when they reflect that they are compelled to sacrifice their pleasure and convenience to learn a religion they care nothing about,—whose only virtue is that it has a good appearance and creates a good impression ; particularly when they reach the age of reason and reflect on the characters of some of those who teach them ; and that people send them there to escape the responsibilities they are supposed to undertake themselves, but never think of doing.

I consider that it would be extremely presumptuous on my part to enter into a dissertation on the opinions children entertain for Sunday schools, but I refer you to Dickens' Bleak House and Mrs. Pardiggle and her children for the moral lesson I frankly acknowledge my inability to write.

<small>Those of us who believe that without the strength and hope of Christianity, this life would be brutalized and this world a desert are given many a heart ache by the charges of meanness which worldlings hurl with only too much truth against employers conspicuous for their goodness on Sunday. Of course, little is said about the sins of men who do not pretend to be any better on Sunday than they are the other six days of the week. The men who force a contrast between their pretensions in church and their practices in business are the subjects of most frequent attack. Business men might hesitate before they identify the blessed laws of their Lord and Saviour with the cruel law of " supply and demand." They make the laws of " supply and demand " their rule of life on week days, and Sunday are foremost in the temples of Him who established the law of love. Yes, and they are liberal givers to the church and to many good causes. The day will come when the church will scorn to take the money of men who cultivate the virtue of generosity, but neglect the scant justice of giving the girls who work for them enough to pay their board. Much that the pulpit says of the press is true, and it is not sparing in its criticism. There is no desire to harshly criticise, but if the ministers of this city did as their Master would have done, the church would be too hot to hold gentlemen who give girls thirty cents for ten hours' work, and allow girls who sometimes handle thousands per day the magnificent stipend of $3 per week.—TELEGRAM.</small>

So far as the above is concerned, I heartily concur in every word of it, and add that there is not a single clergyman in the city of Toronto who would dare to denounce the rascality of a rich member of his congregation, or one who employs cheap labor. The charges against the late Mr. Jeffrey, which broke his heart are too fresh in the minds of clergyman to permit of their running any risks, even if they had the courage, which is extremely doubtful. But the time will never come when the church will scorn to take the money of men who cultivate the virtue of generosity.

A city paper in replying to Rev. Dr. Potts said they could not accept his example as an infallible guide. They cannot evade a public duty by seeking an asylum in generalities—the coward's refuge. Journals are not gifted with the commanding presence or the robust voice of Dr. Potts. And fortunately few of them are able to flee to the past for a retreat from present duty. The esteemed and estimable doctor is a Protestant of the historic school. He avoids making an enemy of the mammon of political unrighteousness by keeping two or three hundred years behind the procession of events. When the Jesuit Bill was calling Canadians to battle for principle against privilege Dr. Potts was knee deep in the Boyne's red flood, or fighting valiantly on the walls of Derry. Protestantism was not calling its soldiers to win at the Boyne, or to man the walls of the maiden city. It urged Canadians to offend party for the sake of principle, and its messsage was unheeded by Dr. Potts and other gentleman like him whose silence was as favourable as his words could be to the cause of aggression.

I do not consider the great and overwelming majority of Protestant preachers of the present day any higher than the lowest and most degraded ward political heeler, whose ambition is to pander to the mob. There are very few who dare go to the length of displeasing the mob, but are ready to do as Talmage very crisply puts it:

"I have as much amusement as any man of my profession can afford to indulge in at any one time, in seeing some of the clerical "reformers" of this day mount their war-charger, dig in their spurs, and with glittering lance dash down upon the iniquities of cities that have been three or four thousand years dead. These men will corner an old sinner of twenty or thirty centuries ago, and scalp him, and hang him, and cut him to pieces, and then say : "Oh! what great things have been done." With amazing prowess, they throw sulphur at Sodom, and fire at Gomorrah, and worms at Herod, and pitch Jezebel over the wall, but wipe off their gold spectacles, and put on their best kid gloves, and unroll their morocco-covered sermon, and look bashful when they begin to speak about the sins of our day, as though it were a shame even to mention them. The hypocrites! They are afraid of the libertines and the men who drink too much, in their churches, and those who grind the face of the poor. Better, I say, clear out all our audiences, from pulpit to storm-door, until no one is left but the sexton, and he staying merely to lock up, than to have the pulpit afraid of the pew. The time has come when the living Jadases and Herods and Jezebels are to be arraigned. There is one thing I like about a big church : a dozen people may get mad about the truth and go off, and you don't know they are gone until about the next year! The cities standing on the ground are the cities to be reformed, and not the Herculaneums buried under volcanic ashes, or the cities of the plain fifty feet under the Dead Sea."

Methodism in Nebraska has been agitated greatly by the trouble in the church at Schuyler, a city of about 2,500 people in Colfax county. The Rev. Henry C. Meyers, a graduate of the University of the north-west, was sent to Schuyler a year ago against the protest of some members, who wished their old paster to be returned. The malcontents proceeded to make trouble for the new pastor, but he proved to be an eloquent and forcible speaker, and drew larger audiences than the edifice would hold. A new church was built, but about a month before the conference was held, his enemies re-enforced by a dozen members who objected to the doctrine of no hell peacher by Mr. Meyers, got up a petition asking that he be not returned for another year. When the appointments were announced it was found that Mr. Meyers had been transferred. This action of the Bishop caused more trouble in the church, and appeals to the presiding elder and the Bishop were made by his friends, but without avail. Mr. Meyers declared he would not be transferred, and the Bishop sent his successor, armed with the necessary legal papers. The new pastor took possession without employing any physical force. The deposed minister has begun the task of building up a church of his own in Schuyler, and his first services, on Sunday, were largely attended.

His letter of declination to the presiding elder of the district has just been made public, and the bitter tenor of it, as well as the charges he makes against the " ecclesiastical bosses," as he calls the church authorities, has created a sensation in the State. In this letter he gives the following reasons for his action :

" First, I can no longer subject my thinking to the thoughts of a few sectarian bosses who thought their thoughts a hundred years ago. My motto is, Reason is the lamp in the light of which every man must walk for himself. The world has outgrown the sectarian thinking of the centuries past, and is now moving in the progressive light of reason's lamp in the present day. The Dantean hell of the past—the pit from which flames of fire and smoke ascended, mingled with the breath of brimstone and the cries and groans of suffering spirits—is a hell no longer reasonable to all thinking men and women of this age. To preach men into hell who do not bow down to the creed of the church, a formula, once possessing a measure of life, but now dead and decaying is as unreasonable as the mind that pictured it. Who made the thinkers of a hundred years ago infallible so that their thoughts possessed a priori and unchangeable principles, and then left all future thinkers to the fate of their human weakness? Did God ? He did if the old doctrine be true.

" Is the creed of the Methodist church an infallible rule ? If it is, then all other creeds are wrong, for it differs from all others. Methodism teaches that there are Christians in most churches, but when men desire to become members of the Methodist church they are rejected unless they believe what Methodism teaches ; from which the conclusion inevitably follows, Chistianity is not Christianity unless it is labelled Methodist. But, says the zealous but misguided advocate of church creeds, Methodism numbers millions. Yes, so did the Roman Government, but the Roman Empire played its last act and stepped off the stage. Number does not prove infallibility. Truth is small and despises show, but moves quietly and unauspiciously forward to the conquest of the world.

" Creeds must shake off their dead leaves before their branches can produce ripened fruit to save and bless the world. Churches, like nations, must move in the direction of ultimate truth or die and decay with the past. As water, standing still, stagnates and produces living organism, so churches refusing to move forward, will die, and from their effete body will rise a new organism instinct with the breath of a broader and clearer light. Good is good no matter whether it is found in character built by church creeds or built by a personal recognition of duty and right with a faithful allegiance to the same. Men are not all on their way to the bottomless pit who do not bow down to creeds composed by a few claimers of infallibility. Is Abraham Lincoln in the bottomless pit ? Where are the greatest men of this nation ? Was Gen. Grant ever on record of the Methodist church ? Where are Clay, Sumner, and Webster ? Tell me and I will be silent.

" My second reason for withdrawing is this : Methodism is controlled by a set of ecclesiastical bosses, and all under-graduates are their tools. All ordinary preachers are instantly crushed to death unless they salute the pope. All kinds of chicanery and infidelity are practised by the leaders under the cloak of ecclesiastical and religious duty. The church guillotine stands upon the platform at every conference, sharpened and ready to decapitate every preacher who prostrates not himself to the gods. Unless they become professional beggars they are immediately relegated to the rear. The man of brains must seek his field for himself, while the beggar rides his circuit gathering supplies for bosses. Millions of dollars annually are collected and carried to foreign fields to build up personal enterprises at the expenses of privation, suffering, and beggary in our home country.

"Where is the $20,000 ship bought and paid for by the American people and placed in the waters of the Congo by Taylor for the purpose of establishing trading posts? What have been the results of $300,000 begged of the children and poor of this country and sent to Bulgaria? What of the millions sent to China? 'The Chairman,' said Dr. Maxfield of Omaha, in a speech made at Stanton, Neb., some years ago, 'will be a Chinaman no matter where he is, or what be the character of his instruction.' This is doubtless true. But why send millions of money needed by the poor and destitute of this country to China to no purpose? We answer: It is to keep missionary secretaries in lucrative positions. To this end the popes of the church will crush out of existence all preachers who do not endorse the movement. Book concerns are run by this gigantic institution, and all preachers are required to purchase their literature from them at enormous prices, so that the Bishops can come and draw large salaries, ride in Pullman palace cars, stop at costly hotels, and build fine mansions. All this comes from the self-sacrificing preachers, who live for the most part upon from $200 to $300 a year. Thousands of dollars passed out of Nebraska during the hardest times ever seen to fields rendering large support to the bosses of the church, while the citizens of Eastern States were appealed to assist the needy to keep from starvation.

"These are but a small number of the reasons I have for withdrawing."

I ask your careful perusal of the foregoing as showing the means church authorities are ready to employ to avenge themselves upon those who adversely criticise their acts, and as proving the absurdity of Protestant claims to liberty of conscience. This man asserts there is no hell, and nine-tenths of the Protestants of the present day agree with him but the Methodist authorities whose vagaries he denounced, took good care to keep him out of the pale of the church, as soon as he showed his independence.

Assuming that Christianity is founded upon the ten commandments, Christ's sermon on the Mount; that St. Paul was inspired of God, and that the bible is true, how many are there who are Christians according to its definition there either clergy or laity? There is not five per cent on the continent of America, and I hold that the clergy is entirely to blame for such a state of affairs. By whose authority does this man or that man preach a "liberal" Christianity, which will permit his congregation to do almost anything so long as they keep within the technicalities of laws made by man to shield rogues and swindlers? for I hold that the man who borrows from me or buys from me and does not pay me, is nothing less than a swindler.

Is there a so-called Christian to-day who would think of obeying the divine injunction which says "if thine enemy smite thee on one cheek, turn thou the other"? There is not one. A preacher will, doubtless tell you that it does not bear its literal interpretation, and let some one cross him, and he will demonstrate how little restraint his Christianity has over him in his frantic attempt to give the person who opposes him a black eye. The passage I have referred to means what it says or it means nothing. So do all the Scriptures.

What is the value of Christianity anyway? It does not appear to elevate, refine or change those who profess it one iota. I have heard ministers of the gospel use the vilest billingsgate in speaking, and if anyone should show a good example surely it is they.

Hon. S. H. Blake recently aroused the ire of the Hamilton brethren by some remarks of his, and the brethren retort in kind. At a meeting of the Ministerial Association, Evangelist Moody and Hon. S. H. Blake were severely rebuked for statements made at public meetings concerning higher criticism. Rev. Dr. Burns said he was much annoyed at the reflection made on the talent of preachers who occupy Hamilton pulpits. Rev. Dr. Lyle said such ignoramuses should be severely censured. If the Lord's work can prosper without the ignorant, the utterances of Moody and Blake, he said, should be hissed down, as they indicated a lack of charity and show "a wicked spirit and much ignorance. The memories of higher critics will live when these wretched, sneering pigmy critics are dead and forgotten."

Rev. Mr. McPherson said he could forgive Moody, on account of his intense enthusiasm. Blake's remarks, however, were very insulting, and Blake should be thoroughly ashamed of himself.

Rev. Mr. Gilmour advised the Association not to put itself on record in the matter, and the discussion dropped.

Hon. S. H. Blake has also said the success of the Sunday car advocates was attributable to those clergymen who openly favoured Sunday afternoon bicycling and boating, and in a measure Sunday cars. The Sabbath was being secularized by witty speeches on prohibition and by the turning of churches into concert halls. Ministers attended such lectures on Sunday afternoons instead of teaching in Bible classes the importance of keeping holy the Sabbath day.

When the time came for the collection at Bond street Congregational church the new pastor, Rev. Morgan Wood, spoke out as follows: "The ushers will now pass amongst you and take up the collection. I get awfully tired of making that announcement every Sunday, friends. I have to ask you for money, but if everybody here would get into the habit of dropping his money into a box at the door there would be no occasion for this. But there is one thing I want to say. Everybody here ought to put at least five cents in the plate.

"Ushers" he continued, addressing himself to the church officers. "I want to say something to you. Watch the people who don't put any collection on the plate. Watch them, look good and hard at them, shame them into it, and if they don't give they'll not come again, or if they do, they'll bring their money with them next time."

Christianity, Christianity, thou hast much to answer for when such things are done in thy holy name.

In another part of this article is a quotation from a paper which says that clergymen all but called one another liars in Montreal and Ottawa.

Listen to this from the Methodist conference:

The Rev. W. McDonagh did not propose to allow this conference or any other body of men to gag him.

Here is another example of similar heroics:

The Rev. Mr. Willoughby was again on his feet in an instant. He would like to know who dared place what he called any obstacles in the way of Manitoba. He was prepared to stand by that country let the worst come to the worst, and he wanted a vote taken immediately to show the world how they felt on the question.

I think the above is about what some hysterical old woman would say. Yet I heard another Methodist divine speak against Mr. J. C. Rykert in a style that would have gladdened the hearts of fish wives all over the world. It might be called a disgrace to Christianity, only Christianity is impervious to disgrace.

When Rev. Fulton came to this city to address audiences on the Church of Rome, he referred to the mass as a roaring farce. And his Christian audience applauded.

The committee which investigated the charges against the Rev. Geo. Nesbit, of the Anglican church, Sutton, found that he was guilty of opening letters of a parishioner, Miss Kathleen Osborne: also of calling the lady an "infernal liar," and finally of having brought the names of some of his parishioners into publicity in connection with the case. A verdict of suspension for one year from his parish was brought in against Mr. Nesbit.

Bishop Cameron, of Antigonish in speaking of some political opponents one of whom was a devoted Catholic, called them "hell-inspired hypocrites."

Personally, I admire the above references, which breathe the spirit of educated ruffianism and ecclesiastical blackguardism, and I ask you what there is in so-called Christianity more than a cloak to hide the vilest traits of human character? Besides which it demonstrates what I contend that clergymen who are presumed to teach us the way of the gentle Savior are not any more fitted to do so than anyone else if we may judge them by the intemperance of their language towards those who are opposed to them.

During the progress of the Equal Rights bout in Ontario some years ago, I confess my inability to understand the vindictive frenzy that a large number of Protestant clergymen worked themselves into, but a residence in Montreal of over a year has completely opened my eyes. First of all, the Jesuits, against whom their venom was principally directed, are never obliged to announce in the press the sermons they are to preach, nor the attractions they are to have, but their church is always crowded to the doors. The reason is therefore, perfectly clear. Jealousy? Certainly not. Again, they have one of the finest colleges in the world, which is attended by the flower of the French Canadian youth, and I never wish to see a more manly-looking crowd of boys than their pupils. The vigorous onslaughts made upon the Jesuits appear to have injured them not at all. Their school is patronized as it always has been, and that is only the logical outcome of events. The people who send their sons there know the Jesuits. They know them well, and what must be the feelings of those blatherskites who traduced them when they found that after the expulsion of all their wind, their enemies are still doing business in the old stand, untainted and serene as ever, and their church crowded as it always has been. My only surprise is now that there was not an immense influx into the Insane asylums of Ontario, when the crowd of windbags found out " how vain how ineffective their designs, while rage their leader and Jehovah Mine," turned out their portion, and what their frenzy must have been, and how little harm they had done.

During the past twenty years science and art have made most rapid progress in their development, and politics have never been discussed with greater energy than at the present day, so it is only reasonable, therefore, that religion too, should have its progress in similar proportion, and be discussed by the different religious teachers with acrimony corresponding to the discussions of partisan politics. Besides competition in religion has become very keen of late years, and it behooves the preacher to enter the field ready to give the moral value for the money, an easy way to heaven, no restraint in morals, but a good show to the world.

Early in 1878 or it may have been in 1877, a Toronto paper published as the opinion of a certain professor the following : " Religion is a great political question, and will die the death of all such questions, after having served its purpose. It has held out longer on account of its adherents, but it will end in just the same way as every other great political question has ended." I wrote to the clergyman who read it but he had forgotten what paper he saw it in but that is the pith of the quotation, if not the exact language.

The speakers on this question are Doctors of Divinity in endless profusion, scattered over the country, and as Max O'Reil says of the title of Colonel in the United States, few escape it. Colleges are abounding all over the country, spreading their nets to catch some victim, to confer the meaningless title upon him, though the victims are in most cases very willing ones. Few indeed escape it.

That Toronto has the ablest pulpit orators in the Dominion is beyond question though that is not saying much, but that there are any intellectual giants among them who, in theology, compare with the

Hon. Edward Blake in law is answered very decidedly in the negative. Sensationalism has, however, provided a most excellent substitute, though it cannot always be said to be a paying commodity. Take as an example the Auditorium. It commenced under circumstances that promised undoubted prosperity. Preaching on Sunday night with an orchestra to accompany the singing, and the modern Samson, who could break a chain by placing it on his arm the rest of the week. If as we are informed variety is the spice of life, then its success should have been assured. It is, however, beyond doubt that the methods adopted by the pastor of the auditorium were not held in that profound esteem which he thought they should have been. It is presumed that in the course of a sermon in the Queen street Methodist church on questionable church attractions the Rev. Manly Benson had reference to the auditorium and its manager. The latter gentleman on the following Sunday replied—not so much to the arguments of Mr. Benson as to the methods employed at the auditorium, but to abuse of Mr. Benson personally. He started with an attack on Mr. Benson's name, and that part of his sermon was interspersed with denunciatory language that would have done credit to a fish-wife or even the disputants in a prize fight. When the affairs of the concern became so far involved that it was impossible to continue the "services" as they may be called, it was closed, and Mr. Wilkinson left for the United States, in connection with which the Globe says:

> Rev. J. M. Wilkinson, well-known in Toronto as the pastor for some years of Agnes street church and later on as an energetic, freehanded evangelistic worker, conducting successful popular services in the tabernacle and elsewhere, received the permission of the Toronto conference to remove to Illinois where he will settle. He has been preaching in Chicago, and has met with such a measure of success there that he has concluded that his field of labour lies there. Mr. Wilkinson is a young man yet, an effective speaker, and an ardent worker. His methods of work have not always been exactly like those of everybody else, a point which will doubtless tell to his advantage in his new sphare of labour.

No one would object to sensationalism to any very great extent, if ability were behind it, or any good cause were served by it but there is none. A worthy Presbyterian preacher some time ago gave vent to some pyrotechnic sensationalism in regard to Aldermen. In the course of his remarks he struck out from the shoulder as a local paper put it, at these who made that their psofession, but toned himself down towards the end by remarking that his strictures did not, of course apply to Toronto. The average reader will doubtles wonder why, then he delivered the sermon. His strictures no doubt were meant to apply to the Chinese or some other Asiatic race, and yet it was subsequently proven that Toronto Aldermen were guilty of boodling.

Men who are so ready to treat of sensational subjects, demonstrate their insincerity when they allow their own adherents to do just as they please in keeping or breaking the rules of the churches, or committing acts of absolute dishonesty.

It is not for the spiritual profit of the Methodist church that its business enterprises should give credit to clergymen who have to be dunned in public for the amount of their indebtedness to a denominational concern. It is rough on a Book Room, when ministers who cannot, or will not, pay up get far in upon the debit side of its ledger. It is rough on Methodism in the Hamilton Conference at least, when a representative of the Book Room rises to reproach the debtors of that institution in words which the worlding will construe as an intimation that all ministers are dead beats. Refusing credit or collecting debts by a process of law might be a hard measure, but saddling a whole class with the liabilities of individuals is not an admirable method of collecting debts.

When clergymen are so lax in enforcing their church discipline, and so tardy in paying their debts, but eager to rush into print or preach sermons that will bring them into notoriety, I think the time is not far distant when a discriminating public will conclude that modern Christianity is a thing they can live quite pleasantly without, on the hypothesis that their spiritual advisers are not any better then they are themselves nor are some of them quite as good.

If opera, tragedy and comedy have their seasons of special favour, and politics its heated discussions, so too religion has its changes and varieties in similar commensuration, and the public have their desires fulfilled and their requirements gratified just as the theatre-goer has his, for the preacher's popularity like that of the theatrical manager or politician is gauged by his ability to keep in touch with the people.

Circumstances not unfrequently occur where opportunities are given for a display of pyrotechnics, and they are always seized upon with avidity by the preachers who wish to make any comments upon them, being duly advertised in the daily papers. As an example take the hanging of that consummate blackguard Birchall. A man may be hanged for murder, and if he quietly submits to it, he is not likely to receive much attention from the preachers, but as this most infamous blackleg who had not a redeeming feature in all his filthy character managed to keep himself prominently before the public, his execution was seized upon by different preachers to attract the crowd to their respective churches, and in reviewing the matter Saturday Night very clearly echoes the general feeling of the public on the subject:

And the parsons, too ! Of course it is perfectly proper that they should preach on current topics, but there is a tendency to sensationalism amongst them, and we always expect Rev. Dr. Wild to have his say when anything is being said. He and Rev. Dr. Stafford both preached from the text, "Thou shalt not kill," both aiming at the same conclusion, that capital punishment should be abolished, though they took different methods to prove the same thing. Both were apparently brought to this conclusion by the educated and interesting nature of the victim, the death of so many common murderers having been passed over unnoticed. As usual Dr. Wild's sermon was as much evolved from the encyclopaedia as from the bible. After pointing out that capital punishment was a relic of barbarism a fragment of the old doctrine of revenge, he showed that besides murder there were eleven other kinds of crime that were punishable with death under the Mosaic dispensation: first, striking a parent ; second, blasphemy ; third, Sabbath breaking ; fourth, with craft ; fifth, adultery ; sixth, unchastity ; seventh, rape ; eighth, incestuousness ; ninth, man-slaying ; tenth, idolatry ; eleventh, false swearing, adding, "now it is a remarkable thing that those who plead for capital punishment never bring forward these and argue that they should be enforced now ; they bring forward that if a man kills another capital punishment should take place because it is written in the bock of Moses."

Dr. Wild is evidently of the opinion that the Mosaic law is not law to-day. I do not remember what his views on the observance of the sabbath are, but I am glad he has pointed out to the modern Sabbatarian that if we are to follow out the Mosaic law in this respect we must put to death those who disobey the Mosaic law something which, by the way, it is impossible for us to observe in this age and under conditions such as we are surrounded by in this climate and country. Possibly he holds that the same modification of the law should be made in respect to Sabbath observance as to murder, that imprisonment for life would be sufficiently severe for those who light a fire on Sunday or journey beyond the specified number of miles. As a matter of fact capital punishment is not retained out of respect for Moses any more than is Sunday insisted upon as a day of rest, because the Great Law Giver made it a portion of his regulations. As a gentleman whom I regard as one of the brainiest members of the Methodist body either lay or clerical in this province, remarked to me, "Sunday should be kept, not because Moses kept it, but because it is an economic necessity," I think we hang people for the same reason, not because Moses did it but because we want to get rid of that sort of people. It is cheaper and safer, and altogether more reasonable to put them to death than to imprison them for life. Of course as Dr. Wild and Dr. Stafford point out, there is a possibility of converting them, but there are so many decent people now who don't need converting in that way, who are left without even prison fare and never have the ministration of a preacher volunteered to them, that I think we ought to take care of them first. and after we get so far advanced that we have no decent people dying for want of simple prison provender then we may take up the problem of making over the murderously bad ones. Until that time comes, if Drs. Wild and Stafford would devote a portion of their energies to caring for honest people who are foolish enough to permit their only crime to be poverty, and have failed to become enterprising enough to be murderers the progress of civilization will not be stayed by the occasional necktie social which sends up to the Supreme Court of the Universe some human malformation in the shape of a murderer.

The great trouble with these preachers and many scientists is they want to deal with freaks all the time ignoring the great mass of uninteresting, but human atoms who live and die without so much as the gentle touch of a missionary's gloved hand. Why should we fret over the freaks? Why should the church especially make its doctrines apply to the exhibits of a dime museum of nature instead of the great surging, sorrowing mass who go into the world and go out of it without any recognition but kicks and hunger? Why should we care for the lives of a few cowardly assassins whom the world is never safe from until the hangman has had them, while gentle women weep and babies cry because they have not been fed, and men gnash their teeth because, without having sinned against the law, or been guilty of any greater crime than being born, they are undergoing a life sentence of humiliation and hunger in the dark cell of social oblivion? It seems to prove that human sin and suffering must be thrust in the eyes and the stench of human wrong-doing held under the nostrils of these leaders of religious thought before they can be made to recognize the existence of anyone but the well-dressed and well-fed parishioners who fill their pews. Death! Why should death frighten these persons? Every day in this land of ours the sentence of death is being imposed upon some innocent child, overworked mother, and unfortunate father. Death! Unmerited death! Death after an imprisonment for life, death after vain struggles to live, death after fruitless appeals to God and his people! Have not all seen it, perhaps helped to inflict it? Our clerical friends could not be silent a moment or rest an instant from their labour and if they felt half as badly about the death of a fellow-being as they would have us believe. Death! Why, this earth is carnival of death. Civilization! Why. it is but another name for the refinement of cruelty in the infliction of death. Death! Was it not the sentence imposed upon mankind for the sin of our first father and mother, imposed upon us before we were born, a sentence which will be inflicted on mankind after we are dead? I can't see why it should so greatly horrify Brother Wild, or unduly excite the eloquence of Brother Stafford.

We remember how, when the Equal Rights Crusade was at its zenith sensationalism was the only accepted form of service that could attract the multitude, and receive any kind of recognition from the press. How many preachers are there in the whole Dominion who have awakened to find themselves famous, surprised beyond expression at the ability they possessed, but never suspected, when this ability was appraised by that portion of the press which could always find space for the snarls of reverend nobodies, suffering from periodical attacks of the spleen or vapours, measuring the universe by that narrow scrap of tape which was the span or their own littleness, and who would never have been heard of did these journals not publish their articles. The airy castles they built of future glory are nothing but the ashes they are sitting in to-day. The rotten foundations of human vanity which the prophet assures us are only shortlived at best, and upon which their hopes were built have crumbled to the dust—the would-be-sensationalist is far and away beyond oblivion. This seems especially sad, since we had the outside assistance of professional haters of Rome, escaped nuns etc., to assist us in the good work. We remember with profound thankfulness of the privileges we enjoyed in listening to these grand and ennobling declamations and recitations from lives of sensual filth written by saintly men and women for the moral and spiritual welfare of mankind, and with no thought of profit to themselves. We remember their righteous indignation with the press of the city in not publishing these stories, and assisting in the propogation of the good work, and the justice of the aspersions they cast upon the press for such neglect of duty we acknowledge to have been well-merited.

It is stated that when Corinne and her merry makers visit the Toronto Opera house, it is almost impossible to obtain seats, and should anyone by mischance go late he is obliged to take whatever seat he can get, and in fact be very thankful if he can get a seat at all. The reason of this is that the suggestiveness of the play and actors are the secret of its popularity. It, therefore, behooved the Ministry in its forethought and wisdom to provide an entertainment equally attractive, and they did so. It will not be doubted, I think, that if the divine Son of God were to make his second coming, he would be surprised and perhaps overwhelmed with the marvellous progress made in Christianity during the past few years. It is equally certain that he would find that those preachers who are supposed to emulate him, would prove that in depth of learning, and theology and the construction of his texts they were'far and away ahead of Him, though the word came through his inspiration, remembering at the same time that any question of miserable sinners on the question of the Great Perhaps is a matter too commonplace to receive the consideration of those eminent Doctors of Divinity, who, like the poor, are always with us, and whose almost supernal ability it would be absurd to question. Perhaps, too, he would feel somewhat abashed and believe that he was not in the running, when brought face to face with the sesquipedalian language and elegance of diction employed by the present day preacher in accordance with the popular demand. Comparing the new testament with the modern day requirements I do not think anyone will for one moment contend, that as a literary effort it is anything to the expressive slang we use in the present day. Like the air we breathe slang is absolutely necessary to our very existence. The man who has no fear of doing so, goes to the opera house to hear and see what he expects to see, but the alleged Christian who is afraid of being boycotted, is compelled to look to the pulpit for such a treat. In order to meet the spiritual needs of his congregation a certain Reverend gentleman made visits to certain houses of ill-fame in an American city, and entertained his hearers with a delectable account of his experience. Besides this he has given us a further exhibition of his prowess in this choice and touching language: "If you or I have any wish to be a little Redeemer." " I can understand some of the angels not in the redemption business loafing along the celestial courts." " Christ has taken out the only patent method of saving the world."

Verily the church of God must have fallen to singular depths.

Toronto has not yet been favoured with a visit from this distinguished gentleman, but it is merely a question of time when she will be, though thus far we have been satisfied with Sam Jones, who has been able to satisfy our requirements, and meet our refined tastes with the most delectable paraphrasing. You will, doubtless remember that we had him and Sam Small here in company, and you will remember that we, like humanity in general, satisfied our cultured curiosity by giving him a reception that would have gratified the ablest statesman who ever lived, after the completion of some important diplomatic triumph. It is not, I think, contended by those who brought him here that they did so on account of his ability as a teacher of the word of God. His vulgarity, which passed for wit; his slangy style of oratory and the delightfully familiar manner in which he spoke to and of the Son of God and God himself, and which gave him a continental notoriety were his drawing cards, and as he fed the popular demand for sensationalism and vulgar slang it cannot be said that he did not earn his money. Those who could have gone to a low theatre and heard no worse than this could feel consistently that their senses were being gratified and no rule of the church was being broken. He, too, must have felt gratified at our open-armed reception and the sycophantic constancy with which we received and applauded his defiling remarks. In speaking of him a newspaper says:

He had been hired to deliver a series of sermons at the Urbana Camp meeting. The secular press freely denounces the management as being more solicitous for the almighty dollar than the salvation of souls. When it was proposed to raise the price of admission to the grounds, there was a vigorous protest, which was met by the "Rev," Sam in the following stirring pulpit expostulation:

"You stingy old devil, you talk of going to heaven Why, you old dog, you are too stingy to get into heaven. You kicked because you thought you had to pay an extra five cents to get into the grounds. I just like to catch an old dog like you and hold him out by the collar and let him kick himself to death."

At another time, when evidences of an unchristian rebellion were manifest, he became equally eloquent:

"A dude," he said, "talks about killing me; why I would just spit on him and drown him."

Refreshing is it not?

I was privileged some few years ago to hear him "preach" at Grimsby Park. He seems to nurse a grievance against Colonel Ingersoll, whom he accused of using most disgraceful profanity in a Railway sleeper where both had passed the night. In a burst of grandeur of soul he exclaimed "I wouldn't let my dog speak to him, I wouldn't speak to him myself." It will be inferred therefore, that Mr. Jones has a dog which speaks, but his announcement of the fact that he would not speak to Colonel Ingersoll himself, suggests the idea that the Prince of Wales for instance, would scarce get over the heartburning that might be caused if some sweep were to announce that he would not speak to him. I understand, though, that notwithstanding Mr. Jones terrible determination not to speak to him, Mr. Ingersoll still breathes. In the course of his observations, Mr. Jones was demonstrating God's love, and he took himself as a living example, "when I go home, and my dog runs to meet me. I pat him and I say 'what makes you love me so?' and he says 'because you so good to me,' and when I go to my horse and feed him and ask him 'what makes you love me so?' he says, 'because you're so good to me.'"

I think that is sublime. A horse that speaks and a dog that speaks. Still in these days of democracy it may safely be inferred that Providence in the selection of his preachers is as lenient as humanity in the selection of gentlemen, though it may be thought that heaven is not very particular who is now preaching for it. I think if pharisees abounded in these days, one might very consistantly say that when such characters are the chosen of the Lord, he stands a good chance of entering the pearly gates on the plea that heaven is not such a desirable place after all, when the characters of its advocates are taken into consideration.

Like all businesses, religion has its fakirs, and a thriving trade is done by some of them. One sect pretends to cure all diseases by faith, but their faith is not shaken by the death of their patients. " If they had had more faith they would have recovered." A celebrated physician cured all illnesses by bleedings and hot water. When a patient died it was because he had not been bled copiously enough or too copious, and the water administered too hot or not hot enough! The theory remained excellent. In the faith cure faké the proselytes are appealed to for funds to found what is called the " Lord's Treasury." When one of the Christian Scientists came to our city, the ungrateful press took no notice of his coming, whereupon some one, I don't know who undertook to lecture them in the Advance, in the following language, though I might say, inferentially, that a few lessons in writing and spelling would do him no harm, if he proposes inflicting any more of it on the long-suffering compositor :

His advent to Toronto is worthy of note, for after a lengthy sojourn in Australia, he has created a stir in the United States, and the silence of the Toronto press, silence, which from a journalistic standpoint is extremely silly—makes it imperative that such papers as the Advance should do this work. I attended the meetings as a skeptic, having no sympathy with what I considered a fantastic interpretation of scripture, supported by fancied or fanciful cures of some weak-minded men and hysterical women. I went to scoff. I remained to the prayer meeting, because I was anxious to hear the whole matter.

His accent is Scotch, he is an Edinboro man, his style of speaking ts very direct—too blunt for some super-sensitive ears. He calls tobacco smokers "nasty stink-pots" he speaks of Job's affliction as " the vile stinking boils that came from the devil's dirty fingers."

Our Saviour would undoubtedly have been more than pleased at this refreshing style of speaking supposed to be delivered in his name. This is a sample of their cures :

At Arger's Hotel Coroner Orr conducted an inquest into the cause of death of a six-year-old lad named Percy Robert Beck, who died while under treatment by a Christian Scientist. Crown Attorney Dewart examined the witnesses. Mrs. Beck, mother of the lad, said he took sick about three weeks before. Mrs. Beer, who had attended him three times before, was sent for. Her treatment was mental, no medicines being used. The Scientists claimed God sent sickness as a punishment for sin, and people merely believed they were sick ; the truth did everything. Mrs. Beer said to deceased : " Percy Beck, you have no illness, you are a child of God, and cannot be sick." Percy became worse and Mrs. Beer treated him by sitting silently beside him. She charged one dollar for each treatment. Thomas Beck, the lad's father, corroborated his wife's statement, and said he had more faith in the Christian Scientists than he had in doctors. Two brothers of deceased said they also were treated in the same way.

When some years ago, the secular society had the effrontery to speak of bringing Colonel Igersoll here, holy Toronto held up its hands in anguish at the idea. A gentleman whose eloquence, high moral character and brilliant intellect have won for him a reputation wherever the English language is spoken, was not fit to speak in this saintly city; yet the Colonel came and lectured, and the house was packed to the doors, yet in his entire lecture there was not the first sign of coarseness or vulgarity; it was a most elegant elucidation of what the lecturer believed to be true. Max O'Rell who enjoyed his hospitality when in New York in addition to many other pleasant things has the following:

Mr. Ingersoll is not only America's greatest living orator, he is a great writer and thinker; the trinity that he worships is the trinity of science, observation and experience. I never heard Mr. Ingersoll say that he did not believe in a God. He will not acknowledge the existence of a Jehovah, the God of the Jews, a God who commanded the people of his choice to exterminate their enemies sparing neither old men, women nor children. Mr. Ingersoll is not the only seeker after truth who has been puzzled to reconcile the idea of the gentle merciful saviour who taught the doctrine of love and forgiveness in Palestine, and bade his disciples put up their swords in the presence of their persecutors, and the idea of this cruel, revengeful, and implacable deity. "I rob Smith" exclaims Mr. Ingersoll in the ironical language he is such a master of, "God forgives me. How does that help Smith?" That which makes this man so formidable is not so much his eloquence, his quick repartee, his sarcasm, his pathos, his humor, it is above all things the life he leads, the example he sets of all the domestic virtues. One must have the privilege of knowing him intimately, of penetrating into that sanctuary of conjugal happiness, his home, before one can form an idea of the respect that he must inspire even in those who abhor his doctrines. His house is the home of the purest joys; it holds four hearts that beat as one. Authors, artists, journalists, members of the thinking world may be met at the Colonel's charming Sunday evenings. Between midnight and one in the morning the last visitor reluctactly departs. On the way home you think of all the witty things that have been said the arrows of satire that have been shot at hypocrisy and humbug, the ennobling humanitarian opinions that have been advanced; and though you may not be converted, or converted or perverted to Ingersollism, you are sure to leave that house feeling fuller of good will toward all men, and saying yourself: "What a delightful evening I have passed."

Now, the lot of Colonel Ingersoll in this world is very enviable, for his profession brings him in a magnificent income. As to refusing his place in the next, what an absurdity.

When Robert Ingersoll presents himself at the pearly gates of Paradise, St. Peter sees that good, open face, radiant with happiness, the doors will be thrown wide to let him pass, and the saint will say:

"Come Robert, come in, thy happy face pleases me. We have just let in a cargo of long-faced folk—Presbyterians I'll be bound and it does one good to look at thee. Thou hast done they utmost to stifle the hydra headed monster superstition, and to destroy the infamies that are in circulation on the subject of the Lord. Come in, friend, thou hast loved, thou has been beloved, thou hast preached concord, mercy, peace love, and happiness; come, take thy place among the benefactors of the human race."

This is the opinion expressed by one of the ablest writers of the day. A gentleman, who, to him, was an entire stranger yet when that same gentleman was invited to visit us as a brilliant orator the Christian people declared unanimously that he should not come and why? Fear, doubtless that he would show their Pharisacial actions up and they would lose the little prestige they now possess. And yet a Christian will complacently inform you that his religion is unassailable.

OF TORONTO THE GOOD. 175

I give you also the following, and do not think I am at all astray in stating that the notice was given by one of the society and furnished to all the city newspapers.

The West Presbyterian church Band of Hope held their regular meeting on Thursday evening and there was an attendance above the average. The behaviour was all that could be desired. One parent brought two of her children, and another sent two, and so the quiet work goes on. The superintendents were in their places and the children were addressed by Mr. George Wilson.

You will notice that we are informed that the *quiet* work goes on, yet I feel constrained to say that if it is quiet, it is not[from any feeling of modesty on the part of the officers or promoters, but is purely and simply the gross negligence of the press in not giving it publicity.

It would indeed be an unanswerable enigma to ask what would the preachers do without the press. Consult any of the Toronto papers, and particularly the Mail, and you will see that quite half the correspondence is from preachers of the different denominations, answering some contemporary, denouncing some adversary, or giving vent to their views on some of the political questions of the day, or criticising the work or sermon of a brother minister.

Let the thoughtful reader reflect for one moment, and ask himself if it were not for the notoriety given them by the press, how many preachers would there be who would be accused of heresy and other similar offences that injures no one, but simply serves the purpose of bringing themselves before the public, and in a lesser degree their accusers? I do not think there would be one where now there is a hundred. As an example take the case of the Rev. Dr. Briggs, his trials before the different synods and assemblies in the different parts of the United States, and what do they all amount to? Simply to let a lot of men air their opinions, and have them published in the press throughout the country, and the very remote contingency of a new religion, belief, faith or whatever you chose to call it, being inflicted on long-suffering humanity. Do you think that the charge of heresy brought against this preacher and that preacher is anything more than mere excuses for newspaper notoriety? If you do think otherwise your abiliy to read human character must be very limited indeed.

If clergymen are actuated by motives Christlike, why was it necessary for the Rev. Dr. Carman of Belleville to rush into print when it so happened that he was not asked to say grace at a banquet given in Belleville in honor of Sir Mackenzie Bowell? Would it not have been far more dignified, without saying Christlike to have allowed the matter to pass in silence? It is quite within the range of recollection of many people that during the time the Toronto Mail was the champion of Protestant rights, the Rev. Dr. Carman was in the habit of writing long letters to that journal taken from some scriptural text. How do those letters compare with the letter he wrote to the Belleville Ontario with regard to his position at the Bowell banquet? In striking contrast to his position appears that of the Catholic priest who was invited to perform the ceremony of saying grace. Mr. Thomas Ritchie explains the whole matter in a letter to the Intelligencer. He accepts the entire responsibility for having requested Mgr. Farrel to say grace, and adds that the latter at the time asked to be excused on the ground that such action might create bad feeling. Mgr. Farrel desired that no bad feeling should be created. What construction could be put upon Dr. Carman's attitude except that he desired to create bad feeling, and whose conduct was the more gentlemanly, without going so far as to say Christlike? The Telegram quite satirically observes of another preacher:

<blockquote>Rev. John Burwash who is upholding Coercion by his presence on platforms and his utterances in print, expresses opinions which would be entirely unimportant if their author did not wear a name adorned by the rare powers of his brother, Rev. N. Burwash, Chancellor of Victoria University.</blockquote>

It giving these delineations of clerical characteristics and my adverse comments on their actions, I consider it my right to affirm thát if clergymen are actuated by no higher motives than newspaper notoriety, they do far more to advance the theories and the march of infidelity than a dozen men like Col. Ingersoll would do. It is a clergyman's place to command respect and by example prove that he really believes in a loving Savior. If they indicate by their actions that their minds have no higher plane than those they are presumed to teach, I contend that their usefulness is gone. There is no class of men who are more ready to rush into print than they, and I hold that when they do so they do so with a loss of the respect their cloth should entitle them to. The frequency of church rows demonstrates my contention that clergymen do not receive, nor merit the respect that clergymen in former times received, and that the fault is entirely their own I have tried to prove by my criticisms.

Years ago when I was attending school, I recollect a young lad of about ten coming into school one morning flushed with importance and swaggering like a triumphant general.

"Did you see my name in the paper last night?" he asked, proudly and as no one answered, we held our breath while he read : "'A young lad by name of John Jones was almost run over last night by Bingham's express wagon, etc.'"

Nothing could exceed the pride with which he read the blood curdling announcement, and whenever I see eccentricities on the part of clergymen and others, which are reported in the newspapers I think of little Johnny Jones and his name in the paper.

Some time ago when I was employed on a city paper the pastor of what was then called, and the present pastor still calls St. Paul's Methodist Church, in preparing his advertisement of the Sunday services, invariably called the church Avenue Road Methodist Church. To the evil minded it might occur that he styled his church the Avenue Road, simply to get it placed at the head of the list of churches, possibly thereby implying its importance, or it might be that a church on that aristocratic thoroughfare would be considered a more fashionable temple in which to worship than common every day St. Paul's. I express no opinion on the matter myself; but call your attention to an observation reported in the Mail and Empire as having been made by this gentleman : "Imagine Jesus Christ standing on the street corners with a cigar or a cigarette in his mouth etc." In view of these matters does anyone presume that so distinguished a clergyman was simply seeking notoriety? By no means, nor could any reasonable being presume that his remarks concerning Christ were in any respect blasphemous, because they were not. Still, what were they?

At a meeting of the preachers some little time ago, a rev. gentleman passed some observations in regard to the hymn " God Save the Queen," implying that it would not be required much longer. He was not immortalized, however, for his breach of good taste, and when he sought fame as a school trustee, unsuccessfully, the ignorant, not to say brutal instincts of the electors, leading them to support men who completely snowed him under. I think this case is especially sad.

A couple of years ago the Industrial Exhibition Association, according to its usual custom I believe, sent passes to a Baptist clergyman amongst others, which the rev. gentleman returned to the President of the Association. No one need complain of that, but why was it necessary for him to rush into print and electrify the world with the announcement that he had returned the passes in order that he might have the right to criticise the show? Some people not endowed with Christian charity might insist that the rev. gentleman informed the public of his sacrifice merely for the sake of the notoriety it would give him. If that view prevails, it certainly has not had any tangible result as far as I can see, for he is still with us, but it is not, of course, by any means certain that he was actuated by any such motive.

Lately I have noticed that the heretics are not so plentiful as they were a few years ago, but I notice that quite a few clergymen are being advertised by the patent medicine dealers, and this may have the effect of reducing the number who might otherwise have sought immortality through heresy.

It must be that ministers rub up so little against the world that contradiction maddens them, and when in Presbytery or Synod they are contradicted by each other the polished violence of their language is startling. There was some excuse for the fathers and brethren who practically called each other liars over an issue important as that tried in the Synod of Ottawa and Montreal. But the language even there was unnecessarily warm, and there were too many accusations of double-dealing to make the debate altogether edifying. And our own Synod of Toronto and Kingston with less provocation, displayed its power to embitter controversy. There was nothing worth wrangling about there, nothing that should have raised any voice above a whisper, but Rev. Dr. Parsons managed to speak of some one "having the impudence" to do thus and so and other reverend gentlemen used language that would have been followed by a reprimand in the secular court, or a call to order from the Speaker of a profane Parliament.

The heresy scheme has reached that point in his history as to become a subject for ridicnle, and will be simply laughed out of court, as witness the following from the Telegram :

THE J. HUSS WAS ABSENT.

A well-meant and earnest effort to start a heresy trial in Montreal collapsed, at least temporarily, in its first stages, owing to the absence of the heretic.

Everything else was in a state of advanced readiness. The intellectual fagots had been cut, and were being dried. The enquirer or inquisitors were prepared to mentally rack the author of "The Perfect Father or the Perfect Word."

But the "intellectual treat" had to be postponed. There was no use for stake or fagot, because there was no John Huss on the scene. The learned professor who was to be the John Huss of the occasion was away fishing in Muskoka, and was not, therefore, to be tried or tortured by his brethren.

It was not thus in other days, when all-powerful orthodoxy decided to investigate a heretic. The heretic was there to be investigated if he had to be carried. The fiery trial of John Huss was not adjourned owing to the absence of the heretic and the brethren in Montreal will do well next time to make sure that they have their heretic before they attempt to try him.

We listen to the melody of "Onward Christian Soldiers," and enjoy the harmonious music as well as the sentiment it expresses, and subscribe with at a murmur to the truthfulness of those sublime lines which state:

We are all united, all one body we,
One in faith and doctrine one in charity.

I have only to ask your indulgence for a moment to demonstrate the truthfulness of this assertion. The Rev. Dr. Workman says, in reply an editorial on his view of Messiahism by the editor of the Christian Guardian:

As the editor of the Christian Guardian has been most bitter and persistant in his attack upon my teaching, I shall first reply to his unmerited and ill-natured strictures. * * In my prompt reply to his *misleading editorial* which, besides the characteristics already indicated, contained two or three *serious quotations* that the editor never acknowledged. * * One of my correspondents writes me "Reading Dr. B.'s criticism I felt compelled to accept his logic, until, carefully perusing your reply, I saw that his premises were wrong, that he misunderstands and mis-states your view" Notwithstanding his *repeated misrepresentation* of my teaching he was publicly reported in a recent interview as saying, "I put no special meaning on his words. I do not even interpret them. I simply assume that in writing plain English sentences he meant what he said." As the editor has made this statement in substantially the same terms two or three times since his first attack was published, I am prepared to prove by overwelming evidence that it is *absolutely false* to the fact of the case. * * That is to say, in every criticism he makes: either his statements or his assumption, or his suggestion or his implication respecting me or my work *are untrue*. In other words he sets up a man of straw and then as systematically knocks him down again.

If anyone doubts after reading this that "we are not united, all one body we, one in faith and charity, etc.," he is simply an idiot.

The quarrels of the churches and the preachers are without number, like the sands of the sea, and recently the Telegram published the following editorial on the subject of church rows:

A LESSON FOR THE TROUBLERS OF ZION.

A good answer was that returned by the Salvation Army officer when asked his reason for quitting an organization which he had faithfully served.

It was clear that he had been aggrieved, and the power to say much if he liked rendered all the more honourable in him to declare that "for the good of the work it was best to say nothing." It almost always is best to say nothing. Parties to churches troubles are too seldom true to the faith as that ex-Salvationist, who is content to let the God whom he has tried to serve judge between him and his adversaries. Virtues which adorn all churches in times of peace are not exactly resplendent in the walk and conversation of church members in times of troubles. Too often all hands are so anxious to stand well in the sight of the world that they wound the cause in the effort to give brethren on the other side a black eye. There will be a good deal of unregenerate human nature when the millenium is nearer than it is now, and the worst qualities of our fallen humanity are too widely prevalent in every church row.

And yet how inscrutable and mysterious seem the decrees of a divine Providence.

Mrs. Margaret L. Shepherd, whose anti-Romanist lecturing tour has been such a complete failure in liberal Ontario, has decided, according to the Toronto News, to abandon the lecture platform and take to the dramatic stage. The experience of several men who have lectured throughout Ontario should have been enough to have deterred her from a course that was sure to have but one result—to get her into bad odor with all classes of the community.

The gentleman who was most prominent in bringing Dr. Fulton to the city, and who led him around to one of the city papers to have his lecture printed, has fallen by the wayside. He bit the dust after a few days illness.

That grand classic and almost sublime work. "Why priests should wed" I never hear of lately.

A recent scandal, in a church of the west end which was freely ventilated in the courts and in which Mr. Massey was interested to the tune of fifteen-hundred dollars, in still fresh in the minds of the public.

Mr. Longley, whose name figured in a possible scandal has left the nation, and the auditorium, where all the escaped nuns etc., used to hold forth is now used for any purpose that will yield a rent. It is strange and incomprehensible.

Rev. Dr. Wild, whose anti-Roman proclivities are so well known, is not now the pastor of the Bond street congregational church, where men have frequently held forth against that church and one pastor Dr. Sims sent in his resignation, on account of the financial condition of the church.

Where are all the illustrious prelates, made famous by the Equal Rights Agitation a few years ago? Sitting in the ashes of the ruins they erected and thought would be lasting. How about those who refused to be mixed up with the cry? Rev. Dr. Potts, who was reproached for his inactivity during that campaign has only just refused one of the greatest honors ever conferred upon a Canadian,—the pulpit of one of the wealthiest and most influential congregations in the United States.

It seems to me simply a question as to how long it will be before the Roman Catholic Church again reigns supreme. Let the unprejudiced unbeliever look at the two bodies of people, Catholic and Protestant, and I do not see how, in the light of reason, he could do otherwise than join the Catholic Church, should he come to the conclusion that Christianity was necessary to his everlasting salvation. No church has received the revilings it has received from every Protestant windbag who considers himself divinely inspired, and yet it seems to thrive in spite of this treatment. Protestant churches are daily showing the world their disagreements, fights, rows, etc., in which each faction is determined to give the other side the worst of it. No such disgraceful scenes ever take place amongst Catholics. A priest or a minister is supposed, I believe, to represent Christ, but in Protestant congregations they decide for themselves which one of Christ's apostles shall preach to them, and the Lord help him if his teachings run counter to their wishes. In the Catholic church a priest goes where he is told as the disciples did in the time of Christ, and the people receive him as their pastor who ever he is, and without protest and without a fight. I do not think there is a case on record where a Catholic congregation ever locked the door of their edifice, and refused the priest sent to them admittance. Yet the same cannot be said of Protestant congregations. Nor is there anything sacred in a Protestant place of worship—it is a place to go for enjoyment and display millinery, where you can go in late if you wish to and if you did as Catholics do, bend your knee before entering the house of God, you would in all probability be laughed at. A Protestant minister is a busines man, who is paid for his services according to his ability and the wealth of his congregation. A priest gets a living and very little more, and sometimes both are very precarious. The profession of one is a business. The other is an incessant sacrifice.

I listened to some young men at a Methodist ordination service, one time, relate the histories of the inspiration by which they knew they were called of God. I do not hesitate to say that every one of them deliberately lied, when he gave such experience. If the conduct of these young men was despicable, how much more despicable it is on the part of that church to require candidates for its ministry to tell such falsehoods? Would it not be far better to do away with such a farce, or let the men come forward like men and say, "I wish to obtain an easy livelihood at a good salary. I think I will enjoy the work, and will do my best to give satisfaction to those who employ me, and endeavor to meet their wishes in whatever way they desire to conduct their spiritual life." It would be more consistent to say the least of it. Why should any man be compelled to perjure himself simply to comply with the absurd theory that he preaches for Christ and that no financial considerations influence him?

Compare the two classes of men, and which is the more Christ like? The Protestant who permits every violation of church discipline, who can arrange his "opinions" to accord with those of his congregation, who is called upon to make no sacrifice whatever, who knows what salary be is to receive wherever he goes, and whose occupation is simply a business, which is well paid, or the priest, who is governed by the scriptures which are the same to all, rich and poor alike, and cannot be changed to suit the wishes or inspirations of his flock, who is obliged to go where he is bidden, and labor for almost nothing, whose life is one long sacrifice.

How many clergymen are there, or clergy and laity together for that matter, who act or attempt to act up to what Christ taught. His disciples in the fifth chapter of Matthew? "Blessed are the meek. Blessed are ye when men shall revile you and persecute you." So said Christ to his disciples, but in the course of my long career, I have never met a man or woman, clergy or laity, who did not do his or her best to administer a thorough knock out to anyone who had crossed them. Christian charity they did not seem to know. I venture the assertion that there are not ten so-called Christians in a thousand who do not expect to make a dying thief repentance, if their wordly acts count for anything. I once stated this to a clergyman, and the only answer he could make me was some inanity like "Judge not, that ye be not judged." The merits of the case he would not and could not argue, knowing quite well that I could have attacked the probity of half his congregation, whose shortcomings he knew would not be safe for him to attack, or he would very soon be taught to mind his own business, and attend to his inane platitudes for which he was paid to preach, reminding me of a joke I once heard some years ago. A preacher had come to a village to relieve the regular incumbent. Before entering the pulpit he was button-holed by one of the elders who cautioned him against saying anything against the hotel keepers. "They contribute to the church sometimes, you know," he said "so don't say anything against them, but give it red hot to the Mormons."

The self-importance and absolute lack of genuine Christian characteristics among ministers and their demonstrations that they are not shining examples of piety to their flocks, have had the effect of producing upon the minds of the people that while it is good form and a passport to respectability to belong to a church, it is by no means necessary that they should follow any of the advice their pastors give them, or do as he says they should do. In fact the very reverse is the case. If I were a writer of fiction I would not wish any other advertisement than that the clergy should denounce it. Its success would thereby be assured. Surely no sane man will say that the literary merit of Robert Elsmere made it famous. I read it, and say that it is just about as prosaic and dull a piece of trash as I ever read, and I have read even one of Mrs. Southworth's and one of Maxwell Gray's novels. But Mr. Gladstone happened to take exception to something in it and wrote against it. The success of the book was thereby assured. Zola's works owe their immense circulations, not by any means to their elegance of diction or anything else that I could ever see, but only to the fact that clergymen have proscribed them. Ouida's works are the same, though it is to be said that they do posssss rare merits in delineations of character. I read Zola's works simply because they had been suppressed by some over sensitive people. I simply wasted my money. I sold the books that I had paid fifty cents for at five cents a piece. It is the same with everything. A party of Christian women passed a resolution that newspapers should not publish lengthy reports of murder and other sensational trials. A murder trial of the present day is like a court reception. Crowds of ladies go there and hundreds are refused admittance because they cannot get seating accommodation. The circumstances show how much influence clergymen and other Christian bodies really have. It is nothing at all.

If clergymen are to have any respect paid to them or their opinions, it must be by noble deeds, as Carlyle says "not by noisy theoretic laudations of a church, but by silent practical demonstrations of the church."

Christianity, or what passes for it, was beautifully exemplified a short time ago by the wife of one of the most prominent clergymen of the city of Toronto, as showing how extremely little there is of practical Christianity at all, but showing what takes the place of such, and is accepted as such. I was in the train from Toronto to Hamilton when this lady got on. She took two seats, and after seating her luggage over one of them, she knelt on the other so that she blocked the way of any impertinent person taking possession, while carrying on a conversation with her husband, who stood in the aisle. You have doubtless seen a dog gnawing at one bone, while keeping his eye on another a few feet away, and noticed how jealously he guarded it? That is the most apt illustration I can give you. When the train started this clergyman's wife was the only one in that coach who occupied two seats, yet when a poor woman with a basket and a child came on board and looked helplesly down the aisle, did she offer her one of her seats? Not by any means. She turned her head away in order that she might not see her, and the woman was accommodated by a gentleman giving her his seat. Now, there was no commandment violated by that Christian lady, I am quite prepared to admit, and anyone who would say she was not going to heaven would be a fool. If "by faith ye are saved" there can be no doubt of the lady's faith in the certainty that she is going to heaven, consequently she is absolutely certain of future reward. Pride, which goeth before destruction and selfishness, which appeard to be this lady's chief attribute, are prominent characteristics of modern Christianity, and I think no one will question the fact that Christ, if He worked miracles when on earth, will have His powers taxed to the uttermost to reconcile the different "grades" of earthly society when they come before him, unless the same orders or degrees of society prevail in heaven as on earth. That lady demonstrated modern Christianity as it is practised more clearly than a volume of theory could do.

Compare if you will the meek and lowly Jesus of Nazareth with the self-sufficient, impudent, proud, overbearing and vindictive Pharisees who occupy pulpits in the majority of Christian churches to-day, and wonder if he came to the earth again, what would he think of them, or would he even be recognized by them?

Christ sat with publicans and sinners. But if there came to the house of God a man with marks of dissipation upon him, people almost threw up their hands in horror, as much as to say: "Isn't it shocking?" How these dainty, fastidious Christians in all our churches are going to get into heaven I don't know unless they have a especial train of cars, cushioned and upholstered, each one a car to himself! They cannot go with the great herd of publicans and sinners. Oh! ye who curly your lip of scorn at the fallen, I tell you plainly, if you had been surrounded by the same influences, instead of sitting to-day amid the cultured and the refined and the Christian, you would have been a crouching wretch in stable or ditch, covered with filth and abomination. It is not because you are naturally any better, but because the mercy of God has protected you. Who are you that, brought up in Christian circles and watched by Christian parentage, you should be so hard on the fallen?

A number of people have lately gone extensively into the business of converting the Jews and Rabbi de Sola, of Montreal, gives them such a scathing and well-merited denunciation that I give it.

At the Passover service in the Spanish and Portuguese Synagogue Montreal he preached a powerful sermon upon Israel's past, present, and future, basing his remarks upon the text, "The right of the Eternal is exalted, the right hand of the Eternal doeth valiantly. I shall not die, but live and proclaim the works of the Eternal." Quoting the words "Ye are my witnesses, said the Eternal, and my servant whom I have chosen," he said: "For thirty-two centuries we have been performing this mission, proclaiming to mankind the sovereignty and over-ruling Providence of the Almighty, and testifying to the supreme excellence of the law committed to our care amid the thunders of Sinai. That law inculcates the morality upon which the fabric of civilized society rests; and as the preservation of our identity as a distinct people is the most conclusive proof of its divine origin and authority, we may well stand amazed at the phenomenal infatuation of men who would remove God's witnesses, who would destroy the living testimony to the divine inspiration of the Bible, by converting the children of Israel from their ancestral faith.

"While I shall be very sorry to charge the supporters of this missionary movement with any hostile sentiment akin to that which animates the anti-Semites, I do unhesitatingly characterize as most insolent the manner in which they talk and write about our people. They speak of their 'work among the Jews' as if the Jews were heathens or barbarian. The Jew has been God's servant in giving to mankind the knowledge of the way of life; he is God's living testimony to the heavenly origin of that law to which all civilized beings bow; and yet men who acknowledge the law of Sinai, and who know that Providence alone has enabled the Jew to outlive all attempts to destroy him, would now induce him to abandon his character and his mission as God's witness. Men who have received religion from the Jew would preach religion to the Jew. But Israel has not been preserved through centuries of trial to meet extinction in this missionary movement. Divinely commissioned, and divinely sustained, Israel will continue to proclaim the sovereignty and over-ruling providence of the Almighty. Let the supporters of the missionary movement pause, and consider these facts —facts that are suggestively emphasized by the admittedly meagre results that have attended what they are pleased to term their missionary labors but which we regard as an impertinent interference with our right as men and as British subjects, to adhere to our religion without molestation. Money is spent lavishly in these conversionist efforts. How much of it is squandered upon people who find conversion pecuniarily profitable? How much better to apply this money to the relief of the misery and suffering of the thousands who know not where to turn for a crust of bread, or for a resting place on which to lay their weary limbs. Convert the Jew? There are others in infinitely greater need of conversion. Convert to manhood the creature who staggers along in a state of drunken bestiality. Convert to civilization those who desolate homes with their murderous deeds. Convert to decency and chastity those who gain a livelihood by prostituting the purity of manhood and the honor of womanhood. With such evils polluting society, is it not the very acme of folly and inconsistency to pass them by, and concentrate missionary zeal upon the Jew? But, apart from the circumstance that the Almighty has constituted in His witnesses and has preserved us for a glorious future, what reason have we for abandoning our ancestral faith? Are the persecutions inflicted upon us for centuries in the name of religion an argument in favor of our adopting that religion? If the patient endurance of outrage be an evidence of true religion, then the Jew has indeed proved that he has nothing to learn. Not only has he borne centuries of persecution with marvellous patience, but he proves how foreign to his principles are fanaticism and intolerance, by proclaiming as a cardinal doctrine of his religion that 'the pious of all creeds share in the happiness of the future state,' that the 'God of the spirits of all flesh' does not restrict salvation to any race or creed. The Jew adheres to those institutions which prevent his absorption by his more powerful neighbors. But he does this simply in order that he may live to proclaim the works of the Eternal. Fanaticism may persecute him, bigotry assail him. He will continue to perform his divinely appointed mission undeterred, with no utterance of rebuke rising to his lips save the golden words, 'Have we not all one Father? Hath not one God created us?'"

In pointing out these foibles of the clergy of the present day, I have endeavoured to do so without malice to any of them, and in using the names of such, I have done so merely to show that all my cases are legitimate and are not the figments of my own brain. In my judgment it seems to me that there is practically no necessity for clergymen at all. They are not better than anyone else, in any single respect. They permit their congregations to do just as the congregations see fit, and I am forced to the conclusion that the religion of the present day is simply that people expect to make a death bed repentance, and expect to go to heaven if they do so, as the case of the dying thief is always held to apply to all sinners. Now suppose this be true, why was there any necessity for Christ to give any instructions to the people as to what they should do, when if a repentance like that of the dying thief is to be sufficient. He might just as well have come to the earth, and been crucified and pardoned the dying thief upon the cross. As an evidence that the clergy are not in any respect respected, let me give you the experience of Mr. Stead in Chicago, when he purposed addressing the workingmen. He was distinctly told that if he mentioned Christianity he would be hissed down and why? Simply because the workingmen knew that in any difficulty between capital and labour, the clergy were with capital every time, right or wrong. Why then should these men entertain any respect for the clergy? Clergymen are simply the tools of their flocks. They preach what will please them, and they preach nothing else. Inane platitudes, pleasing to the people who pay them is the theme for the clergyman of to-day, and let him beware who tries anything else.

As showing the immense influence of Christianity, here is an example of recent occurrence: At Grimsby Park, where well known clergymen, all the most advanced Prohibitionists, and Womens' Enfranchisement Advocates have their full say and which is moreover a place of religious recreation, the following occurred as reported by the Ottawa Free Press:

> Grimsby Park, Aug. 25.—During his preliminary remarks in introducing the Rev. Dr. Potts at Grimsby Park last night, President Phelps caused a wave of excitement to pass through the audience by referring to the fact that the young ladies stay out at night. While walking through the park after midnight he said he was pained to see young ladies and young gentlemen roaming about. At these remarks smiles illumined the faces of the innocent young men, blushes reddened the countenances of the girls and a general feeling of uneasiness was manifested. In indignant tones some of the young ladies were heard to remark that they didn't care a bit as night was the nicest time anyway.

It is superfluous for me to state what every one in Canada knows, namely, that Grimsby Park is the favourite summer resort of the clergy of the Methodist church and the laity as well. I do not propose to discuse whether there was any wrong committed there or not, but I desire to state this much, that if you will find such a flagrant violation of the rules of a park which, state that the lights must be out and people in their cottages at ten o'clock at night, how clearly, it must demonstrate the remarkably small amount of influence, clergymen or there wises, religious or otherwise, have in their own families, and that if such a violation of rules is made there, how much greater must they be in other places, where there is no restarint, and it may consistantly be asked what did President Phelps see that he should make it the subject of a special admonition to the assemblage at the Park.

Besides the class of women who congregate at Grimsby Park every year as well as those who speak there are advocates of that relic of antiquity the Curfew Bell, confirming my contention that these women have no influence whatever over their own daughters, that they know nothing at all of what they are doing, and that they simply desire to shift the responsibility of caring for their morals to the shoulders of some one else. That is modern Christianity.

I submit the following advice, which I think is the advice of a whole-souled Christian woman, and I am sure if women, instead of devoting their time to the ballot and such nonsense, would give some such attention to their daughters, it would have a far more wholesome effect than the ballot will ever have:

Mrs. Alice Kinney Wright, regularly installed associate pastor of the Church of Reconciliation and Prospect Heights Universalist church, New York, has written for the Sunday New York World a sermon to summer girls. Her text is "Keep thyself pure," I. Timothy, v. 22. Here are some selected paragraphs from among the many good things she said: This "one thing needful" is a manly and womanly character, built so solidly upon the foundation of purity and uprightness that not all the demons of society shall cause it to tremble. Carve clearly and deeply in the corner-stone of this foundation the divine injunction, "Keep thyself pure." Strive at all times to live this sentiment; then let the rich young life in you have its full freedom, and you will not only be the sunshine of your home, but will carry with you an influence for good wherever you may go.

Oh, how we all love and admire the sweet, pure girl who says, "I do not believe in allowing my gentlemen friends those privileges which rightfully belong to the man I intend to marry. I have not met him yet, but he is going to be a good man, and I will reserve all rights to myself for him." You girls who do not agree with this idea may call her a "prude" and a "prim old stick." But if she has intellect and grace along with her "prudish idea," she is just the girl that the self-respecting young man wants for his wife. Young woman, when you get so low down in the moral scale that you can when with your gentlemen (?) friends laugh at the obcene insinuation and listen to the questionable joke or story; when you become so careless of yourself that a caress means no more to you than a hand shake would to the modest girl; while you may pride yourself upon being "virtuous, that is, not really bad," you are in the midst of grave dangers; you have fallen to a level where you are subject to any insult, and from which no man who respects himself will raise you to the dignity of wifehood. You do not wish to win for yourself the unsavory reputation of the girl-of-many-engagements, and you should not enter hastily into the responsibilities of wifehood. Be content to wait until you are sure that you are in love—and with a man. Above all things, do not mistake a dude or a bank account for a man, because the result is sure to be disastrous to your happiness. And do not experiment, but be guided, in this matter at least, by the experience of others. It is not wise to venture when the happiness or misery of a lifetime is the stake. God did not create woman and place upon her such grave responsibilities without endowing her with a constitution capable of great endurance. And our weak, waist-contracted, insipid, know-nothing, do-nothing and good-for-nothing society figureheads, instead of being admired, as in the past, should, in accord with the trend of present thought, be looked upon as unnatural monstrosities of the human family. Young women, let us secure our divine birth-right, and carefully guard its transference to future generations. I plead with you, add to your summer amusements a large grain of thoughtfulness and common sense; add to those friendships with your gentlemen companions a dignity that is infallible and at the same time natural and unassuming; then, being prepared in the midst of all your frivolity and fun to repulse any undue familiarity on the part of the man of many engagements, keeping the corner stone of your character foundation uneffaced, you may always look back upon your summer with perfect delight, unmarred by the sight of any dark spots that you wish to cover, but cannot because you were not alone in your wrong doing. Rise, oh! manhood, in your youth and strength, and go forward to meet the real coming womanhood with the whiteness of her purity like a bridal veil about her, and, standing together upon the principles of true living, crush beneath your united virtue that false standard of morality upon which these men of much experience base their vile theories.

Young men and women, let your friendships this summer be pure and helpful; sometimes talk together earnestly about the sober realities of life and the ideals that light up youth's vision. Then your summer's experience together may add to the accumulating strength of our movement towards social purity and sex equality.

Yet, how many girls are there who would think twice of foregoing her present enjoyment by acting upon the advice above given?

Some time ago I had a conversation with a young lady, or perhaps I should say more correctly, a lady who is no longer young, but who is unmarried, who is deeply interested in the cause of Temperance. She is, as she states herself, an advanced Prohibitionist, and in ringing tones she demands the total Prohibition of the Liquor traffic. She informed me that she was greatly pleased to see so many young people taking such an interest in the good work, and Pointed with Pride, as the saying is, to the fact that the Pavilion was always crowded with the young of both sexes.

I could hardly conceal my amazement at her cool audacity in accepting this as a proof of their coinciding with her views.

"Surely," I remarked, "you do not flatter yourself that these young people come to hear you speak, and because they are interested in Prohibition."

"Certainly, I do," she answered promptly.

"Then, I am very sorry to undeceive you," I replied, "if you will take the trouble to see what becomes of these young people after they leave here, you will tell a very different story."

"Why?"

"Because they come here as it is a convenient place to meet at."

"Do you mean to say that this place is made a convenient place of meeting by boys and girls?"

"If you choose to put it in that way, yes I do."

Here was a woman, arguing for the complete prohibition of a traffic which yields one third of the revenue of the country, a social reformer, she called herself, and yet she had no more conception of the proclivities of young people than an inmate of an asylum would have had, flattering herself that these young people came to the pavilion for the purpose of hearing her speak on this subject. It seems to me that social ignorance could go no further, than for her to take to herself the solution of a great social question, and then show that she was preposterous enough to suppose that she could attract a multitude of people to hear her speak when by her own confession she was absolutely ignorant of the customs society has relegated to itself.

Crowds of young people attend these meetings without a doubt, but when the meetings are over how many of them could tell what was said. Comparatively few, if any.

There is this difference between the woman with whom I was speaking and myself, she thinks she knows her subject, and she doesn't, but I have seen, and I speak from experience.

If a young miss asked her mother's permission to take a walk on Sunday afternoon, she might be refused. If she asked permission to attend a temperance meeting she would receive it. If a boy accompanies her home or part way home from a Temperance meeting, it is all right. If he met her in the street and accompanied her home, it might look bad, it is a fine distinction, but it is truth.

THE BAR.

The number of lawyers in Toronto is very large, numbering perhaps away up in the hundreds. Of them comparatively few are in receipt of handsome incomes. Men like Christopher Robinson, Edward Blake, S. H. Blake, Dalton McCarthy and B. B. Osler, are the equal in legal acumen of any on the continent, and rank with the best in the world. The argument of the Hon. Edward Blake before the Privy Council in England on the Boundaries question called forth the remark from the Committee that it was either the ablest or one of the ablest that they had ever listened to. Men of their strength cannot afford to do wrong. They are well paid for their services, and there is no case of any magnitude that comes up that two of the five at least are not engaged in, and they enjoy a prominence enviable, but which has been brought at the price of their own indomitable will, perseverance and remarkable ability, combined with highest integrity. In addition to those mentioned, there are numbers of men of more or less ability who, though clever, have not the calibre these possess.

They have an association called the Benchers of the Law Society, whose place it is to punish those members of the profession who fail to keep themselves free from the sins that would land anyone else in prison.

The following are the Benchers who were elected for the coming five years, and the votes they received :

M. H. Strathy (Barrie), 940; Chas. Moss, 931; B. M. Britton (Kingston), 887; Wm. Douglass (Chatham), 882; Hon. A. S. Hardy, 879; Christopher Robinson, 864; D. B. Maclennan (Cornwall), 852; John Iddington (Stratford), 838; Dr. Hoskin, 836; Colin Macdougall (St. Thomas), 835; B. B Osler, 819; D. Guthrie (Guelph), 804; M. O'Gara (Ottawa), 801; Geo. C. Gibbons (London), 797; R. Bayley (London), 766; A. B. Aylesworth, 730; J. V. Teetzel (Hamilton), 716; A. Bruce (Hamilton), 715; George H. Watson, 700; Wm. Kerr (Cobourg), 681; A. H. Clarke (Windsor), 669; George F. Shepley, 666; John Bell (Belleville), 657; Ed. Martin (Hamilton), 635; D'Alton McCarthy, 621; C. H. Ritchie, 609; W. R. Riddell, 582; W. D. Hogg (Ottawa), 579; E. B. Edwards (Peterboro'), 578; Æmelins Irving, 572.

The Telegram has an article that may be perused with the consciousness that if it were not deserved, it would not have been writen :

No change could make the benchers less useful than they have been, and any alteration must, therefore, point towards improvement. The benchers of the law society constitute a body distinguished for appetite rather than for efficiency in the discharge of public duty. They are more zealous to eat lunches than to maintain the honour of the profession, or to protect the public against the buccaneers who infest too many Ontario law offices. The benchers fail notoriously to protect professional honour or thé swindled public. Their discipline is a farce. Offences that force them to censure lawyers would imprison laymen. They exercise their authority to discipline lawyers only in case of crimes where a non-professional scoundrel would go to penitentiary. Even then conviction follows extreme guilt only when the offenders fail to raise the money to compound the felony. The benchers need to wake up. Official life is to them one long lunch. They are dining away the resources of the law society when they should be running rascals out of the profession. Some lawyers rob clients, but no lawyer ever goes to gaol for the crime.

The above has my heartiest approbation. It is not many years ago that a young lady was swindled out of some money, and though time out of number the case was brought up it was finally discovered that the demands of the people required that the name of the man who swindled her should be struck from the rolls, when it was finally done. That was his punishment. A starving wretch may steal a loaf of bread, but he is sent to goal or the Central.

Lawyers have more chances to be dishonest than other men have. The proportion of sinners among lawyers is perhaps not large, but the man with a wide circle of acquaintance in Toronto is fortunate if he does not actually know of lawyers who have betrayed their trust by crimes that would land a laymen in penitentiary. A list of the widows and orphans who have been impoverished by the dishonesty of lawyers, and the names of the lawyers who have impoverished them within the last few years in Toronto, would astonish the public. Any well informed man about town can without the slightest trouble give five or six specfic instances of fraud by lawyers. There is no help for the infortunate victims. Young children who were left well provided for may go upon the street or become a burden upon relatives. Widows who could have lived confortably upon the estate bequeathed by their husbands, have had their resources stolen or blundered away. Where is the comfort in assurances that the lawyers who have done this work did not intend to do wrong? Gentlemen who have taken other people's money cannot plead their good intentions as a reason why they should not be sent to Kingston. The authority of the benchers is strained to its utmost limit when they compel a dishonest lawyer to make restitution if he can find the money, and let him alone if he has impoverished himself as well as his clients. There ought to be some more powerful agency than the Law Society for the correction of abuses in the legal profession. There should be some tribunal which would sit in public and judge between dishonest lawyers and their victims, and it is useless to disguise the truth that victims of dishonest lawyers are unpleasantly numerous in Toronto.

Ought not the Law Society to provide some easy method of enforcing the regulations which it frames for upholding the honour of the profession which it guards?

The man who is robbed by a lawyer now must not only have a keen sense of his duty to the public, but a good deal of money. If he undertakes to punish the defaulter at his own expense, he is, in fact, twice robbed. The sight of the delinquent stripped of his gown is poor satisfaction to the man who in the first place had to lose the money, and in the second place provide money for the punishment of the solicitor who robbed him. There should be an officer of the Law Society whose duty it would be to investigate all complaints against any practitioner on the rolls. Exposure ought to follow in every case where there has been genuine dishonesty. The individual who has been robbed by one lawyer ought not to be called upon to pay another lawyer to purge the legal profession of a rogue.

How is it that the powers of the criminal law are rarely, if ever, exercised against trustees who speculate for their own profit with funds placed in their hands for the benefit of widows, orphans or too-confiding clients? The facts developed by the processes of civil law at Osgoode Hall leave little ground for hope that the crime of misappropriation is as rare as is its punishment. The practice of using other people's money as if it were your own is altogether too popular. There must be ten betrayals of trust for every one that is recorded in print. It is with authorities to cure, but it is with individuals to prevent, these crimes which rob the helpless. The law ought to punish those who betray a trust, not by the loss of a barrister's gown nor by financial damages, but by terms in jail. And individuals should remember that vigilance is the price at which they can purchase safety for the funds in the hands of trustees. They should not take anything for granted. An honest trustee will invite and welcome the utmost scrutiny. The closest scrutiny should come uninvited to the dishonest trustee.

The report of the committee of the Law Society, charged with the duty of considering whether ex-Alderman W. H. Hall is entitled to retain his rank in an honourable profession, is awaited with anxiety, and will be read with interest. If the committee of the Law Society decides that Mr. Hall has done nothing to forfeit his standing as an honourable practitioner, it ought to supplement that decision by a statement of the offences which a lawyer must commit before the Law Society will expel him. It is well enough that the Law Society should be slow to use its great disciplinary powers. In this particular case the profession has been discredited by the public acts of a public man, who happened to be a lawyer. In other cases the Law Society has not interfered either to protect or avenge clients who have been wronged by lawyers, who still retain their rank in the profession.

Unversed in business matters and unable to read or write was the late Eliza Roberts, an aged colored woman, who lived with Anne Berry for years on Chestnut street. Had this not been so Barrister Joseph A. Donovan would not have been in the county jail. His incarceration is the final act in the long standing suit which Mrs. Eliza Roberts brought against him for the return to her of a lot on the west side of Spadina avenue, above College. Prior to 1890 Mrs. Roberts alleged that Mr.

Donovan persistently visited her and finally talked her into the belief that she was not the absolute owner of the lot, that in fact she only had a life interest in it. Believing this, and knowing that being nearly 90 years of age she could not hope to live but a few years, she was induced by Mr. Donovan to sell the property to him for $300. The deed was forthwith made out, but Mrs. Roberts was described in that deed as the absolute owner. Shortly after Mr. Donovan secured a loan, giving a mortgage on the property for security which mortgage now amounts to nearly $5,000. The trial of the action which the aged colored widow filed resulted in a judgment whereby Mr. Donovan was ordered to remove the mortgage and to reconvey the property to its wronged owner. Subsequently Mrs. Roberts died willing the property, when it would be reconveyed to Anne Berry. Various appeals delayed the case from time to time until a few weeks ago when Mr. Moss moved for and obtained an order committing Mr. Donovan for contempt of court for non-compliance with the court's judgment.

Nov. 21 the order was granted, but the clerk of Single Court was instructed not to issue until after four days had elapsed. On one of these Mr. Donovan was injured by the elevator at 9½ Adelaide street west, the building in which his office is located. The order was then further stayed. Saturday it issued, and Mr. Donovan may be compelled to remain in jail until he purges his contempt. Mrs. Berry is now the owner of the property, which is however still encumbered by the $5,000 mortgage. The order also issued for the committal of Mrs. Donovan, who virtually became the owner of the property by the deed but she is not yet in custody, and it is said cannot be found.

MUSIC AND THE DRAMA.

For many years our ancient and beautiful city has taken unto itself the title of "Musical Toronto." I think the origin of the expression can be traced to the gushing description given by a young man on one of the city papers, in connection with the musical festival held some years ago. With a sarcasm beyond his years, and of which he was entirely unconscious, he praised to heaven everything connected with the festival, though it might be inferentially observed that he probably knew as much about music as a child knows of metaphysics, and appeared to be about as competent to criticise a musical performance as a party of deaf mutes might be expected to give in an opinion on the rendition of one of Mosart's masterpieces. I have no doubt, however, that he sincerely believed it was a criticism, and in the usual and accepted definition of that elastic term, it was doubtless intended to be such.

A fair criticism of a local concert, musicale or entertainment got up under local auspices however, is entirely out of the question. Some, and it is a great many years ago there appeared in one of the daily papers a criticism of a performance by a local organization, and in the opinion of the dramatic editor, there was given what he believed to be a fair and impartial view of the performance, but the leader thereof was furious. He wrote a bitter and trenchant letter to the Managing Director of the journal in question denouncing in unmeasured terms the dramatic editor's action, and threatening all the thunders of his wrath by withdrawing his advertising patronage from it.

I have conveniently forgotten the gentleman's name and that of his organization, but perhaps you can remember it.

However, it is worthy of note that it had one desirable effect, that the press could thereafter depend on having local affairs criticised or rather praised by some of the performers themselves, and you have only to read the musical and dramatic news of any of the city journals to be convinced of the truth of this statement. The following is a case in point, and I think anyone reading it will come to the same conclusion- that I have that the vocation of the critic is a thing of the past, and not a necessity in our present age:

> The concert in the Parliament street Baptist church on Tuesday evening brought out a large audience, who evinced their decided approval of the excellent programme rendered by numerous encores. The chief feature of the programme was the duet "Jesus, I love Thee" which was sung by Mrs. T D. Smith and Mr. Charles H. Thorn in such a manner as to bring down the house. Mr. Kimber's solo, "The Lost Chord," was given in fine style and an encore resulted. Of the playing of Prof. Farrington's orchestra and the singing of the Woodgreen quartette it need only be said that they were as good as usual. Rev. James Grant presided in his usual happy manner. "Alone on the midnight sea" was splendidly sung by Mr. H. E. Davey and won him an encore.

Imigine a sacred Duo, sung in the House of God, *bringing down the house.*

A correspondent addresses the Telegram doubtless being impressed with the idea of the superior merits of "Musical Toronto." and his language his decidedly refreshing, though it may be he thinks he is one of the soloists, Toronto is so rich in :

> SIR,—I suggest that the Philharmonic can recover the prestige of its palmiest days if it selects works which have a reputation and employs local talent as soloists. Neg'ect of these two considerations has alienated public sympathy from this society. Imported talent is not a necessity as our city is rich in solo singers. The public cares little for new works ; let us have some of the good old oratorios and public interest will be revived. The society that would present Haydn's 'Seasons" would draw the largest audience ever gathered in the city. The "Messiah" would be acceptable if sung every Christmas. Follow this the coming year with "Judas Maccabeeas," "Joshua" or "Jephtha" towards spring, and the Philharmonic would work itself back into the affections of the music lovers of Toronto. Try it and mark the result.
> —CATO.

This correspondent like every one else it entitled to his or her opinion, but just where the city rich in solo singers, I confess my inability to see, there is not a tenor in the city worthy the name, and certainly none who could sing "Judas Maccabeeas" or Mosart's "Twelfth Mass." While in soprano there is Mrs. Caldwell, who stands alone without a rival.

It is to be wondered at ?

There is not a competent teacher in the city to undertake the cultivation of voices, notwithstanding the fact of a number of people advertising such. I merely point to the fact that if there are competent teachers where is the result of their work ? I have attended some of the concerts in Association Hall, where embryo artists are wont to exhibit their progress. I listened to a young lady with a somewhat reedy soprano, screeching at the top of her voice in a mad plunge at high C.

If she reached it, she had certainly cause to be thankful, for that was the only meritorious part of the effort, though perhaps it is unnecessary for me to say she was encored. That, however, is the fate of all singers in Toronto. They only require the assurance to stand before the audience. The audience will undoubtedly encore them. Any young lady who persuades herself that she is a second Patti, and will yell to the top of her voice on some classical piece of music, can count upon receiving a most generous reception from her audience, because in encoring her they also express a degree of flattery to themselves, indicating as they do that their cultured tastes appreciate classical music, though they may know nothing at all about it, and generally don't.

As the Telegram says : Toronto has a chorus of musical enthusiasts whose alleged desire for high class orchestral entertainment makes more clamour in the papers than their money makes noise in the box office of the Massey Hall when a high class orchestra is playing inside.

I once attended a concert given by a choir called, I believe the Toronto Scotch Choir, and while I desire to express my appreciation of the meritorious action of the public in turning out to make it a success, I confess that I am at sea as to what induced such lavish encores to music that was only fair at best, and had a programme of some twenty members to detract by its tediousness from whatever might have been good in it. I could understand and appreciate the fact of Mrs. Caldwell receiving a warm reception, and being encored, but to this day I am puzzled to imagine what, unless it were purely mechanical, ever induced them to extend the same courtesy to a gentleman who was called the " Hamilton tenor," and who rendered in his own peculiar way "For a'a that," in a manner that a street gamin would have blushed at, or if he wouldn't, then he deserved to be horsewhipped. The gentleman had no more music in his voice than a peacock, and as for expression, it was entirely out of the question. I make no exaggeration when I say that I have never heard his equal and I have heard some of the worst singers in the world.

On this subject of encores, the Telegram seeing the necessity of calling a halt, has the following :

> Toronto could not afford to be measured by the faults of its concert audiences. Applause, hearty, long-continued and indiscriminate crowns every effort. Encores are too common to be noticed. Orchestras, brass bands, balladists, comic singers and elocutionists are all honoured with an enthusiastic recall. The average audience seems to be possessed by an idea that it is so much ahead of the combination every time that it encores a favourite When the worst song is a triumph and the worst singer is enthusiastically recalled the encore ceases to be a compliment and becomes a nuisance. Besides, many people are kept away from concerts by the certainty that an encore will follow every number on the programme. Like the rain the encore falleth upon the just and the unjust, and the prospect of having to sit till midnight listening to oft-repeated ballads and comic songs is not attractive.

The reasons for this state of affairs are various. One of them is the assertion I made before that instead of a fair criticism being made of the work, nothing but praise rewards the efforts of the so-called artists, and to a very large extent the press is to blame. Does the reader for one moment imagine that the programme of Saturday afternoon music in Association Hall is the unbiassed criticism of the musical or dramatic editor of the paper in which it appears ? It certainly was not in my career as a journalist, it is simply prepared by the institution in question, and sent for publication. This I know to be the case with one paper at least, and I see no reason to doubt the same circumstances exist with regard to the others.

Some years ago Bill Nye lectured in Toronto and people were so delighted with him that they get up and went out. He happened to be under the management of the Press Club, consequently no adverse criticism was made. His recent lecture, however, was dismal a failure, that one paper remarked that Mr. Nye had called the Pavilion a race track, and added that he no doubt would consider it so if he had to sit on the hard benches and hear himself talk.

Mr. Nye was, very possibly, a humorist, and the people who held that view point to the fact that his writings and sayings were copied all over the United States and Canada. That proves nothing. It simply demonstrates how badly off the press is for alleged wit, when they publish such trash.

Blasphemy is wit, wit and irreverence is humour to Bill Nye, and when the people of Paterson strewed his dress suit with rotten eggs after one of his lectures, the fragrant offerings of their enthusiasm may have struck the humourist as so many merry jests.

American humor would have agreably modified the austerity of Puritan nature in the time of the Commonwealth. What would have been a boon then, is developing into something very like a nuisance in these days when the tendency of thought, manner and life is towards a point for removed from undue austerity. Toronto listened to Bill Nye with a courtesy that ill-concealed its weariness. The large audience that came out to hear Robert Jones Burdette on the strength of his deservedly great reputation reached for its hat and wraps with a unanimity that drove the lecturer from the platform. Certainly, Mr. Burdette was the most entertaining of all the platform humorists who visit Toronto. His failure to please is a sign, first, of bad judgment in the choice of a subject and in the make up of his lecture, second, of a revolt against the humorists who assume that more or less picturesque flippancy is a never-failing laugh-maker.

During the winter months the public are satiated with church concerts which are always "grand," musicals and entertainments of every description, and which are, for the most part, the work of amateurs who are praised to the skies for their labour. One of the performers usually writes up the event and is unstinting in his or her praise of the artists; but the good sense, happily. however, of the editor, prevails, and a generous public are spared the affliction of having to wade through a quarter of a column description of how Miss Samantha Johnson-Macbeth scored a grand success in Gounod's immortel aria Annie Rooney, or how Miss Pauline Alexandrovina Dagmar was applauded to the echo in her rendition of Mosart's masterpiece, Maggie Murphy's Home. The following will demonstrate to what the public are, or would be stalled if the sensible editor did not come to the rescue and curtail such effusions.

Last Sunday was the occasion of the holding of the anniversary services of Broadway Tabernacle. The eloquent and impressive sermons were aided in no small degree by the sweet and expressive singing of the choir, who were assisted by Mr Robert Shaw the rising young tenor, and by Misses Kleiser and Brimson, both of whose soprano voices were heard with pleasure. Mrs. R. A. Howson, the organist and choirmaster deserves the thanks of the congregation for the appropriate and effective manner in which the musical portion of the services was rendered.

The concert given Tuesday evening in the Gerrard street Methodist church was a magnificent success. Seldom has a better programme been presented to a church congregation than that enjoyed by the large assembly. Miss Maud Bayne, Miss Clara Wallace, Miss Lily Eaton and Miss Helen May Patterson were exceptionally happy in their selections and sustained their reputations as favourite elocutionists. Mr. Spicer's songs were heartily appreciated, as were also the solo and duett by Mr. and Mrs. Easton of Parkdale. "The cobbler" and the "Fairies" by Miss Coulter of Islington won universal approval and Mr. Dixon's ventriloquism was applauded to the echo. Mr. Morris and Miss Morden also took important parts in the programme.

Just imagine the editor who is obliged to wade through such bosh. One man, who has contrived through the instrumentality of lenient newspaper men to puff his wife's musical pretentions up to the largest capacity by multifarious notices in the dramatic columns, made a habitual practice of coming to the office of the paper where I was employed, and requesting to be furnished with proofs of the advertisements of concerts where the lady was to sing, in order that he might make sure that her name was the most prominent in the list of artists. It might be mentioned that the advertising clerk had received instructions to accept no advertising orders from this man unless accompanied by the cash, or the order signed by some responsible party satisfactory to the manager. He sent a lad into the office on one occasion and requested that the proofs should be ready for him at 11 o'clock, to which the clerk, myself, paid no attention whatever, and as he was to be acting clerk that night, he was prepared for him,

At 11 o'clock or a little later he appeared, and in his most grandiloquent manner stated his business:

"I sent my office boy in here to order proofs for the advertisement of the ...... concert to be ready at 11 o'clock."

"Yes," the clerk responded, "and I think the boy was informed that it would be necessary for him to have an order from Mr...... who has signed the orders for the advertising."

"Good God!" he exclaimed, "you don't mean to say the advertisement is not set up yet."

"It is quite likely it is set up, but as to getting proofs for you, you know that is out of the question."

"Is Mr...... in?" mentioning rhe dramatic editor.

"Yes, I think he is."

"Is the elevator running?"

"No, I think not."

He hurried away up stairs and the clerk heard him walking up the stairs. As a matter of fact it was within the power of the clerk to have proofs if he wished, but the pleasure one always feels on sitting down on a cad was too strong and he took advantage of his position to refuse to accommodate him. I give you these particulars gratis, so that if you know the person referred to you will know also how it comes that her name was made the most prominent in the list of artists. It was not that the was the leading personage on the programme as might be imagined by the unsophisticated, but merely an act of grace on the part of a good natured editor.

Appropos of the prominence given to the lady in question, it is within the memory of Torontonians that on the opening night of the Academy of Music, the particulur star was Miss Nora Clench, and an artist of more than ordinary ability, and justly recognized as such; but Mr. Whitney Mockridge, who is not that heaven born singer he would like to have people believe he is, felt himself so deeply aggrieved by Miss Clench's name being set in larger type than his own, that he did not wish to sing, and the concert was consequently delayed for an hour on that account. If Mr. Mockridge really possessed any special ability it would perhaps be excusable, though in any case it was perfectly absurd, but to compare himself as a vocalist with Miss Clench as a violinist is so ridiculous that he may be easily pardoned for the smallness of his soul in making an ass of himself, if that be possible, in such a matter.

You need only read the papers of any of the large cities to see the "arts and graces" employed to obtain newspaper notoriety which now passes for fame, by actresses and singers. When Miss Claire was to sing in Toronto, the papers were filled with the chivalric devotion of her fiance, and the scandalous actions of Miss Lilian Russell in the recent encounter of the two singers in Boston. I think there is nothing more delightful than to have your private affairs brought before the public through the newspapers, and I feel sure that you will agree with me that it is in excellent taste.

Inasmuch as notoriety and fame are synonymous nowadays, I presume when some charming young debutante makes her bow, and the expectant world is informed that her worthy mother was a prize-fighter, the generous public will rush to see her, and give her a warm reception in commemoration of the feats of valour performed by the notorious mother.

On one of my visits to Toronto, I was invited to a concert to hear a gentleman who lays claim to being more than an ordinary tenor, sing, and was really surprised at his efforts. "He can't read a note," my friend exclaimed exultantly, as though this were something to be proud of. To Blind Tom it is quite natural to refer as being unable to read music, as in addition to being blind he is likewise an idiot, but that a man in full possession of his faculties, who has been a public singer for years, and music constantly before him, can truthfully say he cannot read music at all, proves himself to be less than a blind idiot.

I have often thought that Toronto audiences were extremely generous or profoundly stupid, though perhaps it is a moderate combination of both. When a new song is introduced by some comedian such as "Near It," "I tried with my voice to enchant Her," and others less pleasing, those who have not heard them from the lips of the singer who originally introduces them, will certainly bear me out. As a matter of fact a teacher like Emilio Belari would not condescend to teach in Toronto, but even were he disposed to do so, after he had fought through the opposition he would have to encounter, he might feel like giving up in disgust. When a gentleman came from Boston to give a season of lessons, one of the city papers whose critic is also one of the musical professors, I believe, proceeded to deprecate in a general way people who came to the city for a few months' course thereby undoing, if that were possible, what had been done to build up these voices by careful training, &c., &c., and stating that these people never came to the city a second time, though with a delicacy of feeling that was commendable he did not state that some of these pupils were so well pleased with their teacher that they underwent the expense of going to Boston to receive instructions there. However, you may conceive the mental capacity of the writer of this article when in criticising of a certain play, he had sufficient regard for the truth to say that one young lady on the bills in a certain play, was forty years of age, when she was certainly not more than eighteen.

Again in the case of the Scotch choir I mentioned the press had nothing but the highest praise to bestow upon it, which as I previously pointed out was entirely unwarranted by the performance. So, too, in the case of the Balmoral choir which visited us some years ago. It was lauded to the skies, though, and I speak with all sincerity, it had no advantage over any other organization of a similar nature, though it is not saying much for it. Yet it received eulogies that even the great Patti herself might have envied. Hence my contention that newspaper criticism is unreliable is fully borne out by the facts. It is to be remembered that in the cases of these two organizations, members of the press were in some way connected with them. In the first they were members of the Scotch choir, and the Balmoral choir was under the patronage of the Caledonian Society which numbers amongst its members quite a large number of journalists. Is it, therefore, likely that they would give an adverse criticism, or in fact give a criticism at all?

Of the drama itself it seems unnecessary to speak. The three opera houses all cater for the best possible custom, and their efforts are well rewarded. The aim is to provide the very best talent on the continent, and a really good play or opera is well patronized. The Grand, the Princess, and Jacob's & Sparrow's each has its respective class of plays and comparative prices, and very rarely an inforior show comes to either.

In a recent benefit at which Manager Sheppard of the Grand made a speech, the public were told that theatrical companies always said that if a Toronto audience approved, they were successful elsewhere. This seems to be a popular way of flattering any town or city into the idea that its tastes are fastidious. I have heard Ottawa people say the same thing, St. Catharines, Hamilton and Montreal as well. In one of Roland's Reed's plays there is a scene in an asylum, and the stereotyped remark made by every one incarcerated is: "You know *I'm* not in here because I'm insane, it is only to see a friend of mine." And after soothing the patient the motherly matron says to herself: " Poor fellow, that's what they all say." See any connection ?

Great and multifarious are the means employed to advertise this or that singer or artist. Take as an example young Kavanagh, who appeared in the Metropolitan church. The public were informed that he had been introduced to the divine Patti, who after hearing him sing " Angels ever bright and Fair," and " In verdure Clad," expressed her appreciation, and kissed him.

Quite frequently I am at a loss to understand what theatrical managers are thinking about when they are forming their companies, and employing the actors and actresses for the different characters. In some cases it would seem that the law of reversion was pursued with a total disregard as to how it looks on the stage.

As a fair example take the play " Struck Oil," I think it is, where a girl of innocence and principle is supposed to be embodied in " Nan." It is only supposition, however. A great, coarse looking woman of about thirty-five makes the character a laughing stock. Similarly in Alvin Joslin, as played by some Company other than Charles L. Davis'. A crisp looking damsel is stated in the programme to be a "fashionable lady," and it is well that the programme says so, otherwise the public would be in profound ignorance of it. A woman on the shady of forty, thin and attenuated, whose appearance betokens a distressing familiarity with the wash tub is in perfect good faith advanced to us as a lady of fashion. Even if nothing else did so, her costumes would belie the character. The same deficiency exists in regard to Irish pays, particularly Joe Murphy and Scanlon. The first time I heard Joe Murphy I was dumbfounded. The press had been prodigal in its praise of him. His first song was Milloy's " Kerry Dances," and I never, I am happy to say, heard it rendered similarly before nor since. It was absolutely murdered. The first bar contains a G, but since Joe Murphy cannot do an impossibility he did not attempt to touch it. He went over the words in a sing-song fashion, without either accuaracy or expression, and it is perhaps, not necessary for me to add that he was encored. I do not think I am in any respect deviating from the truth in stating that neither Joe Murphy nor Scanlon can sing. It is true they go over the words but the music is changed to meet their voices, the high notes they never attempt, and so far as there being any music in their voices it is absurd to pretend it.

QUACK DOCTORS.

Owing to to the protection afforded by the Medical Act, Canada generally is free from these curses of modern civilization the quack doctors ; but if they are not permitted to practise, there is nothing debarring them from the boon of advertising and the credulity of the pubiic, which is a marked characteristic of the human race, frequently exhibits itself in this country. The quacks or medical imposters to whom this chapter is devoted live upon credulity, and do all in their power to encourage it.

OF TORONTO THE GOOD.   199

Some of these people live in Toronto, and a great many more in the United States, and they offer to cure any and every manner of disease. Some offer their wares for a small sum, others charge enormous prices. Frequently one of these men will personate half a dozen different characters. The newspapers are full of their advertisements, some of which are really unfit for the columns of a respectable journal. Besides this, they send thousands of circulars through the mails to persons in various parts of the country, setting forth the horrors of certain diseases, and offering to cure them by their remedies. The circular contains an elaborate description of the symptoms or premonitory signs of these diseases and a very large number of persons reading these descriptions really come to the conclusion that they are affected in the manner stated by the quack. So great is the power of the imagination in these cases, that sound and healthy men are sometimes absolutely led to believe themselves in need of medical attention. A short conversation with their regular physician would soon undeceive them, but they foolishly send their money to the author of the circular in question, and request a quantity of his medicine for the purpose of trying it. The nostrum is received in due time and is accompanied by a second circular in which the patient is coolly informed that he must not expect to be cured by one bottle, box or package as the case may be, but that five or six or sometimes a dozen will be necessary to complete the cure, especially if the case is as desperate as the letter applying for the medicine seems to indicate. Many are foolish enough to take the whole half dozen bottles or packages, and in the end are no better in health than they were at first. Indeed, they are fortunate if they are not seriously injured by the doses they have taken. They are disheartened in nine cases out of ten, and are at length really in need of good medical advice. They have paid the quack more money than a good practitioner would demand for his services, and have only been injured by their folly.

It may be said that no honest and competent physician will undertake to treat cases by letter. No one worthy of patronage will guarantee a cure in any case, for an educated practitioner understands that cases are many and frequent where the best human skill may be exerted in vain. Further than this, a physician of merit will not advertise himself in the newspapers, except to announce the location of his office or residence. Such physicians are jealous of their personal or professional reputations, and are proud of their calling. They use their knowledge for the good of mankind, and are prompt to make known their discoveries, so that all the world may enjoy the benefit, they themselves being rewarded with the fame of their invention. Not so with the quacks. Some few have some medical knowledge, and are even graduates of regular colleges, but the majority have neither medical knowledge or skill. They know their remedies are worthless, and they offer them only to make money. They know that in many cases their nostrums will inflict positive injury upon their victims, but they are careless of the harm they do. They live upon human misery. The reader may rest assured that not a single physician who conducts his business by means of circulars or advertisements is really competent to treat the cases he professes to cure, and that no one knows this better than himself.

Some time ago a firm of physicians so-called, with a great emblazonation of advertisements, anounced "They are coming," and again "They are here," and how in the world they managed to dupe the public or obtain a foothold is absolutely incomprehensible. One of the city newspapers, however, can tell the profound manner in which they were duped, and how payment for the glaring advertisements has never been made to this day.

As a general rule the various medicines advertised as specifics or panaceas for various ills, are humbugs and are utterly worthless. Many of them are made up of harmless drugs, which can do no harm, if, as is almost certain, they do no good ; but others again are composed of very dangerous substances. The remedies advertised for "private diseases" rarely fail to make the patient worse either by aggravating the disease itself or by permanently injuring the constitution. Vital fluids and others of that ilk, generally contain mercury to a large extent, and anyone conversant with the properties of this substance can easily understand how great is the danger in using them. The various bitters which flood the country are only cheap whisky or rum and water, made nauseous with drugs. They have no virtue whatever as medicinal agents, and merely injure the tone of the stomach ; their chief result being to establish the habit of intemperance; they are more fiery than ordinary liquors, and destructive in their effects. The various medicinal wines that are offered for sale are decoctions of elderberry juice and kindred substances and are more hurtful than beneficial. The hair dyes advertised under so many different names contain such poison as nitrate of silver, oxide of lead, acetate of lead, and sulphate of copper. These are fatal to the hair, and generally injure the scalp. The ointment for promoting the growth of whiskers and mustaches is either perfumed and colored lard, or poisonous compounds which contain quicklime or corrosive sublimate, or some kindred substance. If you have any acquaintance who has ever used this means of covering his face with a manly down ask him which came first the beard or a trublesome eruption.

Different newspapers often contain advertisements like the following : "A retired physician of forty years' practice having had placed in his hands a certain cure for consumption, bronchitis, colds, etc., and will send it to all sufferers on receipt of a three cent stamp. &c., &c."

A single moment's reflection ought to convince any sensible person that the parties thus advertising are frauds, if they remember that it costs a great deal of money to advertise; and as the announcements referred to can be seen in scores of papers, it is safe to say that they spend thousands of dollars a year in advertising. Letters come asking him for his valuable prescription which he sends and notifies the party asking for it that if the articles named in it cannot be obtained by him at the drug store convenient to him, he will furnish them at a certain sum, which he assures him is very cheap as the drugs are rare and expensive. Again a great many people have a reticence in going to a city drug store where they may possibly be known, with such a prescription, and will frequently send the money to escape such comments as the druggist may possibly make. I was reading a few days ago of a man who had been entrusted with a secret prescription for the cure of something or other by a physician who was on his death bed, and gave it to him for the benefit of suffering humanity. I laughed when I read it, and thought how gullible must be the public for a fake like that to succeed.

Another matter that will strike the reader is the fact that if he once sends his money there will be no end to the number of people who have similar remedies, and he will wonder where they got his name. It is very simple. They are perhaps one and the same person or firm, and if not they have possibly purchased the names from another house. How it is done is not a matter of much consequence, but it is certain that when once a name is given to these sharks they seem to have the faculty of having it pretty well advertised that you require the treatment they deal in, and if they cannot sell you the goods themselves they will try to find some one else who can.

Men have grown rich in the business, and it is carried on to an amazing extent in particularly American cities, and to a certain extent in Canada, but the advice given in regard to quack doctors holds equally good in respect to patent medicines.

Some time ago a young friend of mine was suffering from a disease of a private nature, and answered an advertisement inserted by one of the druggists in the city, who, after giving him some medicine, instructed him to perform an act upon his own body that almost killed him, besides the grossly immoral nature of the act. I do not know what redress the young man could have got, but it would have been infinitely satisfactory to me to have seen the druggist punished for his advice, which could have been actuated only by the most morbid ideas. To the general public it might seem that the patient might have known better, but that does not in any respect excuse the action of the druggist in advising an act that at that particular time would have been most disastrous had not the constitution of the patient been able to withstand it, but it demonstrates my point that no one suffering from any disease of a serious nature or any disease at all, for that matter, should consult a druggist or use quack medicines for its cure, as you are almost morally certain to be humbugged.

In the preparation of this article, I wrote to a large number of so called patent medicine dealers for circulars explaining their remedies, and I have given you the pith of what they contain, but the following is really too good to cut down, so I give it in full, and while I do not say anything against it, I submit it for your careful consideration. It is intended to show the reliability of the house issuing the circular, and if you will take the trouble to analyse it, you will see that the fullest information was afforded the brother to transmit to his applicant. The bank account is reported as being fat, and being kept at three banks, and in respect to that I must confess that bankers must be peculiar people in the United States if they will give their customers' business away in that style.

The following is the letter :

My Dear Brother :—Your letter only received, and I have delayed writing until I could answer your inquiries regarding the ... fully. You know when I start to do a thing, I generally do it right. I devoted a whole day to this investigation and make the following report : I first visited the offices, which extend the whole length and width of the large building they occupy. There were, I should judge, about twenty persons employed there as clerks etc., all seemed very busy. The manager showed me all through their establishment, explaining their method of filling orders etc., it seems that all orders are filled the same day as received. I next visited the consultation office, where the physician in charge explained the actions of the appliances they manufacture. To demonstrate the superiority of the articles he has in the office samples of every kind manufactured in the U.S,, and by means of the .... he convinced me that their manufacture gives four times as much strength as the others. Two of the rivals that sell so high he proved give no strength whatever. He showed me hundreds of testimonials from all parts of America. He also showed me orders from every part of the world, Europe, Asia, Africa, Sandwich Islands, Brazil, Australia, Mexico and Japan. I was perfectly satisfied from what I saw that their goods were all that they represented them to be, and that they did an immense business. I next visited their bankers to find their financial standing. I find that they own real estate in this city, worth I should judge, about seventy-five thousand dollars ; that they have a fat bank account at three of the leading banks, and are without doubt perfectly responsible. In conclusion, brother, I would by all means advise you to try their treatment, and I feel sure from what I have seen that you will find their goods just what they represent them to be and also that you will be honestly dealt with.

Your, affectionate brother,

....

I submit the following, which I think will strike the common sense reader us being the maudlin raving of a drunken ass, if anyone outside of the office of the concern wrote it :

An earnest man who had suffered, hesitated, then put it to the test, writes thus :
" Well, I tell you that first day is one I'll never forget. I just bubbled with joy. I wanted to hug everybody and tell them that my old self had died yesterday and my new self was born to-day. Why didn't you tell me when I first wrote that I would find it this way ? "

While there will not be any question of the desirability of having the medical profession as rigidly exact as possible, it may strike a great many as being too rigid in its discipline with its own members. For instance, a medical man is not permitted to advertise himself any more than his address and his speciality if he has one. Breach of this rule permits the council to deal with him as it may think proper. Some years ago Dr. McCully used to advertise quite extensively in the daily papers, and make very frequent assaults on the general hospital, which he irreverently stigmatized as the "old mill." The council at that time, I believe was unable to reach him, but one would imagine that the law courts might have afforded redress. One hallow e'en some of the brilliant medical students congregated in front of his residence and showered it with stones. Dr. McCully showed his appreciation of this compliment, and fired into the crowd. For this he was summoned and discharged, and at the same time I have no doubt he received the thanks of thousands of Toronto's citizens for his courage. The students in council assembled a few days later drew up a heroic resolution of sympathy with one of the young men, who received the charge from the doctor's gun, but tradition does not say that in addition to their bravery any one of them acknowledged himself as having thrown stones at the Doctor's house. Such bravery as that would probably be too much to expect. The resolution of condolance was as far as their chivalry could go. It might be thought by the uninitiated that the powers of the Doctors are sufficiently great, or that they might be somewhat curtailed. The judge who tried the prisoners in the Sharon poisoning case had the hardihood to say that the expert medical evidence was absolutely valueless, as it would seem to him, that any evidence a lawyer wished to procure, the doctors would give him, and that it was utterly worthless. No one knows that the Medical Council passed resolutions condemning his aspersions. It may be that they were well founded. Besides it may be remembered that one of the leading physicians, or at least a man who considers himself such, gave a permit for burying an abortion, when the latter was alive. This matter was ventilated by the leader of the Opposition in the Ontario House during a recent session. Perhaps it might be in the public interest if the doctors had some restrictive legislation passed for the benefit of the public. However that is a matter for the public.

The fact of the matter is simply that doctors wish to maintain a monopoly, and all their heroics to the contrary would not change my opinion one iota.

Similarly with the druggist. They have so long enjoyed the monopoly of charging the public twenty cents an ounce for water, that when Eaton and Simpson decided to give the public the benefit of low prices the latter was promptly brought up on a charge of violating the Pharmacy Act and fined. Any other than an unworthy motive, did not prompt this display of spleen. Mr. Simpson had a licensed chemist to work for him, who could probably compound drugs just as well and probably considerably better than those who incited the prosecution.

Daniel Boyer, the Markham curer of cancer, was tried at the Police Court on a charge of having infringed upon the provisions of the Medical Act by treating Miss Rose Cates, of Wilton avenue, for fibroid tumor in March last. The Crown called Miss Cates, who swore that, having become afflicted with the tumor and fearing that it would develop into cancer, went to Markham to consult Boyer. The latter is the inventor of a patent plaster which when applied to a cancer " draws it out by the roots." She stated her case to him and secured several plasters and, as her mother was a woman of nervous temperament, she decided to remain at Boyer's house while undergoing treatment. For board for eight days and for the plasters she subsequently paid him $13. In all her evidence it did not appear that he had tendered her any medical advice. He simply sold the plasters as a patent medicine. Moreover she was cured. The case fell through.

The News observes " If the Markham man who was in court yesterday has a plaster that can cure tumors, as a patient swore in her testimony, it is an outrage that he should not be allowed to sell it to the poor sufferers without being prosecuted for it. Surely the health— even the life of a person—is of more consequence than the maintenance of medical ethics."

SITUATION AGENCIES.

There are inserted, almost every day, advertisements for help wanted, but just how far they are beneficial is a matter for those interested to judge, but before you invest your money, carefully peruse the following article, and decide for yourself:

Of all the investments known the one least likely to produce any return is the fee paid to an employment bureau for assistance promised in securing a position. The possibilities held out by the agent are immense. The probabilities are not so great. The number of situations secured in comparison to the number of applications received are diccouragingly small.

All employment agencies are licensed. A by-law regulates the fees allowed to be charged. The books used in transacting business are all open to public inspection. These are perhaps the greatest evils. Intended, as the by-law was, to be a safeguard to the public. it only inspires confidence, it affords no protection. This is an industry that prospers best in times of adversity. The bird of action grown fat when death is in the land. The employment agent succeeds best when the bread-earner fares worst. When work is scarce applications for aid to find it are many. All applications are accompanied by the necessary fee. The unemployed are kindly received in these places. These agents, philanthropists are their friends. The fees charged are as follows for domestics, 50c ; for governesses, female bookkeepers, clerks, stenographers, etc., $1 ; for laborers, 50c ; and for coachmen, male bookkeepers, clerks, etc., $1. If a situation is procured the whole amount paid is kept. If the attempt is fruitless, as is too often the case, half the amount paid is returned to the applicant. The applicant is promised the assistance of the agent. The assistance consists in registering the name in a register for the purpose and permitting the person seeking employment to drop into the employment office occasionally for a period of ten days. The last is no great privilege as the usual furniture for such offices is one table and one chair, or per adventure two. One may, of course, lean up against the wall.

" We do not," said one of these agents, "guarantee that we will get any applicant a position. We merely promise to try."

" What does your trying amount to ? "

" We are in correspondence with many large warehouses and factories ; that is we advertise."

" About what percentage of the applicants do you find positions for ? "

" I am not prepared to say, but that has really nothing to do with the business."

The mention of advertising recalls an incident which happened at the time of the Industrial Fair last year. One of the employment bureaus advertised for girls to work on the Exhibition grounds. At least two of those who applied and who paid the necessary fee were directed to a fictitious address. They returned and demand d the money back which they had paid. This was refused and was only received by police interference.

There is another case where men were advertised for to go to the lumber woods. When they went to the woods to which they were directed, they found there was no work for them.

This sort of thing should be stopped. There is nothing meaner or more contemptible than this trafficking on the necessities of the poor and unemployed. Faint hopes are presented. The unfortunate snatch at faint hopes. A little reflection would show the employer of labour need not apply, and as a matter of fact do not often apply to these agencies to fill these positions. The very large majority of them have any number of applications always on hand and they find it an easy matter to select men to fill vacancies.

Barnum is said to have remarked that people like to be humbugged. So long as this is true it would be scarcely charitable to rob the public of such a fruitful source of amusement, and this is perhaps the only apology for the existence of employment bureaus.

Several well-dressed, respectable young men called at Police headquarters and reported a contemptibly mean swindle that they claimed had been perpetrated upon them. According to their statement they answered the following advertisement which appeared in the evening papers :

WANTED—50 men for the lumber woods, wages, $26 to $35, board and fares paid. Apply 45 Wallace avenue, near Dufferin street, after 5.

At the address indicated in the advertisement they met a man who represented to them that he had received instructions from a lumberman to engage that number of men. He taxed all that he engaged

25 cents as his commission, and ordered them to report at the Union station for transportation, only to cause them to meet with bitter disappointment as there was no one there to meet them. Some of the young fellows smarting under the sad experience went to the house, intending to have a reckoning with the individual who made the engagement, but found the house empty, the bird having flown. A warrant was issued for his arrest.

SWINDLERS.

Of the various schemes resorted to by mankind to swindle his brother it would be impossible to say which in the worst, or where they originate, but one would think that with the oft-recurring warnings of the press, people would learn to beware of such people. The following affair seems so patent on its face that one is surprised at people of intelligence biting at it :

According to an advertisement that had appeared in several rural weeklies, a new weekly paper called the Cosmopolitan Advertiser was about to be issued in Toronto. The publisher was stated to be W. Armand, Box 2,537 Toronto P. O. He offered as a premium for a subscription price of $1 for six months a solid gold watch made by the Charles Stark Company. The postal authorities entertained a suspicion that the deal was not all right and an interview with Inspector Stark followed. He detailed a detective to watch for the person who took the letters out of box 2,537 and W. R. Wood, a young man employed as clerk in the Budget office, 64 Bay street, called for the letters. He was promptly escorted ever to the police headquarters where a consultation with Inspector Stark took place. Wood stated that he held a power of attorney from Armand, whose address he did not know, but who, he believed, resided in the States. He met him through answering an advertisement. He claimed that Armand was at present negotiating with Toronto printers to publish the new journal. He received thirty four letters the previous day and another large number the day of his arrest. These letters were all handed over to Inspector Stark, and $24 of the money previously received. The balance he said he had turned over to Armand who had been in the city the day previously. He also surrendered the key to the Post office box. The Charles Stark Co. repudiate having any business dealings with either Armand or Wood.

F. E. Handy was the first witness called for the prosecution. He testified that he enclosed a dollar addressed to box 2,537 Toronto. He sent money to William Armand. He had an idea that it was a fraud but he made up his mind to try it anyway. Detective Stark identified the letter written by Mr. Handy as having been among the stock of letters the defendant Wood had handed to him. He recounted the details of the interview that took place between Wood and himself, in which the former admitted that the scheme looked like a fraud, but he was dragged into it through an advertisement. The Magistrate committed Wood for trial on his own bail.

Advertising is essentially one of the best means for the swindler to use for his purpose, and no matter how vigilant the newspapers may be it is impossible to check the different schemes they invent.

Wanted—Treasurer for dramatic company, long engagement to the right party, must have $200 cash security. Apply box 204 Telegram.

Such was the advertisement that met the gaze of Mr. Fred Barrow, a young Englishman who has been a short time in Toronto, and has been anxious to obtain some employment. Straightway he hied himself to the Telegram office and answered the advertisement. In reply he received a note asking him to call upon Mr. M. J. Marshall, at the Arlington hotel. He was received by a stoutish man of forty-five or fifty years, standing, perhaps, five feet eight. This was Mr. Marshall the gentleman who had inserted the advertisement. Mr. Marshall plunged into business. He had organized, he averred, the Zoe Gayton variety troupe which was to begin an extended United States tour. Everything was in readiness, but alas, he had been disappointed in getting a treasurer. He was, however, delighted to find that his wandering advertisement had struck so promising a young gentleman as Mr. Barrow, and hoped they would come to an understanding. The scheme was talked over and finally an agreement was drafted on a sheet of paper by Mr. Marshall. By its terms Barrow was engaged as treasurer at a salary of $18.50 per week, with board and travelling expenses. He was to give two weeks' notice of his intention to leave, and was to be given the same time to prepare to relinquish his post should he not prove satisfactory. If both parties were suited, Mr. Barrow was to hold the job for six months. As an earnest of good faith he was to put up $100 security in Mr. Marshall's hands.

"But," said Mr. Barrow "I shouldn't like to put up that much."

"How much can you deposit?" asked Marshall.

"Well, I'll put up fifty dollars," was the answer.

The complaisant Mr. Marshall agreed to this—it was only a matter of form, Mr. Barrow knew. The sheet of foolscap was signed without witnesses though, and Mr. Barrow put it in his pocket. Then he handed over to Mr. Marshall the fifty dollars. Arrangements were then made for the pair's departure for Buffalo on Sunday at 1.10. Mr. Barrow packed his trunks, and at the time appointed was at the station. Mr. Marshall was not there. He was not on the train when it pulled out of the station, and he was not at the Arlington when the excited "treasurer" drove there. He had gone, and accompanying him were Mr. Barrow's fifty bills.

A correspondent from Montreal says:

Montreal has had her lottery plague, and as the promoters of these illegitimate concerns are throwing up the sponge in every direction and asking permission to close up quietly without further expense, our citizens are now turning their eyes westward and rightly ask protection from the faking prize institutions which infest the city of Toronto. As far as this city is concerned, it is safe to say that more hard cash has been filched out of Montreal's capacious pocket by these Toronto prize swindles than by the miserable five and ten cent lotteries which for a short time flourished in our midst. Our city papers have been teeming with advertisements, all of which come from the city of Toronto, inviting people to read correctly certain stupid rebis, and promising that the first answer will bring the winner anything from a Shetland pony to a door mat. As a matter of fact these fakes can be deciphered in three seconds by the dullest 18 months old baby in the Montreal blind asylum. Consequently the crop of fools who are thus taken in in Montreal alone must be enormous. It happens very frequently that a young man or a young woman learns from the Queen City of the West that he or she has read the fake correctly, but in order to be placed in possession of the diamond ring or the gold watch a sum of money must be sent to headquarters, and, in fact, all fakedom is marvelling over the great good luck of our poor deluded Montrealer. The latter then throws away three cents more by writing a protesting note, saying that the advertisement in question made no mention of any such stipulation. The Toronto fakir replies that if his Montreal friend does not see fit to respond, the firm in question will be the gainer and this is about all the satisfaction he receives. He is willing to lose the postage stamps which were enclosed with the answer and congratulates himself that he escapes so easily. One man, however, who sent $3, reports that the diamond received was the size of a pin head, and the ring adorns the small finger of an infant lately arrived. Not long since a lady who had been victimized by one of these swindles, placed the matter in the hands of a city detective, who in turn referred the matter to an officer of the law in Toronto. The western detective replied that the whole concern was a fake and a swindle, but the people who were carrying them on invariably submitted their advertisements to able lawyers, and he regretted to say that he could not reach them. If this be the case the victims in this province think the law of Ontario should be changed and that in short order.

Detective John A. Grose, of the Canadian secret service agency gives timely warning to the public against what he terms fake advertisements. The officer has just received the following, clipped from an Ottawa paper, which reads as follows:

WANTED—A permanent office assistant, either sex, salary $750; fare paid here; enclose address and stamped envelope. Secretary, Box ——— Montreal, Canada.

The remarks below this ad. read as follows : " Sir, the above taken from an Ottawa paper speaks for itself. It is a fraud and the lessees of the box deserve to be brought to justice. Any one by reading the above advertisement " says Mr. Grose, " will see at a glance that it is a fraud. The very idea of paying a female assistant $750 per annum and then paying her fare to this city is enough. The result of this, however, is that many a poor girl who imagines she is fit for the place addresses a reply to an advertisement, and in return she is told to send three or four or five dollars as the case may be, which will pay for the enquiry to be made into her character, and if this is satisfactory the place will be granted her. There are, perhaps, a hundred applicants. If they send in $3 each that means $300 to the advertiser, and nothing in return to the individual who has been long looking for work, and expects a reply to this gilded advertisement. I could enumerate instances by the score where widows and orphans have applied to this office for some redress, stating that they paid to certain employment agencies sums of $3 or $5, with the hope of getting situations in return, and that their hopes have been blasted after numerous trips to the alleged managers of the concerns in question.

Toronto has not yet arrived at the stage of perfection that New York has been generally accredited with possessing where the bogus auctioneer holds sway, but it ought by this time to be well known by every one, that watches are not sold in these places for fun. I was amused once by a farmer coming into one of these auction rooms on King street, and handing over a timepiece, he had bought at the establishment a short time previously.

"I want you to take this watch back," he explained to the auctioneer.

"What for?" he was asked in surprise.

"I don't want it. You said when I bought it if I couldn't get twice the amount I paid for it from a pawn broker, I needn't keep it."

"Well, you needn't, I don't care what you do with it." And then he laughed.

The farmer cast one look of indignation, and walked out.

In addition to the foregoing, we have the newspaper fakir who offers premiums to those who guess the lucky number, find some words in Scripture, or some such other scheme, and in this connection a correspondent addressed the Weekly Mail, and asked if the advertisers carried out their promises, if the fake was bona fide and if he would recommend the correspondent to send his money. To all of which he answered "No." The correspondent thereupon cut the answer out of the paper, and forwarded it to the advertiser. The latter called upon the editor, and demanded to know if he had written the reply, etc., and he answered that he had.

" Do you know that I can sue you for libel?" he demanded.

" Oh, yes," the other answered carelessly, "I am aware of that but I don't think you can get judgment. You see I know what I'm writing about."

The libel suit was not entered, but the advertiser withdrew his patronage from the Mail.

Another case is where a gentleman having sent his good money to a firm of publishers was informed that he had drawn a piece of silverware, and that twenty-five cents would be required for postage and packing. This amount he sent, and received a "silver" spoon worth about ten cents, or say so much per ton, and the postage was two cents, the packing consisting of a little box made of pasteboard.

In connection with these gift enterprises the public have no conception of the number of complaints made to the Post Office Department against them, and one is surprised that people of good sense can be so easily gulled. An advertisement appeared in the Montreal Star some time ago, in which a complete parlor suite was offered for one dollar. A man in Ottawa sent his dollar and received his furniture, which occupied a pasteboard box size about 6 x 8 inches. He complained to the Post Office Department, which however could give him no redress, but the Star, on finding out the character of the concern, discontinued the advertisement.

CONCLUSION.

In conclusion I wish to tender my sincerest thanks to those who have followed my fortunes from beginning to end, and while there may be some of the subject matter which will not meet with your acquiescence, it is to be remembered that the work is founded on truth, and is entirely truth, hence the cause, doubtless of some of its unpopularity. I desire to express also my sincerest thanks to the press, particularly the Telegram and Saturday Night for the many clippings I have taken from them, and for many of the thoughts their articles have inspired. My thanks are equally due to Monsieur Gabouriau, and other writers of fiction for expressions I have found in their works suited to the case I happened to be dealing with, and equally to different physicians whose works I have consulted in dealing with " morbid anatomy." Exception may be taken to some of the chapters of this work, but it is to be remembered that inasmuch as they are a part and parcel of the city, it would be incomplete without them. The peculiar nature of the work has been the foundation for the hope of its success, and I think I am correct in saying that there is no doubt these hopes will be realized There is nothing in it that is not correct and truthful, and this must be my excuse, if any were needed, for the chronicling of unpalatable facts. I have long considered a work of this class a necessity, being as much a social teacher as any newspaper or minister in the country to-day. It gives what the newspapers dare not give, and what they do not know, a faithful and correct account of such things as might be considered unwholesome truths. If in any case I know that any reform has been accomplished through my efforts I shall feel that my work has not been in vain. It is customary in writing of a city to praise it. I have done no such thing. I have told you of the city as I have found it, and if it is not palatable, it is the city's fault and not mine. I am not in any respect offering an apology for my work. I have given what I know to be true, and could prove anything I have said in a Court of Justice. As I have pictured the Social Evil, so I have found it, and no remarks that I have made in that connection are overdrawn. I ask criticism of men who are competent to criticise—the judiciary, and magistracy, clergymen, policemen, members of Parliament can scarcely be expected to give an unbiassed opinion. If they were to agree that certain laws might be amended, they know that every Pharisee who could do so, would league himself and herself against them. Methodist ministers have the persecution of the broken-hearted Jeffreys always before them as an object lesson,—a man whose mortal sin consisted in that he did not believe in Prohibition.

To the press and to different novelists, from whom I have taken extracts I desire to return my sincerest thanks.

THE END.

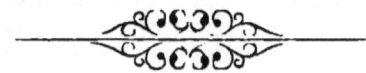

www.ingramcontent.com/pod-product-compliance
Lightning Source LLC
Chambersburg PA
CBHW020825230426
43666CB00007B/1105